STUART CUNNINGHAM

Stuart Cunningham is Professor of Media and Communications at the Queensland University of Technology and Director of the Australian Research Council Centre of Excellence for Creative Industries and Innovation.

In The Vernacular

A Generation of Australian Culture and Controversy

STUART CUNNINGHAM

UQP

First published 2008 by University of Queensland Press
PO Box 6042, St Lucia, Queensland 4067 Australia

www.uqp.com.au

© 2008 Stuart Cunningham

This book is copyright. Except for private study, research,
criticism or reviews, as permitted under the Copyright Act,
no part of this book may be reproduced, stored in a retrieval system,
or transmitted in any form or by any means without prior
written permission. Enquiries should be made to the publisher.

Typeset by Post Pre-press Group, Brisbane
Printed in Australia by McPherson's Printing Group

Cataloguing-in-Publication Data
National Library of Australia

Cunningham, Stuart.
In the vernacular : a generation of Australian culture and
            controversy/Stuart Cunningham.

ISBN 9780702236709 (pbk.)

Culture – Study and teaching – Australia.
Social sciences – Study and teaching – Australia.
Australia – Social conditions – 20th century.
Australia – Cultural policy.

306.071094

To Jo Clifford – always already amore

Contents

Foreword	ix
Acknowledgments	xv
Sources	xvii
Screen title availability	xix
Introduction	xxi

Part 1 Australian film — 1
Chapter 1 The decades of survival: Australian cinema 1930–70 — 4
Chapter 2 Approaching Chauvel — 25
Chapter 3 Apollonius and Dionysus in the Antipodes — 50
Chapter 4 Hollywood genres, Australian movies — 61

Part 2 Australian television — 69
Chapter 5 Style, form and history in Australian mini-series — 73
Chapter 6 Kennedy–Miller: 'House style' in Australian television — 94
Chapter 7 (with Liz Jacka) Australian television in world markets — 122

Part 3 Diasporas and media use — 147
Chapter 8 Theorising the diasporic audience — 149
Chapter 9 (with Tina Nguyen) Actually existing hybridity: Vietnamese diasporic music video — 161

Part 4 The cultural policy debate — 183
Chapter 10 Cultural studies from the viewpoint of cultural policy — 185
Chapter 11 Re-framing culture — 203

Part 5 Creative industries and beyond — 215
Chapter 12 The creative industries after cultural policy — 218
Chapter 13 What price a creative economy? — 231

Notes — 267
Index — 287

Foreword

As leading academics and policy advocates go, Stuart Cunningham is a cheeky bloke. When I agreed to write a few words for this book, by a scholar well-known in recent years for his passionate and flamboyant use of creative industries jargon, I had no idea that a volume called *In the Vernacular* would land on my desk. Startling! For in one of my favourite memories of Stuart as a public speaker, I heckle him a little for informing an assembly of Humanities professors that cultural production and consumption are blurring into 'prosumption' in today's participatory techno-culture: why, I ask (as a friendly adversary), does he have such a cheerful fondness for these obsolescent 'weasel words' of globalising policy-speak? With a fortitude befitting one of Australia's most effective institution-builders and activists for cultural education, he replies that, 'weasel' though such words may sometimes be, during what is often their relatively short shelf-life as markers and definers of an area of policy concern, they establish spaces of opportunity in which it is possible to make things happen that might not otherwise come to pass. Having also fought, on occasion, to affirm the exuberant life-force that is neologism against the puritanical word police of our public media culture, I thought this a wonderful answer – so much so that the moment is still vivid for me. But I would not have described Stuart Cunningham's personal contribution to a generation of Australian culture and controversy as being 'in the vernacular' – as performing, as well as participating in, a local and popular cultural idiom.

Within a few pages of the Introduction to this intellectually gripping book, the rightness of the word 'vernacular' to define its approach, as well as its theme, became clear. Ranging across many topics in Australian cultural history – from the work of Charles Chauvel and other filmmakers of the mid-twentieth century 'survival' to television production in the golden years of the 1980s, on to Vietnamese diasporic media practices and to debates about the role of cultural criticism and education in the 'creative economy' today – this is also a book about the historically shifting grounds of a long-term struggle to create and sustain Australian modes of popular cultural expression. It is a book about how this struggle has been shaped, as much in Chauvel's time as in the heyday of the Kennedy-Miller television mini-series, in the current formulation of creative industries policy, by Australia's relative economic as well as geo-political dependency on larger and greater powers, and by the condition of openness to competing international forces and currents that follows in culture from this. Consistently, too, *In the Vernacular* is a book about those moments in our cultural history in which artists, producers, policy-makers, entrepreneurs and academics, as well as local cultural communities, have been able to make transformative *use* of 'imported' materials in a such an idiomatic and innovative way that an imaginative sense of nationality is nourished by their creativity – and is sometimes, if not always, both embraced by Australian audiences and exported to find acclaim elsewhere.

In this respect, the multi-faceted, entrepreneurial and aesthetically 'weird and wonderful' career of Charles Chauvel remains, with all its avowed colonial baggage, an enabling historical model for Cunningham's way of thinking about how Australians might best make use of the always challenging, always changing conditions in which we go about making vernacular culture. Bringing the globalising rhetoric and concepts of current thinking about a broadly creative economy (as distinct from an economy in which cultural and creative industries remain a special sector) into a dialogue with this deeply *national* enabling model is one of the inspiring achievements of this book. Reading, in sequence, these essays written over a generation of Australian critical debate about culture has allowed me to see how the value of the rhetoric and concepts for Cunningham is all about, once again, their vernacular *uses* in and for a country which has, over the past twenty-five years, raised the policy-based approach to producing and administering culture, and to academic thinking about culture, to a fine art by international standards, which has seen accompanying levels of recognition being accorded (especially in China and the Asia-Pacific region) to the scholarly work and institutional experiments of adventurous pioneers such as Stuart Cunningham. Having read this book, when I hear the word *prosume* in future I will immediately think 'vernacular!' instead of reaching for my revolver.

A more serious way to put this is that I see *In the Vernacular* as defining a profoundly coherent and generative intellectual project that will resonate both in and beyond Australia. As rapid technological change combines with a deep transformation in the worldly conditions in which governments must define their role in relation to culture and education, scholars and cultural activists in many countries are confronting the *imaginative* challenge of what to do with their own national histories of cultural aspiration and experiment. In the developing and post-colonial worlds, as well as in 'strange dominions' like Australia, these histories are often still only partially written, or, if they are written, then they are not always taught and passed on with honour for future generations to transform; the conditions of colonialism shade easily into those of globalisation when it comes to the institutionalised forgetting of vernacular enabling traditions in cultural and intellectual life. From my point of view, Stuart Cunningham's special achievement in editing and reframing the work of many years into a single volume is most strikingly to show us how to produce a sense of emotional as well as intellectual continuity (that is, a sense of belonging) between the projects of the past and those of the present, while pragmatically taking scrupulous account of all the things that are changing and have changed. His eloquent work in Part 3 on the 'globalisation from the margins', that can be grasped by studying diasporic media use, is fully consistent with this.

Cunningham narrates his own journey in other ways throughout the course of this book, preferring often to present himself as moving 'away' from one activity (say, writing the authoritative critical texts in Australian film and television history that appear in Parts 1 and 2) and 'towards' another (the moment of cultural policy advocacy, revisited in Part 4) and then yet another (creative industries) which must generate in turn another 'beyond' (Part 5). In the heat of controversies gone by, I have called Stuart an incurable dialectician and a diehard avant-gardist; no longer wishing to annoy him, I still affectionately think this to be the case about his ways of telling a story and putting an agenda on the table. What really matters, though, is the power of the story to give true stimulus and encouragement to new ideas, and the usefully provocative force of the agenda put forward. With *In the Vernacular* he has excelled himself in both of these respects, most significantly for me when he calls in his Introduction for an 'anchoring' of cultural and especially screen history through 'consistent attention on Australia as a primary object of study, over time and despite changes ... which can demand attention to the international to the exclusion of the local'. The great achievement of this book is precisely to bring this quality of attention *consistently* to bear on a wide range of problems, cultural materials, historical contexts and vernacular idioms of Australian public life, in such a way that others are given tools and precedents to help them both to extend and to extrapolate, dissent, and deviate from Cunningham's own account.

In this, as in other respects outlined by the essays which follow, Stuart Cunningham is the very model of a serious cultural critic working as an 'engaged advocate' of particular positions and directions in contemporary cultural life. This happens to be a deeply ingrained, institutionally rational, and imaginatively enabling tradition of how to make a difference as an intellectual in Australia. At the level of 'big book' production, where valuable scholarly essays and controversies of initially small circulation can reach new and wider publics, that tradition has sometimes appeared to be fading in recent years. It has been, shall we say, a long time between drinks, but the state of my spirits after reading this book is most definitely festive. Three cheers for cultural history, policy advocacy and fruitful public controversy – with an extra toast for cultural prosumption!

Meaghan Morris

Lingnan University, Hong Kong
Centre for Cultural Research, University of Western Sydney

Acknowledgments

In preparing these essays for publication, I have sought to retain them as complete texts, except where repetition, redundancy or confusing signs of datedness make it necessary to edit for readability and clarity. I have not sought to modify views that I no longer hold. In all this, I have been assisted greatly by the editorial ministrations of Harvey May, who has worked with me to prepare these texts for contemporary consumption and, I hope, enjoyment.

Given the spread in time of these essays, this is a wonderful occasion to acknowledge the debt of friendship and the concourse of ideas I owe to many colleagues. This is the short short list. My early encounters with Australian film and TV were greatly enhanced by Albert Moran, Tom O'Regan and Liz Jacka. The stimulus of encountering Toby Miller at that time has not abated. My experience of working as a policy analyst and public interest advocate was made possible by the support of Kate Harrison and Cathy Robinson. The stimulating engagements during the 1990s were often focused around the ARC Key Centre for Cultural and Media Policy and crucial to those collaborations were Tony Bennett and Graeme Turner and, again, Tom O'Regan. Working on major projects at the same time occasioned the deepening of the collegium with John Sinclair and, again, Liz Jacka. The most recent collaborative environment during the 2000s, with the formation of the Creative Industries Faculty at QUT and the research centres that I have led (Creative Industries Research and Applications Centre) or do lead (ARC Centre of Excellence for Creative Industries and Innovation) have depended on the good offices of John Hartley, Terry Flew, Greg Hearn, Brad Haseman, and more recently Terry Cutler and Jason Potts. To all these colleagues, and many, many more, I owe a great and continuing debt of gratitude.

My thanks to my employers over this period, Griffith University, the Communications Law Centre and Queensland University of Technology, for their strong support and encouragement.

Last, and most, thank you to my family, who have cared for and about me – Jo, Hugo, Ben and Vivien.

Sources

Permission was obtained from the following publishers for reproducing the essays from the original works: Allen & Unwin, the Australian Centre for Photography, the Australian Film, Television and Radio School, Oxford University Press, Routledge, Penguin, *Arena*, Currency House and the *International Journal of Cultural Studies*. While all reasonable efforts were made to secure permission, where necessary, for the republication of these essays, the publisher would be glad to hear from anyone we have been unable to contact.

Part 1 Australian film
'The Decades of Survival: Australian Cinema 1930–1970', in Albert Moran and Tom O'Regan (eds), *The Australian Screen*, Penguin, Ringwood, 1989, pp. 53–74.

'Approaching Chauvel', in *Featuring Australia: The Cinema of Charles Chauvel*, Allen & Unwin, Sydney, 1991, pp. 5–29.

'Apollonius and Dionysus in the Antipodes', *Photofile*, vol. 6, no. 2, 1988, pp. 41–6.

'Hollywood Genres, Australian Movies', in Albert Moran and Tom O'Regan (eds), *An Australian Film Reader*, Currency Press, Sydney, 1985, pp. 235–41.

Part 2 Australian television

'Style, Form and History in Australian Mini-Series', in J. Frow and M. Morris (eds), *Australian Cultural Studies: A Reader*, Allen & Unwin, Sydney, 1993, pp. 117–32.

'Kennedy–Miller: House Style in Australian Television', in Elizabeth Jacka and Susan Dermody (eds), *The Imaginary Industry*, AFTRS, North Ryde, 1988.

(with Liz Jacka), 'Australian television in world markets', in John Sinclair, Elizabeth Jacka and Stuart Cunningham (eds), *New Patterns in Global Television: Peripheral Vision*, Oxford University Press, New York, 1995.

Part 3 Diasporas and media use

'Theorising the Diasporic Audience', in Mark Balnaves, Tom O'Regan and Jason Sternberg (eds), *Mobilising the Audience*, University of Queensland Press, St Lucia, 2002, pp. 266–82.

(with Tina Nguyen) 'Actually Existing Hybridity: Vietnamese Diasporic Music Video', in Karim H. Karim (ed.), *The Media of Diaspora*, Routledge, London and New York, 2003, pp. 119–32.

Part 4 The cultural policy debate

'Cultural Studies from the Viewpoint of Cultural Policy', in G. Turner (ed.), *Nation, Culture, Text: Australian Cultural and Media Studies*, Routledge, London, 1993, pp. 126–39.

'Re-Framing Culture', *Arena Magazine*, issue 7, October/November 1993, pp. 33–5.

Part 5 Creative industries and beyond

'The creative industries after cultural policy: A genealogy and some possible preferred futures', *International Journal of Cultural Studies*, vol. 7, no. 1, 2004, pp. 105–16.

What Price a Creative Economy?, Platform Paper series, Currency House, Sydney, July 2006.

Screen title availability

There are welcome developments in the availability of Australian screen content that support the publication of studies that bring them back into the general and student readership 'frame'. Many historical film classics as well as much of the big-budget, 'quality' end of television drama from the 1980s and 1990s have been released on DVD and are readily available. Vietnamese music video, as Chapter 9 suggests, is available only through specialist Vietnamese language outlets.

Part 1 Australian film
The following films are available for hire for educational use from the National Film and Sound Archive (NFSA): *Captain Thunderbolt* (in a 16 mm version), *The Back of Beyond* (DVD), *Eureka Stockade* (VHS and 16 mm), *Jedda* (DVD), *In the Wake of the Bounty* (16 mm and VHS video), *The Overlanders* (16 mm), *Walk into Paradise*, *The Restless and the Damned* (under the alternative title of *The Dispossessed*), *Forty Thousand Horsemen* (16 mm and VHS video), *Pearls and Savages* (16 mm and VHS video), *The Jungle Woman* (VHS video), *Starstruck* (16 mm and VHS video),

SCREEN TITLE AVAILABILITY

The Man from Snowy River (16 mm and VHS video), *Mad Max* (16 mm).

The Back of Beyond Collection – 50th Anniversary Edition is available to purchase as a two-DVD set from ABC Shops. The following films are available for sale as a VHS video from the distributor, ScreenSound Australia: *Jedda, Mike and Stefani, The Rats of Tobruk, Forty Thousand Horsemen*. *They're a Weird Mob, The Man from Snowy River, Mad Max* are available for sale on DVD from Roadshow. *Phar Lap, Mad Max 2*, and *Mad Max 3: Beyond Thunderdome* are available for sale as DVDs from Warner Bros. *Starstruck* is available as a DVD sale from AV Channel.

Part 2 Australian television

Against the Wind, Melba, and *Shout!: The Story of Johnny O'Keefe* can be accessed by authorised institutions and individuals via the NFSA. *Against the Wind* is available to purchase as a DVD boxed set from EMI. *1915* is available for sale as a DVD from Roadshow. *Shout!: The Story of Johnny O'Keefe* is available for sale as a DVD from AV Channel. *The Petrov Affair* is available for sale as a DVD from Shock.

The early Kennedy–Miller film corpus has been covered above. *Dead Calm* and *The Witches of Eastwick* are available as DVD sales from Warner Home Video, *Babe: Pig in the City* is available as a DVD sale from Universal. *Happy Feet* is available as a DVD sale from Roadshow. Most of the Kennedy–Miller mini-series of the 1980s are now available in commercial DVD form for sale from Roadshow Entertainment. The six main mini-series: *The Dismissal, Bodyline, The Cowra Breakout, Vietnam, Dirtwater Dynasty* and *Bangkok Hilton* are a 'Great Australian Stories' boxed set.

Introduction

This book brings together a selection of writings over a period of twenty years focused on Australian screen production, criticism and culture, allied with broader policy concerns that run right through to the present and beyond. It ranges from the neglected heritage of Australian cinema before the 'revival' of the 1970s, through to the 1980s–90s golden age of television drama, both domestic and export quality, across the vibrant margins of the multiculture of the country, to the policy controversies that have animated academic and broader debate for many years and helped to define directions in cultural, media and communication studies.

You might immediately ask: what relevance does such a historical run of work have for contemporary readers? The short answer is simple. Australia doesn't seem to have much sense of its cultural history – in many of its particularly popular manifestations – and this might be getting worse, not better. And the varieties of critical engagement with it – fandom, serious journalism, scholarship of both a critical and an archival bent, and curriculum materials and teaching – do not complement or reinforce each other. The culture wars of the last decade have chilled the enthusiasm and confidence of creative people; and the waning of cultural nationalism from its high points of the late 1980s (especially around the bicentennial of European settlement) and the ineluctable integration and globalisation of cultural expression have all contributed to this situation.

There is a second answer which traces a history of the present: the industrial and social trends in media, communications and culture are outstripping the academic frameworks that have been erected to deal with them. Media and cultural studies have to run to catch up with these developments. This leads to a third purpose, which is to reconnect disciplinary debates about Australian media, communications and cultural studies to the future of the disciplines, which is to say the students who study them. I have built this introduction around these three propositions.

Tom O'Regan, in *Australian National Cinema*,[1] talks of three competing personae for the critic: the cinephile or fan, the critical intellectual and the cultural historian. To these I would add the engaged advocate. In some ways, the field of cultural, media and communications studies has fractured around these different forms of address and around different approaches: there are those who focus variously on textual analysis, or genre coverage of popular culture, on the politics of media representations, or on policy. Each of these voices, and the knowledge claims they invoke, are legitimate practices of education and research in the cultural, media and communications space. The structure of this book, and the progression of the essays in it, embodies the movement of my critical persona from the cinephile and historian and my practice of textual analysis and cultural history to that of engaged advocate for policy change.

It might be assumed, from the controversies that have been engendered by these shifts, that I seek a normative realignment of the disciplinary field. However, as argued in the next part of this introduction, the horizons (or what used to be called the 'available discourses') of critical sense-making are foundational. Without a robust critical climate, enriched by the discourses of the enthusiastic fan and the historian, and seriously engaging with the actually existing situation of culture in the country, there is little for the policy-minded to advocate for. You will notice a kind of recursion to the need for critical understanding in the latter stages of this book, where, in Chapter 13, the explosion of user-created content and the related affordances of web 2.0 are traced and it is suggested that industry and policy makers need to run to catch up with what fans, peer-to-peer dynamics and innovative cyberati are producing in terms of both the content and the structure of communication.

Cultural, media and communications studies thrives on a healthy pluralism; it also needs constant reappraisal of its methods, its relevance, the contributions from other knowledge fields and the world out there – with all the speed with which it poses new questions to a field of inquiry that wants to understand – in the words of two leaders in the field fifteen years ago - 'the whole way of life of a social group as it is structured by representation and by power'.[2]

Generations of popular culture: reclaiming the past

In 2007 there was a high-profile campaign around the decline of teaching of Australian literature in our universities. With the retirement of Professor Elizabeth Webby at Sydney University, there was no longer an occupied chair of Australian literature. Rosemary Neill, in a series of articles in *The Australian*, used this as an occasion to chart the decline of OzLit teaching in both school and higher education.[3] An Australian Literature in Education Roundtable was organised by the Australia Council in Canberra and, in an unusual move for the Howard government, which rarely tired of saying the university sector had never had it so good, then Education Minister Julie Bishop announced

$1.5 million direct extra endowment funding for a Chair in Australian Literature.

So far, so good. But what about chairs of Australian film, Australian television, Australian popular culture? As far as I can tell, there have never been named chairs in these fields, despite their evident popularity with students and the vibrant scholarly literature that has been generated around them. Why does it sound slightly wacky to even propose such a thing?

Without wishing to reopen the whole popular culture debate, I need to register that there is a great deal at stake in what counts as Australian cultural history. In contrast to the visual arts, literature and possibly music, Australian popular cinema and television are rarely accorded the degree of regular reflection and reframing, the dealing with what Meaghan Morris[4] calls their 'positive unoriginality', that is, their indebtedness to international influence while at the same time adapting or appropriating such influence to produce, with variable capacity, distinctly Australian work that resonates with generations of Australians. Numerous institutions are dedicated to this public cultural work – art galleries, festivals, some museums and the many specialist and broadsheet press outlets – but, apart from the exception that proves the rule (the Australian Centre for the Moving Image in Federation Square in Melbourne), there are no institutions dedicated to the critical curatorship and presentation to the public of the Australian screen heritage. Even when the will and opportunity is there, it would normally take a back seat to the expectations of a contemporary cosmopolitanism which tends to dictate a dominant international diet. (This was the response of Robert Dixon, Chair of English Literature at University of Sydney, who responded to the OzLit crisis by saying that Australian literature was alive and well and living in the interstices of crosscutting approaches and an expansive international canon.[5])

In the case of Australian screen, there is a 'thinness' about the institutions that carry the weight of translating past cultural achievement to contemporary audiences. This thinness ultimately is based on a lack of critical variety and depth and a broad brokerage culture, including traditions of press and other media coverage and, of course, formal curricula, which make up the ground base of and for cultural institutions.

Much of this has to do with the problematic standing of popular culture and how to value it. Despite the long campaign that cultural and media studies has waged since the 1950s (with international front-liners like John Hartley[6] often coming from an Australian angle), to have popular culture valued in aesthetic and socio-political terms, it remains one of the knottiest problems in both cultural heritage and contemporary debate.

The book's early chapters, discussing Australia's early popular cinematic culture, rehearse the great difficulty that critics have had in coming to terms with filmmaking which was so out of character with the predominant traditions in the country and which crash-merged Hollywood melodrama and welded highly specific, location-based filmmaking with extremely local historical and cultural reference points.

Evidence for the difficulties of grasping our screen cultural heritage in this case is that there has been very little concerted work that takes issue with or seeks to consolidate the arguments around the status and career of Charles Chauvel that I made some twenty years ago.[7] (The main exception to this was Mudrooroo's reflections,[8] which develop important perspectives on Aboriginal masculinity in respect of Chauvel's race-and-romance melodrama *Jedda*.) Filmmakers (like Tracey Moffatt in *Night Cries*) and film organisations (such as the Brisbane International Film Festival's Annual Chauvel Award and the Chauvel Cinema in Paddington, New South Wales) have been more significant than the film historians in maintaining the Chauvel heritage. And my argument in Chapter 3 ('Apollonius and Dionysus in the Antipodes'), that Frank Hurley and Charles Chauvel embody two contending traditions of cultural engagement with Australia's status as both a product and a progenitor of colonialism, has rarely been taken up.[9] (A welcome development on the cultural heritage front is that many historical film classics, as well as much of the big-budget, 'quality' end of television drama from the 1980s and 1990s have been released on DVD and are readily available.)

But it must be said that the problematic positioning of Australian popular culture has not inhibited the growth, quality and success of academic cultural, media and communication studies in this country. Several surveys[10] point to interrelated fields of inquiry which have emerged strongly over a generation and now occupy positions of consolidated popularity among students (Putnis's and Molloy and Lennie's surveys have shown since the 1970s the growth and solidity of the student demand for coursework in these disciplines[11]) and strong standing in research accomplishment. A recent analysis conducted by the Australian Research Council of research in the 'Humanities and Creative Arts discipline grouping in 2004'[12] found that the disciplines with the strongest international profiles and distinctiveness internationally were philosophy; cultural, media and communication studies; and Asian studies. In this survey of international and national leaders in a range of humanities and creative arts disciplines, cultural studies, and within it cultural policy and creative industries research, were consistently featured as a distinctive and leading element of Australian research strengths.

Having said that, however, it may be something in the breadth and mutability of cultural, media and communications studies that contributes to this thinness. Built-in to the 'inter-discipline' (or what Graeme Turner[13] has called the 'undiscipline') of cultural, media and communication studies is no special fealty to national boundaries around its objects of study. Indeed, as pointed out in declarative terms in Chapter 10 ('Cultural studies from the viewpoint of cultural policy'), it has often been driven by a normative neo-Marxist internationalism which decries any untoward attachment to nation or nation-state. When this critique of cultural nationalism is combined with the latter's waning as a social and cultural force since the 1980s, the result is a double whammy in the potential relevance of the discipline field to this country's understanding of itself.

The 'rigorous mixing'[14] within the force-field of cultural, media and communication studies has made them extraordinarily open and largely accepting of insights from neighbouring disciplines, which have surely strengthened and renewed them over time. This mixing has been not only theoretical (Frow and Morris's point concerns Australian scholars' ability not to be held to primordial doctrinal disputes, but overcoming them in hybrid practice) but also disciplinary. Obviously, literary studies has been a major contributor, but there have been significant intersections with anthropology (Eric Michaels), history (Bridget Griffen-Foley), sociology (John Sinclair) and political science (Murray Goot, Rod Tiffen, Ian Ward). (The key discipline that has not been engaged sufficiently is economics – about which more later.)

However, it has also meant an inevitable degree of 'trying out', a tendency to 'move on' rather than consolidate hard-won disciplinary ground. Several of those who published key contributions in the fledgling sub-disciplines of cultural and especially screen history in Australia have 'moved on'. But it is the proposition of this book that one main way of anchoring the discipline – and contributing to its relevance and currency – is through a consistent attention on Australia as a primary object of study, over time and despite changes in the 'inter-discipline' mix and academic politics which can demand attention to the international to the exclusion of the local. This 'site' may be the occasion for widely varying approaches and concerns: those of the aforementioned cultural heritage building; or, at the opposite end of the spectrum, an action research involvement with the emergent contours of youth cultures (thus engaging with the lived and felt experiences of the main clients of our scholarship); or addressing the 'commanding heights' of policy formation and decision making.

Whatever else might be claimed for the rigorous mixing of the 'inter-discipline', this is a project I have consistently set myself.

Of course, cultural, media and communication studies has often been attacked for postmodern relativism, the bogey term *du jour* after many years of the so-called culture wars. It lacks settled objects of study, agreed agendas and, perhaps most of all, an organised notion of what constitutes cultural value. As John Frow argues, 'the very force of its initial refusal of the normative has become a problem for it, since it occludes those questions of value which lie at the heart of the practices it seeks to theorize'.[15] The issue of normative aesthetic judgement in popular culture is never far from the surface of debate in media and cultural studies, and has been to the fore recently in the work of several Australian leaders in the field, including Alan McKee and Graeme Turner.[16] In his *Australian Television: A Genealogy of Great Moments* and *Beautiful Things in Popular Culture*, McKee seeks to establish canons of great moments and 'bests'; this is the fan/telephile discourse at its strongest. In *Australian Television*, he attempts to construct a cultural heritage for Australian television where it barely exists. Turner periodises the history of local TV current affairs as one of (possibly terminal) decline from its high point in the 1960s and early 1970s. He defends this 'decline from a golden age' valuation strenuously in terms of the formal and regulated as well as the fundamentally ethical and political role current affairs TV should play in maintaining a public sphere in an open, democratic society.

Normative judgements about cultural value are redolent in all discourse on media and popular culture. This has its own history, arising from the necessity of defending and differentiating the field from those forms of heritage culture that came with sometimes centuries of encrusted value. Media and cultural studies should not shy away from this constitutive normativity but embrace it by making the bases for such judgement explicit and therefore contestable. But normative judgment, if it is not to become wooden and authoritarian, needs typically to be made intra-generically.

That is to say, different types of cultural content should be assessed against their own terms and conditions of production and reception. Both McKee and Turner provide sterling service in this mission; and I look to do the same in the treatments of the historical mini-series format in Chapters 5 and 6 of this book. This paradigmatic output – more than fifty of them, mostly across the 1980s – ranks as constituting one of the undisputed golden ages of television drama. Yet the most achieved use of the form, by the Kennedy–Miller company, was subject to extraordinarily illiterate criticism of the company's aesthetic and historical representation strategies, as I show in Chapter 6. But *within* the genre, there was wide divergence in the quality of aesthetic and historical representation, as Chapter 5 ('Style, form and history in Australian mini-series') essays.

Generating controversy: history of the present

The emphases of my work have certainly changed over the period this book covers. There is also a consistency, however, based on an interest in the policy frameworks required for local culture to thrive. I have taken an interdisciplinary approach to policy analysis and policy advocacy, where the economic, the legal and other dimensions of specialist knowledge need to be brought together with cultural and communication policy. However, governments and state policy apparatuses are typically technocratic in their orientation, and controlling in the way that they interact with non-government players, including policy analysts, and they must deal with well-organised, effective big business lobbies, especially in the media and communications space. My background in cultural studies predisposes me to focus on content and the social sphere, with cultural consumption and production to the fore. Policy and industry often have little understanding of the dimensions of social and cultural change in the sphere of cultural consumption and production. Such change is posing increasingly large challenges for policy and industry today, and not only in the media and cultural fields. Some of this vernacular creativity or DIY (do-it-yourself) culture has attracted the, admittedly ugly, neologisms of 'produser' and 'prosumption', capturing the blurring of the previous structural boundaries between consumption and production of the old linear model on which pretty much all cultural, media and communication studies had relied. These burgeoning cultures clearly threaten big business models, as well as many professional production cadres, which usually depend on big business distributional clout to transmit their product to market.

These principles and practices are informed, for me, by a value orientation of tracking and promoting cultural and social change that embraces consumer–citizen empowerment, while not perpetuating a doctrinaire divide between the consumer and citizen aspects of such empowerment. This position, of course, evokes the shades of many core debates in political economy and cultural studies. The work of John Fiske, John Hartley, Nicholas Garnham, Peter Golding and Graeme Murdock[17] and many others are the reference points here about where the balance between the area of content and social *agency* and the area of ownership, control and *structure* exists. It is the nature of such foundational debates that they are not summarily resolved; indeed, they are usually structured as to be effectively unresolvable.

But the social and cultural policy point is to find and build an alignment of interest between small business enterprise cultures, the not-for-profit sector, state-supported culture in the communication and cultural field (such as public service broadcasting and other elements), corporates committed to good citizenship, progressive investment strategies and labour practices, and the social or participatory DIY culture movements. The potential of such alignments have been analysed, for example, by Yochai Benkler[18] in *The Wealth of Networks*, a major work on participatory culture and its implications for notions of power in the contemporary world.

This framework I have offered provides a scaffolding across Parts 4 and 5 of the book, and suggests a good degree of continuity between my role in the cultural policy debate of the 1990s, stirred in part by my book, *Framing Culture*, and my advocacy of creative industries in the 2000s. Chapter 10 has a short version of the argument of *Framing Culture*, an essay which Graeme Turner called 'a particularly uncompromising and thoroughgoing critique of contemporary cultural studies that is not easy to dismiss'.[19] Chapter 11 contains a response to the many critics, both positive and negative, of that argument.

If the cultural policy moment was an occasion for controversy, the development of the creative industries proposition has caused a great deal more: media, cultural and communication studies' critique of the concept of creative industries has been as consistent as it has been negative. (On the other hand, the business disciplines, and to a lesser extent economic and cultural geography, have worked with the concept quite productively.) The broader controversies raised by creative industries have had much to do with the fact that the policy proposition had been examined and adopted by a wide range of government and other actors in the ten years since the framework was first outlined by the British government in 1998.

The gap between the remarkable enthusiasm with which it has been taken up in policy circles across many parts of the world and at many levels (national, state, regional, inter-governmental) and the depth of opposition to it academically marks it out as a major contemporary instance of the gap between policy and critique – which, ironically enough, was the point of departure for the cultural policy debate. I will take stock of the contemporary debate in dialogue with two of the most trenchant critics within cultural, media and communication studies, Nicholas Garnham[20] and Toby Miller.[21]

Garnham's critique centres on an extensive commentary on the core intellectual lineage of the information society and its fatal links to creative industries. Creative industries ideas are a kind of Trojan Horse, secreting the intellectual heritage of the information society and its technocratic baggage into the realm of cultural practice, suborning the latter's proper claims on the public purse and self-understanding, and aligning it with inappropriate bedfellows such as business services, telecommunications and calls for increases in generic creativity. Garnham rests his case on the normative imperative to return to the 'cultural industries' policy focus on distribution (critique of multimedia conglomeration) and consumption (smoothing of the popular market for culture for access and equity) of which he was a main proponent in the 1980s.[22]

Garnham is right to say that the creative industries approach is about linking culture to discourses of information, knowledge and innovation. He is wrong to assume that the latter trumps the former in each and every case, or indeed that it has to be seen at all as a zero sum game. There are two key variations on Garnham as we look at the take-up of creative industries around the world. The first is a dramatic shift from an alleged top-down, central-government-directed truimphalism. In almost all instances of its take-up elsewhere, it has been more tentative and exploratory, allowing for more regional variation, and adaptive to local circumstances. It is the very lack of certainty (*pace* Garnham's 'It assumes that we already know, and thus can take for granted, what the creative industries are, why they are important and thus merit supporting policy initiatives'[23]) that has meant constant definitional wrangling and regular recasting of what counts in the creative industries – in general, a productive ferment rather than preordained certainty.

The second is that the 'unquestioned prestige that now attaches to the information society and to any policy that supposedly favours its development'[24] is quite unevenly engaged. When it is, it takes two forms. In the first, in developed countries, it can be about softening the technocratic orientation of the information society, as it is about taking the creative industries discourse beyond the cultural and media sector and into digital content and the creative economy fields. In the second, in the global south, it is to leverage support for the development of basic infrastructure, the unquestioned prestige of which absolutely cannot be taken for granted but is still very much in the process of being laid in. (Elsewhere, I have suggested four main global variations on the creative industries theme as it has travelled around the world in the United States, Europe, Asia and the global south.[25])

For Miller, the position of critical cultural policy studies – won in part through my arguments in the 1990s – has now become the benchmark from which to judge the extent to which a creative industries approach has fallen short of a posture of acceptable criticality.

Miller is in concert with Garnham in charging that the creative industries idea is a 'neo-liberal' sell-out. However, for Miller the alternative is not necessarily a return to the cultural industries moment of the 1980s in the West, but a spatial displacement to what he regards as the exemplary politics of Latin-American cultural activism. He recommends programs of education and engagement through 'the lens of subalternity and transterritorial as well as local social identities with an emphasis on cultural policy'. In a clarion call to remain 'vibrantly independent', Miller enjoins the cultural studies community to engage with social movements and their potentially positive articulation to government rather than having any truck with corporations.

But at this point it is necessary to question the crude binary of us (critical) and them (neo-liberal) which prevents a productive engagement with the wide range of shades of ideological colour of governments, corporations, social movements and bureaucracies. This is in part to remind readers what Garnham himself argued in the inaugural issue of the key journal *Cultural Studies* in the 1980s: most people's cultural needs and aspirations are being – for better or worse – supplied by corporations in the market as goods and services.

A key feature of creative industries discourse is an 'enterprise' approach to business development. This seeks to take account of the vast preponderance of small business or small-business-like entities that populate the sector in most countries, and addresses what we might call the 'economic subalterns' in our midst. This is a sector running on tight margins and facing high rates of failure, in need of flexible and in many cases experimental forms of state facilitation, and which rarely figures on governments' cultural policy radar. The point is that much of the independent creative enterprises sector (games, design, web development, fashion, music, audiovisual) is organised in this way and spans the commercial and the subvented, complicating the binary thinking that seeks to exclude the commercial from anything other than critique. A significant subset of this phenomenon, which is covered in some detail in Part 3, is the whole area of small commercial firms underpinning minority populations' cultural economy in multiethnic societies – and the distance these economies maintain from official state cultural policy. Small business enterprise or entrepreneurship, and policies to support it, often have to run the gauntlet against much more powerful vested interests, which I have nominated previously[26] as Big Culture, Big Business and Big Government.

From this perspective, the limits of both neo-Marxist critique and Keynesian subvention come into sharper relief. Our current effort in the ARC Centre of Excellence for Creative Industries and Innovation injects an economic 'third way' into debates about the emergent nature of the creative economy and contrasts Schumpeterian approaches with Keynesianism and neo-Marxist political economy.[27] Schumpeter, in 1942 in *Capitalism, Socialism and Democracy*, argued that Marx had 'no adequate theory of enterprise' and failed to 'distinguish the entrepreneur from the capitalist'. Schumpeter 'told of capitalism in the way most people experience it: as consumer desires aroused by endless advertising; as forcible jolts up and down the social pecking order; as goals reached, shattered, altered, then reached once more as people try, try again'. He knew that 'creative destruction fosters economic growth but also that it undercuts cherished human values'. For admirers of Schumpeter, he tells them what capitalism 'really feels like'.[28]

This approach, outlined in brief in Chapter 13 ('What price a creative economy'), gives us a better handle on what is happening at this present moment of 'creative destruction' of the time-honoured models of production, dissemination and consumption in the media and cultural fields offered by new, mobile and interactive digital media and Internet-based modes of communication and distribution. There is now a veritable wave of proposal, analysis and prognostication addressing this question.[29] Rather than foreclose the question of *how* significant a challenge to business-as-usual with the political economy nostrum that monopoly capitalism will always-already triumph, I look to explore new opportunities for content creation and distribution that arise in this turbulent space and explore new theories which attempt to deal with these new emergent realities. This is a cultural politics between, rather than beyond, left and right.[30]

Generation next: pedagogy, precarious labour and the future

It is no surprise that the leading advocacy in Australia for a creative industries approach to education and research has come out of an applied technology university such as Queensland University of Technology (QUT). QUT has a mission to address the vocational aspirations of its students and has had a very strong track record of placing graduates in jobs in Australia over a significant period of time.

There is a certain ethics that subtend the pedagogy in the humanities and creative arts in such a university. It is a matter of core pedagogical ethics to refine critical stances in the disciplinary traditions in the cultural, media and communications studies traditions to take account of vocational aspirations, workplace trends and the broader structure of the economy into which students will be moving and will be looking for career opportunities. Engaging students in the nature of work and labour, involving the exploration of the notion of the portfolio career, self-employment, the expected multiplicity of career directions in any one person's working life, especially in these fields, is *sine qua non*. There must be a balance between a 'glass half full' and a 'glass half empty' analytics and pedagogy. The conditions of precarious, flexible labour, which is a growing focus of research in critical communication studies and forms the basis of much of the critique of creative industries, needs to be addressed as a current reality, to be neither celebrated nor critiqued *tout court*.

The key textbook in the creative industries field is edited by a QUT team led by John Hartley.[31] Along with the more celebratory or dispassionate analytics, the book features Angela McRobbie on exclusionary employment trends in the creative industries, Toby Miller and colleagues on some of the lessons on the politics of labour to be learned from their study of global Hollywood, as well as the links of the creative industries discourse to social movement politics (Graham Meikle, Geert Lovink) and multiculturalism (Nestor Garcia Canclini). It might equally have featured Andrew Ross on the exploitative nature of labour in the new economy.[32]

But I don't think the toothpaste can be squeezed back into the tube, the egg unscrambled. The nature of work in the cultural, media and communication fields, as fields typical of much knowledge work today, is characterised by the increasing occurrence of contract labour, by multiple career pathways, by increasingly global opportunities and challenges, and by the diminution of the 'market organiser' roles played by many large (often public sector) agencies in mentoring, apprenticeship and structured whole-of-career pathways of progression for creative workers. In Australia, for key creative positions in the screen sector, this was a role once played by the ABC, by Crawfords or by Film Australia. In most cases, 'learning-by-doing' apprenticeship opportunities, such as these organisations used to provide, have declined significantly.

Journalism is greatly affected by these changes. The rise of contract and freelance journalism and the increased blurring of the boundaries between professional and pro-am journalistic practice make journalism a classic instance of 'new economy' work practices. An International Labour Organisation survey conducted for the International Federation of Journalists in 2007 found that about one-third of journalists in the developed world are now working in some form of contingent work – as freelancers, casuals or contractors. The traditional journalist workforce is declining (in the United States there was an average 3 per cent reduction in print journalism jobs each year from 2001 to 2006) while the increase in online jobs only partially compensates.[33]

The Australian film industry is an industry of first-time directors and is more and more thoroughly integrated into global talent-scouting and production opportunities and threats. Of the forty-eight features released in the first three-quarters of 2007, according to the Australian Film Commission, thirty-six, or almost 75 per cent, are from first-time filmmakers. This figure is not new; the trend has been well established since the 1990s. Compared with earlier times, relative failure is far less countenanced, and relative success is far more rewarded (usually with an offer you can't refuse, to leave the country and work in one of the global production centres). Australian cinema is a highly effective R&D lab for dominant cinemas such as Hollywood, and the celebratory tone of the Australian media's iterative coverage of 'Aussiewood' papers over the difficulties posed by attractive global opportunities for locally trained and nurtured creatives in a global business.

If the top end of creative employment is global, the industry sectors or application domains into which creative graduates go are highly diverse, requiring a pedagogy that prepares for such diversity. Our detailed research that goes behind the official statistics shows that, compared with other employment, particularly in the traditional professions, creative employment disproportionately occurs outside the creative industries themselves. In other words, creatively-trained people are more likely to be working outside the specialist creative industry sectors than inside them. This is the case for many countries, including Australia, and has been so for some time. The diversity is greatest in the many design occupations: 60 per cent of the employment of designers in Australia occurs outside of specialist design industry sectors. (People occupied as designers are present in 260 out of the possible 440 categories of industry activities across the Australian economy.) In Queensland at the 2001 Census, almost twice as many designers were working in the broader economy than in the specialist design consulting firms.[34]

Creatives need entrepreneurial, sole-trader and associated business skills to cope in the labour markets into which they are going. Across all people employed in the Australian creative industries at the 2006 Census, 12 per cent were sole-practitioners compared with 7 per cent overall for all other service industries. Sixty per cent of employment in the industry classification for Creative Artists, Musicians, Writers & Performers is self-employment. There are four other creative industries sectors with self-employment rates twice the average: photography, craft jewellery, music (and other sound-recording activities) and other specialised design services.[35]

In a study of graduates one year out from graduation from QUT's Creative Industries Faculty,[36] Ruth Bridgstock found that the four strongest predictors of self-reported notions of success were whether the respondents had good career-building skills, previous paid work in their preferred fields, an effective support network, and a passionate belief in the worth of their creative activity. The respondent group was a majority of the graduating cohort in 2005 and were not simply a group of aspirant dreamers – 80 per cent were working in a field cognate to their discipline background. These value orientations need building on in pedagogical frameworks, and critical analysis should inform rather than deconstruct them.

Our discipline's critique of precarious labour strikes me as a bit like David Gauntlett's[37] acerbic point about media studies academics belatedly discovering what has been obvious to their student populations for some time about online worlds. It seems to me that building into cultural, media and communications studies curricula the analytical and practical skills (including 'left' knowledge and skills about rights at work and critical knowledge of corporate citizenship or lack of it, for example, and 'right' knowledge and confidence of global 'creative class' opportunities) to survive in the tough but rapidly growing creative economy is a self-evidently necessary balance between critique and vocational realism.

Part 1 Australian film

The problematic status of our popular cultural heritage is the underlying rationale for Part 1. These chapters – about the Australian cinema before the revival of the industry in the 1970s, during the 'decades of survival' – are a test case for claims made about the thinness of Australian cultural history, which has been somewhat neglected in scholarship and institutional curatorship. As the first essays show, this has much to do with the conundrums of analysis and criticism.

Each of the first three essays attempts to bring together the yin and yang of film studies: semiotic text analysis on the one hand and industry history on the other. The governing question is: why does a society like ours develop industries and make movies like it does? What works as the lynch pin, the analytical Holy Grail as it were, of the analytics of these essays is the colonial-dominion status of the country. The continuities linking them are organised around the 'competing imperialisms', or, more precisely, American media imperialism and British colonialism, as they structured the Australian cultural imagination as well as its polity, industry fortunes and social structure. It is emphasised that this does not render the host as passive recipient of overweening cultural influence; there are always strategies of negotiation of the status of Australia as an 'import culture'. These strategies are rarely smoothly negotiated; however, the competing and contradictory filmmaking responses within the country are highlighted by the comparison between Frank Hurley and Charles Chauvel, the 'Apollonius' and 'Dionysus' of early Australian cinema.

Arguably the greatest creative force of the decades of survival was Charles Chauvel, whose oeuvre, weird and wonderful as it was, remains one of the most difficult to come to terms with aesthetically, culturally and socially. His films pose challenges and intrigue viewers to the present day because they take on the big cultural questions but with a naive aesthetic that seems so antithetical to modern sensibilities.

Even when the revival cinema is under consideration, regimes of cultural criticism and commentary are routinely nonplussed by whether to embrace or eschew the 'dissolve' of an assumedly authentic and procrustean Australian culture against cosmopolitanism and the embrace of a hybrid, evolving and dynamic culture. The so-called film revival of the 1970s was regarded as a definitive break from the cultural cringe and a general beholdenness to all things British or American. But, as Meaghan Morris's notion of 'positive unoriginality' and Tom O'Regan's ideas on import culture[1] show, Australian film of the 1980s was in a constant dialogue with the 'dominant paradigm', playfully and energetically making local meaning within the enabling aesthetic framework laid down by Hollywood. Chapter 4, 'Hollywood genres, Australian movies', should be read in the light of this ongoing meme (Richard Dawkins'[2] felicitous term for a basic unit of cultural information), and also in the context of the question of genre cinema, which is being played out to this day.

Starstruck (director Gillian Armstrong, 1982) is the major film discussed in Chapter 4. Being one of the very few musicals in the contemporary Australian cinema (*Strictly Ballroom* may qualify, but it is less 'traditional' a musical than *Starstruck*), it raises the general issue that local movies have not traded in traditional genres. Again, 'authentic' national cinema and mainstream genre movies tend not to mix in the production and critical lexicon. Perhaps the best example of this gap today is the horror genre. (It is estimated that well over 100 horror films have been made in Australia since the 1970s[3] but, with exceptions such as *Wolf Creek*, they rarely break through into the mainstream, circulating through alternative production and distribution channels.)

There is usually seen to be a limited repertoire of options for filmmaking in Australia. Should the strategy be about making 'grown-up' films[4] (addressed to the adult metropolitan middle classes with some potential for their sale to art house circuits internationally), making genre retreads (which can circulate in broader demographics, including cult circuits, but have lower status and less potential for government backing), or prioritising higher budget and therefore mostly internationally financed and owned projects which have industry development effects locally? These debates are still very much with us during the 'perpetual crisis' of the Australian film industry.

Chapter 1

(1989) The decades of survival: Australian cinema 1930–70

To think of the forty-odd years from the end of the silent period to the beginnings of the contemporary Australian cinema is to be reminded of how fragile are the indigenous traditions on which the so-called 'revival' rests. Taking simply feature films, the period since 1970 has seen easily three times the number made in Australia during 1930–70. Also, feature-film output in the silent period had at least a consistency, variety and continuity about it. The four decades under question here were the 'decades of survival', a long period during which feature production might be said to have *persisted* in the face of, at times, severe constraints. The reasons advanced to explain this are usually variations of the so-called 'media' or 'cultural imperialism' thesis. Australia and its cultural production have been the losers in an unequal exchange with dominant economic and cultural powers, principally the United States. Studies of the Australian cinema, especially those of John Tulloch,[1] have demonstrated a much greater and more interesting complexity of relations of domination and subordination than this thesis would allow.

One of the most intriguing ways that this thesis has been modified is by a more searching attention to the means by which a 'dominated' culture's negotiation of its status is registered in the products of that culture themselves. This chapter pays particular attention to a selection of films from the 'decades of survival', chosen for, among other reasons, their varied but always engaging strategies of negotiation, of making sense, of the (itself historically variable) status of Australia as an 'import culture'. It can be no more than a selection, and a selection based on an internal division of the period that emphasises breaks and changes rather than thematic continuities across this long time-span. Each section begins with a brief justification of the purpose of the subdivision, and proceeds to discuss the films selected.

The 1930s: The Empire connection

One of the ways in which the media imperialism thesis oversimplifies the struggles of the Australian film industry is to construct a bilateral 'David and Goliath' scenario, the places respectively taken by Australia and the Hollywood 'octopus'. Instead, we need to note Tulloch's characterisation of the industry of the 1920s and 1930s as existing in a triangular relationship subtended by 'competing imperialisms', or, more precisely, by American media imperialism and British colonialism.[2] Indeed, notwithstanding the ever-present weight exerted both industrially and stylistically by Hollywood in Australia, the cinema of the 1930s should be seen as a moment of resurgent British, and Empire, influence. This, to be sure, was a 'last hurrah' for Empire, or, as Tulloch puts it, alluding to the Depression and the rapidly shifting allegiances that the Second World War would occasion, 'Australian cinema of the 1930s was especially articulate in its voicing of the British connection, precisely because the transparent value of that connection had for the first time been seriously thrown into doubt.'[3]

Nevertheless, the last hurrah yielded some significant voices. Basically, the 'Empire connection' should be seen as developing in fertile soil: Australia, along with other British dominions such as Canada, New Zealand and South Africa, and other settler societies such as Argentina along with neighbouring South American nations was, and is, positioned in the world politico-economic system as a 'second world' nation, a society established on, and drawing from, the social and cultural heritage of its founder nation of the 'first world', but positioned economically in ways that closely resembled 'third world' nations. It is to be expected that an enduring characteristic of such societies would be overcompensatory displays of allegiance to a displaced heritage found jostling with an uncertain degree of subversion of it. Much of the social debate that the fledgling cinema industry aroused, around questions of censorship for instance, centred on the degree of erosion of 'British' values that it constituted. These kinds of debate were at the forefront during the Royal Commission into the Moving Picture Industry in 1927–28.

This Royal Commission was also important in that it was the first in a decade-long series of attempted and mostly abortive state interventions in the film industry that sought to follow Britain's, and other European countries', lead in the establishment of quotas and other legislative and production plans as 'nationalist' responses to the (by the late 1920s) achieved international dominance of Hollywood. New South Wales and Victoria, which by the 1930s were the only states in which feature production was pursued, enacted quota legislation, following the precedent established in Britain and New Zealand. Through the 1930s most Australian features reached the British market under the protective umbrella of its quota legislation (Cinesound, Greater Union's production company in the 1930s, based its international marketing strategies almost entirely on these conditions) and many of the problems associated with the New South Wales legislation in particular concerned confusions over possible non-reciprocity for British films in the Australian market.

British film production underwent a marked resurgence in the aftermath of its late 1920s quota legislation, its market share in

Australia reaching 27.1 per cent in 1934, after several years of strong growth.[4] This revival fuelled dreams of coordinated 'Empire' production and preferential marketing; several large-scale plans for such a strategy involved well-placed British loyalists in Australia. Perhaps the most elaborate of these plans to come to a degree of fruition was the establishment of National Productions and National Studios in 1935. The National plan for wide-ranging reciprocal arrangements with other local independent producers and with Gaumont-British in England conjured up a 'last colonial dream'[5] of Empire solidarity in the face of the dominance of Hollywood.

Such instances of the 'Empire connection' in the 1930s could be multiplied. What is significant about them, however, is the way they underline an active, albeit predictable and limited, negotiation on the part of a small and vulnerable industry for the places it might occupy on the screens and in the boardrooms of an 'import culture'.

The films of the 1930s have often been regarded as the most conservative of a generally conservative film heritage. Beneath their bland surfaces, however, a good deal of textual perturbation and negotiation of cultural process takes place, much of it concerned to articulate Australia's colonial or dominion status. Several are simply set in England, or have narratives concerned with inheritance or heritage in which characters journey to England or vice versa: *Diggers in Blighty* (1933), *Two Minutes Silence* (1933), *The Silence of Dean Maitland* (1934), *Clara Gibbings* (1934), *Splendid Fellows* (1934), *It Isn't Done* (1937). Others play out, often as comedies of manners, displaced British class values within Australian (or, as is the case in *His Royal Highness* (1932), fantasy) settings: *The Hayseeds* (1933), *Lovers and Luggers* (1937), some of the Dad and Dave series of films made by Cinesound. Some films, such as those of Charles Chauvel, attempt to essay large-scale worlds of colonial endeavour across very different settings: *In the Wake of the Bounty* (1933), *Heritage* (1935), *Uncivilised* (1936). Let us consider some of this range of films in more detail.

Chauvel's films are the most explicit projects from this period exploring the conditions of colonial existence. The singular connection between Chauvel's 'naive', overreaching or 'high melodramatic' style of filmmaking and the difficult and paradoxical conditions of colonial identity produced three extraordinary films: *In the Wake of the Bounty*, *Heritage* and *Uncivilised*. *In the Wake of the Bounty*, for example, is a 'moral tract'[6] that tells the story of the mutiny on the *Bounty*. It essays the argument that the attempt to sever the tie with the mother country in order to establish an autonomous society in 'utopia' will result in dystopic distortions and an overcompensatory reinvestment in the values of the mother country. (*In the Wake of the Bounty* is explored in Chapter 3.)

A similar, if less wide-ranging, 'colonial' theme can be observed by turning to the most prolific and successful filmmaker active in the decade. *It Isn't Done*, a 1937 Cinesound film directed by Ken Hall, concerns the fortunes of one Hubert Blaydon, an Australian farmer who unexpectedly inherits an English baronial estate, and his family's relation to British social values – what 'is' and 'isn't done'. The film appears a solid, routine Cinesound vehicle for one of its more accomplished male leads, Cecil Kellaway, and features Hall's well-established light entertainment, the 'comedy of manners', the narrative turning on 'fish out of water' routines. Certainly Hall, in reminiscent interviews and during the time of production of his seventeen features for Cinesound, forswore any explicit commitment to projects of 'national definition', which were relegated to categories of 'art' and uncommercial indulgence. However, notwithstanding Hall's disclaimers, the output of Cinesound during the 1930s, with Hall at the helm, deals consistently with metropolis–colony relations, if only, in many films, at the level of the 'comedy of manners'. There may not be as strong a claim to be made for the authorial, when considered with the social and industrial, weight behind such a project as may be claimed for Chauvel, or indeed for charm and eccentricity, when compared with Beaumont Smith. Nevertheless, in a film such as *It Isn't Done*, a complex interweave of such relations, central to what counts as 'Australian' cinema, is inscribed.

Consider the symmetry of characterisation. Hubert is paired with Lord Denvee as respective 'national' patriarchs, Min Blaydon and Lady Denvee as their wives, and the 'false' Australians the Dudleys are paired with the Ashtons, lower-class English who demonstrate 'Australian' values in the course of the narrative. But it is the transformations and substitutions that provide the motor of the narrative, and the discursive claims that emerge from it. Hubert, played by Cecil Kellaway in one of the most achieved performances of 1930s cinema, moves from unassuming Australian farmer to English lord and back again, largely carrying the film's shifts of tone – comedy, farce, drama, sermonising – with him. He is indisputably the rightful heir, although the contingency of the inheritance is significantly stressed. However, in the central of many neat paradoxes in the film, he 'bastardises' himself in order that his daughter might attain an inheritance in her new 'home' country, by falsifying his mother's name, thus delegitimating his place in English class society. The script does not shy from a piece of rather radical Australian humour in implying, in as explicit a fashion as possible, that the real bastardry here is the English class system. 'Natural' lord is substituted for class lord.

Patricia Blaydon, Hubert's daughter, moves across the national and class divide, but the film's argument is that this will involve an 'Australianising' of the class system. She rejects the 'false', class-oriented, Australian Ronald Dudley and marries the English 'working man' Peter Ashton, after he has passed Hubert's test of what counts as 'class' in Australia, thus assuming Hubert's inheritance. To balance this 'loss', the returning Blaydons gain Jarms, the quintessential English butler turned Australian egalitarian.

However, the final reconciliation is not achieved around comic substitutions and mannerly upstagings but around what was believed to 'truly' effect dissolutions of class and colonial difference: war. *It Isn't Done* trails gestures towards this theme and then secures it at the end when, unbeknown to each, the Denvees and the Blaydons commemorate the deaths, on the same day in the First World War, of their soldier sons Jeffrey and James. This, the film invites us to believe, is the ground on which a 'legitimate' commonality can be found.

The symmetries are not absolute, of course. The (colonial) paradox of this film is that, even though it is the Australian characters, or those who assume a delegated Australian identity by marriage (Peter Ashton) or by superior insight and identification (Jarms), who undergo transformation, and are thus those on whom the narrative turns, it is the English upper classes whose moral universe remains 'unmoved' and, moreover, who have 'hosted' the transformations. It is only by meeting this universe on its own *terms* that the derived moral universe of the Antipodes can be affirmed. Any reciprocal shift presaged for the metropolis is displaced 'outside' the film, into the future, in the marriage of Patricia and Peter.

The 1940s to mid-1950s: Australian innovation

The 'Empire connection' did not, of course, evaporate in the decades following the 1930s. Indeed, as we will see, the influence of the so-called British documentary movement was determinative during this second period. However, the thematic preoccupations of Australian features certainly shift markedly after an understandably necessary high point of Empire concerns during the Second World War. We will find more consistent articulations of discourses of nationality disengaged from their moorings in Empire–colony concerns. Along with thematic considerations, however, the stress in this section is placed on stylistic innovation. It is a 'bounded' innovation characteristic of an import culture, to be sure, derivative of international ensembles themselves struggling to mark out a place over against the

Hollywood paradigm, but innovation that had a remarkable effect of expanding the conceptual and stylistic horizons of the Australian cinema.

It is important to stress this aspect because the recurring metaphors writers have employed to characterise the period after the war and through the 1960s focus on failure and emptiness: 'the long stagnation' (Lawson), 'interval' (Molloy), 'into the void' (Shirley and Adams), 'bust' (Pike).[7] It is true that the severity of production circumstance during this period cannot be gainsaid. Rationing, emergency measures and loss of personnel to the war effort occasioned virtual cessation of feature production in the years 1940–45. Later, financial restrictions instituted by the new Menzies government in 1951 put paid to a number of promising feature projects, including those of the doyen of the 1930s, Ken Hall. Factually representative of the period were the start and deepening of conservative rule under Menzies and its attendant cultural blackout and mass exodus of film and other cultural talent from Australia; the direct and more covert effects of Cold War anti-leftism on both documentary and feature workers; the exits of the powerful Australian exhibitor Greater Union and the innovative British company Ealing from systematic production plans in the late 1940s and early 1950s; the effects of television and of international financial control and interest in the local distribution–exhibition sector producing an even more entrenched indifference towards support for Australian production than before; and the highly symbolic scandals of certain American 'location' films, particularly *Kangaroo* (1952) and *On the Beach* (1959), dangling the carrot of Hollywood largesse before largely excluded local film workers.

The culmination? During the years under consideration, around two or three features, on average, were made annually, and many of these were produced, directed and/or financed by the English, Americans or, later, the French and the Japanese. This output was constant for nearly thirty years, or more than one-third of the time films have been made here. However, these elements still don't secure a verdict of achieved 'cultural imperialism'. The factors of locally induced breakdown, as well as locally inspired adaptation and resistance, are too significant to overlook.

There is, considering that severely limited output, an exciting range of film style, format and experimentation compared with earlier periods of more sustained feature production.[8] This can be attributed to two influences: the integration of classical documentary methods and approaches to thematic material, and the first marked effects of the international art cinema on Australian filmmaking. Harry Watt's first two ground-breaking films made for Ealing in Australia, *The Overlanders* (1946) and *Eureka Stockade* (1949), Ralph Smart's *Bitter Springs* (1950), again for Ealing, and the feature documentary *The Back of Beyond* (1954) by John Heyer were hallmarks of the first influence and Ron Maslyn Williams's *Mike and Stefani* (1952) was an excellent example of the second. Putting these two vectors together with a more explicit socialist humanism than usually informed them produced two of the most politically and stylistically innovative reworkings of nationalist archetypes both for the time and subsequently – Cecil Holmes's *Captain Thunderbolt* (1953) and *Three in One* (1957). And through this period the great 'stayer' of the Australian cinema, Charles Chauvel, was making his greatest films: *Forty Thousand Horsemen* (1940), *Sons of Matthew* (1949) and *Jedda* (1955). Australian features were never more bridled with industrial uncertainty, yet never more innovative!

The Back of Beyond is an outstanding feature documentary: it traces the journeying of Tom Kruse, the mailman on the Birdsville Track in one of the most remote areas of white settlement in Australia. It is well accepted that the film belongs within the stylistic category of that form of documentary inaugurated by the 'British documentary movement' while being, in the words of Ross Gibson, 'a very peculiar adaptation' of that tradition.[9] But the *theme* of the film is wholly concerned with adaptation as well: how does white Australian frontier society survive in this most inhospitable of ecologies? So, let us play on the word 'adaptation'. *The Back of Beyond* is a superb example of an import culture's adaptation of the conventions of its master stylistic ensemble, the British documentary, insofar as it has found a means of adapting its style to the theme of adaptation.

The Back of Beyond works within the stylistic perimeters associated with the British documentary. These include 'voice-of-God' narration that organises a conventional hierarchy of sound over image, the idea that the 'core' or 'slice' of Australian society that forms the story material of the film is somehow representative of the whole nation, and praise for civic responsibility as a moral 'given'. However, it works significant adaptations of them. Gibson calls its narrative 'minimalist, humble';[10] it could be called 'delegated'. Within a world where survival turns on the necessity to 'tell stories', there is a concerted attempt to delegate authority *from* the God-like narrator *to* the humble storytellers within the film's world (the mailmen, the succession of women who 'communicate' with Tom and his offsiders by two-way radio to the next station, Malcolm, the Aborigine, who retells his past in the area, the Birdsville policeman entering in his diary). Delegation is tied up with an awareness of a gap between the conventions of the British documentary (which produce a romanticisation of heroic civic toil, a heightened degree of typification of character, narrative linearity, and the clear authority of the narrator) and the social and geographical conditions under which these people live their lives. 'Adapting' an aesthetic of romanticisation, there is a consistent *de-dramatisation* carried in the characters' social gestures. Characterisation itself is minimal in the extreme. The superstructure of narrative is classically linear, but the digressions within that superstructure are roomy and at times scarcely motivated by narrative imperatives. A result of these adaptive strategies, as has been asserted, is a degree of delegation of authority to the actual people who survive in this world. *The Back of Beyond* has found stylistic gestures appropriate to the theme of ecological minimalism in the Australian environment.

Consider an example of this de-dramatisation. This is the sequence where the mail truck is bogged en route out of Marree. Tom and his offsider, William, are travelling at night. The headlights train on a world of threateningly ghostly gum trees. The truck is bogged. The musical motif of the film, the surreal carefree Tin Pan Alley record, plays on the soundtrack, accompanying the men's equally carefree reminiscences about breakdown disasters and their ironically makeshift remedies; shot scale, camera placement and editing position them and their situation as the objects of predatory gazes and among symbols of extinction – the dingo and snake, the cattle skull. Like all major transitions in this film, the reprise to end this sequence is a marked enlargement of shot scale that drives a wedge between the narrative situation and the spectator's grasp of a vast environment – in other words, of involvement *in*, or placement *outside*, the drama of character and situation. The little drama of the predators is not sustained; indeed, we find out much later, when Tom is talking to Jack the Dogger, that he has taken full cognisance of the presence of the dingo, and thus the characters' vulnerability during the 'night bog' sequence has to be reread retrospectively. And this is the case in a number of sequences in the film.

No better example than *The Back of Beyond* can be offered of Elsaesser's notion[11] that social and historical conditions in a particular nation might create conditions for a negotiated difference from the prevailing stylistic paradigm – in this case, the British documentary. However, documentary-dramas, most notably *The Overlanders*, display a similar reframing of the British tradition.

Harry Watt, *The Overlanders*' director, had been a major contributor to the British documentary tradition. During the war in Britain, and then later in Australia for Ealing, he had pursued recreations, fictionalisings, in short, dramatisation of the classical documentary, for which he was criticised by the tradition's 'purists' in both countries. On the other hand, he was no ideological and stylistic fellow-traveller of the classical Hollywood style, injecting a strongly collectivist-cum-socialist spirit into both his Australian films, *The Overlanders* and *Eureka Stockade*. In this, he was certainly in concert with the ethos of 'Australian innovation' in the postwar cinema. Let us look at the way *The Overlanders* steers a path through these two import ensembles in the creation of a 'classic' Australian film.

The film, set in 1942 in northern Australia, details the story of a 'mass migration unique in history', the movement of cattle herds 2400 kilometres from north-west Western Australia to central Queensland so that they would not fall into the hands of the Japanese. In gross, the film could be read as a western adventure story; certainly there are enough sequences of 'action-spectacle' centring on the hazards of the drove and the courage and toughness of the cattlemen and women. However, the film is at pains to distance itself from its Hollywood generic 'cousin'. To a young Scottish sailor ('Sinbad') struck by the romance of the project, Dan McAlpine (Chips Rafferty) retorts that 'we don't carry guns to shoot up rustlers'. When the same neophyte drover attempts to drive cattle out of a bog, instead of dismounting and walking them out, Dan shouts at him 'Don't try to be a cowboy!' And, in the film's dramatic climax which involves a stand-off between the thirst-crazed mob and three of the drovers, the company's comedian, Corky, is heard to mutter about Dan, 'What the hell's he waiting for, the whites of their eyes?'

But *The Overlanders*' distance from Hollywood can be more thoroughly measured structurally. The film is as intent on imparting information (remember the British documentary's notion of civic education) as it is on captivating with spectacle. Thus, Chips Rafferty's role is split between fictional crux of the narrative, the laconic man of few words and emphatic actions, and documentary voice-over, dispensing detailed knowledge of the technicalities of droving with an earnest loquaciousness. (Rafferty was considered, on the basis of this and his earlier wartime film roles in Hall's documentaries and Chauvel's *Forty Thousand Horsemen* and *The Rats of Tobruk* (1944), as 'the Australian Everyman, in speech, action, and character'.[12]) Moreover, the characterisation of Dan McAlpine does not push masculine individualism to its limit, as would be expected in imitations of the western genre. Watt is very careful to incorporate an active 'bush heroine', Mary Parsons, into the core droving group, and to privilege her horse-riding and droving prowess in certain set-piece action sequences such as her race to the departing plane. In general, the importance to the project of the women, the child Helen Parsons and the black drovers Jacky and Nipper are underscored at various points in the narrative, nowhere more emphatically than during the breakaway of the cattle mob when Sinbad is hurt and Mary and Jacky save the day.

Indeed, the main characters are formed, across the duration of the narrative, into a de facto social microcosm that 'allows' the film to demonstrate the need for a collectivist approach to issues of national development and response to emergency. Apart from the incorporation of age, gender and racial sectors already mentioned, the white males in the 'collective' – Corky, the English remittance man, Sinbad, the disaffected Scottish sailor, and the individualist Australians Charlie and Bert – are either 're-educated' to participate functionally or 'shown the door'. The 'national importance' of such a project of overlanding is emphasised, not merely by the prologue but by the inscription of classical documentary tropes into the fictional surface. Dan proceeds on his overlanding adventure only with the commission of the company's administrator; the need for administrative intervention (the plane with the inoculation officers) is treated not only as grudgingly necessary but as the occasion for potential assistance when Sinbad is injured; and the government minister's speech at the end is shot in such a way as to provide an appropriate contextualisation of the project. Perhaps most emphatically, it is Dan's reply to Corky's 'get-rich-quick' scheme for a 'Northern

Territory Exploitation Company' that secures this national collectivism: development, he argues stridently, is 'a national job, too big for little people like you'.

The Overlanders' stylistic strategies also work to negotiate a path between fictional modes and documentary modes. Concerning the latter, you might observe the intensive location shooting, to the extent of the difficulty of *seeing* what is happening during the cattle breakout scene, which was shot night-for-night. Then there is the principle of rarely framing closer than mid-shot and more usually in three-shot and long shot, which de-individualises and de-dramatises while undergirding the notion of collective characterisation. Finally, the film has an episodic narrative structure which foregrounds the task-by-task overcoming of obstacles rather than individual psychologies.

Compare the one occasion when the close-up is employed as a crux of camera work and editing to dramatise events, the climactic stand-off between the drovers and the mob, with a very similar sequence in *Red River* (Howard Hawks, 1948). In the latter, a climactic stampede scene is shot with its wide shots 'on location' but its close-ups of the principals in process or studio shots. The drama is an opportunity for the characters to demonstrate riding prowess; the principals of *The Overlanders* dismount to face their major narrative test. The Hollywood film characteristically 'over-dramatises' the natural test by having a main character trampled in the stampede; the threat in *The Overlanders* is survived with a laconic joke.

The strength of the experiments in documentary-drama during this time is borne out in a range of further features, such as *Mike and Stefani* and *Sons of Matthew*. However, this intensity of innovation trailed off in the later years of the 1950s under the pressures of industrial uncertainty and the marginalisation of feature production in Australia.

The mid-1950s and the 1960s: International co-production

This period is usually regarded as the lowest point the Australian cinema reached. In some ominous years in the 1960s not one feature was made. Even the sort of 'positive' reframing that this chapter attempts would typically read the 1960s, for instance, as a time in which the groundwork for the 'revival' was being developed, rather than a period of production as such, just as the late 1950s would be considered as the beginning of a new audiovisual culture with television rather than the end of the second generation of feature film production.[13] A good many of the general industrial parameters pertinent to this period have already been canvassed in the previous section. Continuing the focus on feature production, a general consolidation of factors noted earlier may be seen: feature film faded from agenda-setting debates as television appropriated centre stage; there was further reduction of independent exhibition and even the remotest interest in local production as the major conglomerates, Greater Union and Hoyts, rationalised operations in the 'long siege' with television;[14] and a similar consolidated dominance of now almost exclusively American distribution interests completed the picture 'in the trade'. Even the potential difference of 'quality' art cinema (quaintly dubbed 'Continental' at the time) was diffused and marginalised by indifferent and misconceived marketing.

How, then, was it conceivable for Australian filmmakers to go on working? Never forgetting that film production during this period consisted for the most part of commercials, newsreels and sponsored documentaries, the most significant model established for the feature was the 'co-production'. It is not that this model necessarily produced the 'best' films of the period, but that it was a model in which local production concerns and principals enjoyed more than marginal engagement, and for this reason, and that such films have received scant attention in writings on the Australian cinema, the model repays consideration.

Of interest here are the co-productions entered into by the Southern International company, later Australian Television Enterprises, of which the principals were Chips Rafferty and Lee Robinson: *Walk into Paradise* (1956), *The Stowaway* (1958) and *The Restless and the Damned* (1959), and a much later example of the model in which both Rafferty and Robinson figured, *They're a Weird Mob* (1966). The Robinson–Rafferty partnership represents the first ongoing Australian engagement with international co-production: a significant development in the wake of the slow demise of the Hollywood studio system and the emergence and acceptance of different modes of film production and practice. The Southern International project should be clearly distinguished from the varieties of 'location' filmmaking in Australia in the period (the Ealing features *The Overlanders* (1946), *Eureka Stockade* (1949), *Bitter Springs* (1950), *The Shiralee* (1957) and *The Seige of Pinchgut* (1959), and the American films *Kangaroo* (1952), *Summer of the Seventeenth Doll* (1959) and *On the Beach* (1959) and others) in terms of the degree of production control exercised by the local protagonists.

The paradoxes of this project, however, indicate something of the continuing relevance of our theme of cultural dependency in an import culture. Production control was exercised by Australians in partnership with French (not British or American) interests, but was turned definitively away from local exposure in the light of negligible exhibition potential. The demise of what was initially a successful project was due more to financial overreaching and the internal management of the co-production arrangements than to any more global 'cultural imperialist' notion of disempowerment of Australian film production. It is a project, essentially, of 'exploitation' filmmaking – exploitation of the antipodean as exoticism which nevertheless bears important elements of nationally specific concerns, such as the fortunes of Chips Rafferty's career, Australia's only 'international film star'[15] before the contemporary period. Made for the lower end of the international film market, the films nevertheless had lavish budgets by Australian standards. Basically 'formula' dramas, they still contain traces of the documentary 'look' that infused the more arresting features of the late 1940s and early 1950s. The problematic industrial status of *Walk into Paradise*, *The Stowaway* and *The Restless and the Damned* is clearly underlined by fascinating stylistic disjunctions. Each film involves a story of white colonial adventure against a 'backdrop' of exotic South Pacific locales, which are treated in stylistic terms as a form of documentary spectacle. But these films are far from the 'integrated' documentary-drama style of some of the earlier films discussed. They, and especially the latter two, employ the overwrought character and narrative structure of the sub-genre known as the 'family' or 'domestic' melodrama current during the 1950s in Hollywood, but insert it into a kind of travelogue scenography that works decisively against the hothouse drama typical of this sub-genre. There is a lugubrious predictability about the staging of each dialogue scene (occasioned partly by the necessity of shooting simultaneous dual language versions for the French- and English-speaking markets) that is broken only by the foregrounding of the panoramic documentary 'look' of their locales – the New Guinea highlands, Panama, Tahiti.

Take *The Restless and the Damned* (known in France as *L'Ambitieuse* and as *The Dispossessed* in Britain). It concerns the story of Dominique, a character-type straight from the domestic melodrama, who plots in extraordinarily complex ways to take over the mining operations of her husband George Rancourt's family in Tahiti. To achieve her 'ambitions' she must seduce, plot and finally kill and be killed. One of her first moves is to befriend and indebt to her Timothy, the foreman at the phosphate mine run by Buchanan, a potential rival to the Rancourt business, whom Dominique must neutralise (she later 'allows' Buchanan to seduce her to further her plans). But before this narrative premise is clear a scene ensues in which Dominique takes a sick child across a sea, through jungle and finally to the hospital, where she collapses from the enormous exertion! This is a scene of high drama, but it is not staged as such. Instead, the documentary 'look' dominates: languid cutting, with no analytical editing to emphasise facial gesture, extreme long shots of the tiny boat at sea, no 'mood' music. It is a long scene of eviscerated drama, with no narrative premise until we learn, in the succeeding scene, that the child is Timothy's grandson!

Or consider a central psychological strut of the film, the marriage of Dominique and George, the 'ambitious woman' and the 'weak husband'. The marriage undergoes the 'usual' (usual for the Hollywood model on which it is based, in films such as *Written on the Wind*) peripatetics, tied into affairs, seductions, business fortunes, and to abrupt shifts of emotional tenor. Its dissolution builds to a climax as George demands a divorce, Dominique faints and falls to the floor, comatose, and the unrepentant husband squashes a cockroach next to his prone wife! Dominique, reckoning that her financial ambitions cannot be realised if George succeeds in divorcing her, plots his death against the 'background' of beatific natives going to church! George goes out hunting goats, and the blood of these over-determined symbols of slaughter is mixed with that of their hunter as Dominique shoots him. Dying, he shoots her. However, the emotional crescendo having been reached, the characters are positioned in a series of extreme long shots as they stumble to their respective deaths across a 'spectacular' rocky redoubt. The melodramatic denouement becomes the sweeping look of the travelogue.

The character of Dominique, as a reviewer remarked, is a 'complicated' one,[16] but the cinematic articulation required to represent psychological density 'fades' and is displaced in *The Restless and the Damned*. Moreover, the colonial situations that comprise the worlds of all three films are rendered as little more than 'colourful' background material, when they are not the premises for a quite distressingly perfunctory racism. Although the narratorial prologue to *The Restless and the Damned* claims that in the midst of a rapacious and debasing white presence the 'natives' retain their dignity, this is contradicted throughout the film in the way such 'dignity' is treated merely as perfunctory 'background', and 'local colour' as intersequential linkages between the central narrative of white depradation. So, on both counts – articulations of documentary and drama, and the essaying of the colonial situation – the co-productions seem less achieved, and for good reason, than other projects discussed here.

In many ways *They're a Weird Mob* (1966) presents a very different set of issues of co-production from those of the Southern International ventures. Its British principals were the *auteurs manques*, Michael Powell and Emetic Pressburger, treating an established Australian popular novel by John O'Grady (Nino Culotta). A strange amalgam indeed, but the film commands attention for the way it was carried on such a groundswell of local support. Pike and Cooper remind us that:

> no criticism from the press could erode the novelty for Australians of seeing a home-grown entertainment. After a long 'drought', with no substantial local involvement in Australian feature production for about seven years, the film was eagerly awaited and received much free advance publicity. The film became the focus of a new wave of pressure on the government to provide financial support for the industry.[17]

So *They're a Weird Mob* is a fitting film with which to conclude our discussion of the 'decades of survival', pointing as it does, Janus-like, backward to the international co-productions of the late 1950s and forward to the kind of creature of state subvention that the films of the revival were.

Despite primarily British creative control, the film was promoted and received as an aggressively 'Australian' feature. But such cultural assertion could probably be read from hindsight as muted and qualified. The film, following the book closely, concerns Nino Culotta, an Italian emigrant to Australia who has to take work as a builder's labourer when his profession, journalism, is closed to him in the film's humorous opening sequences. His orientation to the social mores, linguistic peculiarities and work routines of his 'mates' provides further broad comedy. His romance with Kay Kelly, once he overcomes the misgivings of her father, blossoms into marriage plans.

'They're a weird mob'? The film's address is uncertain; at times it is an unsettling ethnographer's gaze at the rituals that bind a social fraction together, at others a wholehearted endorsement of the authenticity of such rituals, all bound together with the ironic self-deprecation of 'Australian' humour. The film might be read as an early harbinger of the yet-to-be officially inscribed discourse of multiculturalism, with its point of enunciation being the estranged view of Nino trying to come to terms with both cultural displacement and class displacement. It could simultaneously be read as a forerunner of the 'ocker' film of the early 1970s in terms of its aggressive yet self-deprecating endorsement of the 'Australian way of life'. It doesn't, however, attempt to separate out these potential frictions, but binds them over into a comic assimilationist utopia of class and ethnic harmony.

The film also resembles the early revival films stylistically, its thin weave of episodic narrative around the romance of Nino and Kay allows for ample displays of cultural idiosyncrasy and an allied profusion of cameo appearances by Australian show-business names. But the episodic quality of the main body of the film makes no claims to a principle of narrative difference in the direction of the art cinema, as the early revival 'period' or 'costume drama' films do. Rather, the meandering ethnographer's purview is displaced in the film's denouement by a strong sense of narrative closure.

Nino goes to get permission to marry Kay from her father, played by the icon of 'Australianness', Chips Rafferty, who, it has already been established, resents 'dago' migrants with a passion. Chips, framed in threateningly exaggerated low angles, is won over by the Australian directness of the 'new Australian'. 'The

Pope a dago!' Chips hurrumps. 'Christ was born in a stable', Nino counters. Father admits he started as a bricklayer, just like Nino. Nino expounds the Australian dream: in a 'new' country, a man can be whatever he likes. Nino wants sons. Father approves. Kay wants daughters. There is then an 'answering' scene when Kay, the 'rich girl', meets Nino's working-class mates, who try to impress her with their attempts at couthness. This scene resolves itself into an 'egalitarian' booze-up. These two symmetrical scenes knit together frictions of ethnicity, gender, the generations, religion and national identification in a 'successful' negotiation and presentation of a 'weird mob'.

Chapter 2

(1991) Approaching Chauvel

In order to approach Charles Chauvel's career and his films, adequate models of film history and Australian culture are needed. What are the relationships that exist between culture and society, the film industry, an individual production career, and film style? The question of Australian cinema history must also be addressed, to assess the industrial and stylistic consequences of the international dominance of Hollywood from the late 1910s, and to place the Australian cinema in the world context.

What is Chauvel's place within the Australian cinema? Is his 'voice' a distinctive one? Do his career and films typify the conditions under which the cinema has existed in Australia? And what are the connections *between* his career and his films, beyond a mere 'life and works' approach?

Film history

Film history has been called a 'narrow discourse' and has been likened to a pre-paradigmatic or primitive science.[1] Robert Allen,

Edward Buscombe and others[2] have presented the problems and challenges arising in the reconstruction of film history. These are usefully summarised in David Bordwell's conclusion to his study of Japanese film history.[3] Primary data (studio records, trade and fan magazines, government documentation, film reviews, and so on) need to be researched and assessed. No longer can film history be constituted by the accretion of directors' career surveys. Social histories of film fail on two counts. By considering that films merely reflect society, they assume too much, and by seldom addressing industrial and textual specifics, they explain too little. According to Bordwell, what is needed is a 'totalized view' that embraces 'the complex interaction of economic and cultural factors that define cinema as a social practice'.[4]

We can get a good sense of the lie of the land by considering the strengths and weaknesses of a textbook aimed at the burgeoning area of film studies, Robert Allen and Douglas Gomery's *Film History: Theory and Practice*.[5] Though a textbook, it is also a polemic against what hitherto have passed as introductions to film history:

> Our subject in this book is the historical study of film itself . . . Our students were all too eager to regard what they read in film history books as the single, indisputable truth, and most of them thought it heretical to question the film historian's methods, philosophical orientation, evidence, or conclusions. Survey texts contributed to the problem by remaining silent as to the process by which historical questions are posed, research conducted, evidence analysed, and generalisations drawn (pp. iii–iv).

While Allen and Gomery's book provides a clear blueprint for a new approach to film history, significant gaps and omissions are apparent in the approach the authors adopt. They quarantine contemporary developments in film theory from a full engagement with film history. Their brief two-page discussion of 'Semiotics and

Film History' merely notes that 'semiotics is not a theory of film *history* per se, but its acceptance as a theory of film in general among film scholars over the past decade has far-reaching implications for film history.'[6] Important psychoanalytic approaches to film studies are separated from this presentation of semiotics and installed in a chapter on 'Social Film History', partly, no doubt, because the challenging links established by psychoanalytic film analysis between the film text and its reception would have threatened the authors' own distinction between aesthetic and social film history.

This approach leads to a kind of smorgasbord offering of *separate* avenues of inquiry into film history. Attempts to relate film industry, text, reception and society to each other are put to one side in the book. For the most part, it centres on the exposition of four 'traditional approaches to film history': the aesthetic, the technological, the economic and the social. Only in the final chapter, an extended case study of cinéma vérité in America, entitled 'Reintegrating Film History', is there an attempt to bring these approaches together.

It is also notable that the authors concentrate almost exclusively on American film history and the historiography of Hollywood cinema. Primarily, this is in acknowledgement of the historical centrality of Hollywood's economic, aesthetic and cultural impact.[7] The question of non-American film history is broached rarely: only histories of film *reception* in the Third World are solicited, in order to combat cultural biases that conflate film history with film production in America and western Europe.[8] Films such as *La Hora de los Hornos* are cited merely as examples of Third World 'reactions' against Hollywood style.[9]

National cinemas

The dilemmas of film history become more evident when the question of national cinemas is considered. In traditional histories, national cinema is a category into which an imprecise jumble of 'great' auteurs and 'great' stylistic innovations are lumped. The history and the social and cultural structure of nations playing host to these outstanding directors or styles often appear irrelevant in these writings. Further difficulties arise when the evolving international structures of film distribution and, to a lesser extent, film production and exhibition are considered – without mentioning the major critique of nationality as a historical and theoretical given in the political analyses inspired by Marxist internationalism.

Well-known moments of national cinema (for example post-revolutionary Soviet cinema, French impressionism and the new wave, Italian neo-realism, the British documentary and 'Free Cinema', German expressionism and the new German cinema) were more or less marginal to mainstream film production, distribution and reception within their respective countries and times. It seems that the more aesthetic apogees are emphasised in traditional histories, the less emphasis is placed on a systematic political economy of film for these various nations and, by implication, on a political economy of film as such.

However, the concept of national cinema remains necessary, and useful, as long as it is delivered from this parlous state. It can be stiffened with programmatic political intent, as happens in Third World cinema theory inspired by the revisionist Marxism of Gramsci and Fanon. In this tradition, nationality has been posed as the proletarianisation of cinema practices by transnational capitalism.[10] It also can be used to 'break down' American cinema by focusing on Hollywood's hegemonic position in relation to independent practices *within* the United States and, further, by stressing the synthetic nature of Hollywood's aesthetic regimes, its bower-bird appropriation of the stylistic innovations and the personnel of various national cinemas. But, as a general principle, the concept of national cinema is best enhanced by highlighting the differing and often contradictory *constructions* of nationality in film practices.[11]

Much new film history has centred, for good reason, on Hollywood as the international paradigm of industrial organisation and textual form since the late 1910s. In one of the major works of this kind, David Bordwell, Janet Staiger and Kristin Thompson demonstrate that this cinema has been most successful in achieving a thorough and lasting synthesis of industry and text.[12] As Buscombe puts it: 'Such is the domination that Hollywood had imposed over world cinema that at times Hollywood appears to be . . . no longer a national cinema but *the* cinema, just as at a certain stage of development for the son the father is not a man amongst others but manhood itself.'[13]

Buscombe suggests that any history of Hollywood might validly include discussion of the structured dominance of its preferred modes of production, distribution and exhibition for countries that fall within its virtually universal sphere of influence.[14] But this equation of structured dominance could equally well be reversed, with histories of national cinemas recognising the extent to which their object is the history of the reception and adoption of Hollywood film style, modes of production and dissemination.[15]

The relationships between national cinemas and Hollywood should be advanced in a more subtle fashion than the widespread tendency to regard non-Hollywood filmmaking either as poor imitation or brave independence. Hollywood then may be seen as the crucial 'background set' for most other feature filmmaking, and

> . . . we can start to grasp intertextual relations beyond the hackneyed divisions of nation, movement and school. A conception of norms and deviations lets us study the extent to which, with differences in devices, there was an international 'classicism' of narrative cinema that dominated the period from 1920 or so to the present and the extent to which national schools and individual filmmakers contributed to or reacted against that norm.[16]

Hollywood not only provided the stylistic norms, it also formed an inextricable element of the 'social imaginary', the cultural horizons, of filmmakers of the world.[17]

A central concern of this book is to mediate between film theory's emphasis on analyses of an indefinite series of individual texts and traditional social film history with its overly simplistic relating of text and society. On the one hand, the notion of a 'social imaginary' operating within a particular filmmaker's work moves us beyond textual boundaries. On the other hand, historicised textual criticism is well positioned to address the theoretical dilemmas of social film history, aptly summed up by Allen and Gomery in the following terms: 'Films are certainly cultural documents, but what they *document is* the complex relationship among reader, fictional text, author, and culture.'[18]

Australian film history

How does writing on Australian film history shape up in the light of these concerns? It can be broadly divided into three modes: the traditional approach, the transitional, and the theoretical.

The *traditional* mode of writing Australian film history could be characterised as excavatory, celebratory and polemical. Eric Reade's books *The Australian Screen, Australian Silent Films, The Talkies Era* and *History and Heartburn* and John Baxter's *The Australian Cinema*, along with the archival compilation films on early film history, *Forgotten Cinema, The Pictures That Moved, The Passionate Industry* and *Now You're Talking*,[19] saw themselves as relaying a story too long untold, to an important extent untold because of the lack of surviving film texts, especially from the silent period.[20] Baxter declares, 'The inflexible rules of chemistry have robbed us of our film history'.[21] These histories often take a polemical stance towards the relevance of such excavation, compilation and story-telling to the times and conditions in which they were writing, specifically the situation of the film industry in the late 1960s and early 1970s. A celebratory tone is evident in their belief that, since Australia once had a thriving indigenous industry, it can have one again.

Underpinning traditional histories is the notion of a boom-bust-boom cycle spanning the eighty years of the century, encapsulated in the words of Andrew Pike:

> The past, in terms of Australian feature film production, is a distant one. After a short burst of activity between 1910 and 1912, the production of feature films declined sharply and continued at a level of rarely more than 10 features a year until World War 2. Efforts to revive production after the disruptions caused by the war failed, and during the 1950s and 1960s *only* a few locally-made features were completed ... This period of inactivity ended abruptly, however, in 1970; new people had come to dominate production, beliefs in the nature of a viable industry had altered, and the films being made bore little resemblance to earlier work.[22]

While the facts cited in support of this cyclical topography are accurate, the argument is simplistic and distorting. By focusing exclusively on feature production, it fails to consider the complex relationships between feature, documentary, newsreel production and adjacent practices such as theatre, vaudeville and television. The so-called period of 'bust' in the decades after the Second World War was far from being one if the development of documentary in this period, and documentary's subsequent fruitful feeding into feature production, is considered. Further, this argument shows a limited conception of the various antecedents of contemporary Australian filmmaking. The so-called revival might have owed more to the success of the international art cinema, and to evolving government underwriting of the arts in Australia, than to a once-thriving film heritage.

This type of historiography also strikes a celebratory note in writing Australia into world cinema history in terms of particular aesthetic and stylistic high points. Australian film history was found to include neglected masterpieces (*The Sentimental Bloke*), great directors (Raymond Longford), action directors (Charles Chauvel), a popular production house (Cinesound in the 1930s), a front-runner in the international 'firsts' stakes *(The Kelly Gang*, 1906, for first feature film), and a peculiarly indigenous genre popular with audiences (the bushranger films).[23]

The transitional mode of writing Australian film history includes Sylvia Lawson's 'Toward Decolonisation', Susan Dermody's studies of industry and text in the early sound period, and Graham Shirley and Brian Adams's general history of Australian cinema.[24] Such work is transitional in that it exhibits characteristics of both the traditional and the theoretical modes.

John Tulloch's studies of Australian silent cinema, *Legends on the Screen: The Narrative Film in Australia 1919–1929* and *Australian Cinema: Industry, Narrative and Meaning*,[25] recast the assumptions governing traditional and transitional modes of writing history in a third, *theoretical*, mode. His declared interest is to shift the ground on which early Australian film history has been understood as the outcome of 'media imperialism'– as a series of courageous and often brilliant but ultimately ill-fated attempts to establish an indigenous industry in the face of increasingly effective American global dominance. The David and Goliath story minus the biblical consolation! The principal effect of this 'myth' of the Australian cinema is to mask the systemic means by which the early industry was organised to facilitate, indeed embrace, such dominance.

According to Tulloch, the media imperialism thesis has insufficient explanatory value:

> The dependent cinema industry needs, itself, to be considered as a working social system, composed of a dynamic interaction of goals, groups and traditions within it. This will enable us to look for conflict among its dominant groups, cracks within its dominant meanings, which the media imperialism thesis has hidden.[26]

For Tulloch, the media imperialism thesis 'tends to represent the dependent industry as a passive recipient rather than as a working system', thus downplaying the complexity of the local struggle. It tends to be monolithic and homogenising, minimising the differences of power *between* dependent countries. 'There was nothing automatic about Hollywood's ultimate control of Australian cinema. It was the result of competing imperialisms *within* Australia.' The Australian film industry was as much the object of British colonialism as of American imperialism. Finally, the thesis 'does not explain how the meanings of films are generated within the context of the film industry, even where it assumes the transmission of covert values and ideology'.[27]

The media imperialism thesis is rendered more subtly than in earlier accounts. Such imperialism was not generally understood or represented as imperialism by participants, but was consistently thought of as in the best interests of the industry, however much those interests shifted as a function of imperialising initiatives and responses to them by indigenous industry elites. It is the effective alignment of Australian interests with British and American interests, even as those latter interests shift and enter into competition, that characterises the Australian cinema's 'Second World' status.

It is necessary at this point to step back and consider Australia's status as a 'Second World', 'semi-peripheral' or 'dominion capitalist' nation in the global political economy. A major model in political economy that seeks to understand global asymmetries in economic and cultural exchange is dependency theory.[28] Developed for the most part to account for First World–Third World relations, dependency theory has demonstrated that linear models of imperialist domination of Third World countries by the First World are unable to account for the degree of penetration and absorption of First World values of practice by Third World cultures, or of the way in which such values are made over into what effectively function as Third World values. Further, dependency theory shows that, rather than unilaterally inhibiting the economic and cultural development of the Third World, First World–Third World exchange promotes a 'systematic development of underdevelopment': Third World countries may indeed, on many indicators, enhance their economic and cultural profile through First World–Third World exchange, but this simultaneously consolidates their dependent status in a global political economy.

Dependency theory can be modified to account for countries such as Australia, which are of neither the First World nor the Third World.[29] Australia has evolved, quite recently, into a post-colonial society, but, unlike many Third World nations, it is not post-revolutionary. Unlike Third World countries, dependence and political-economic development in Australia were not mutually exclusive. Likewise, complex relations of dependency, which cannot simply be posited as relations of domination and inhibition, informed fields of cultural production, such as the cinema, at every level.

Dependency theory thus provides a framework in which to pursue implications for national cinema histories. National cinemas are not aligned one with another in a uniform relation with Hollywood. They also enter into relations among themselves. The most pertinent of these relations for Australia was as a colony or dominion of the 'mother country' (Britain), which had significant effects for the Australian cinema, especially during the 1930s and 1940s. These effects are charted on the production career of Chauvel, as well as on the 'social imaginary' informing his film-making strategies.

Charles Chauvel and Australian film history

How might a theoretical account of the career and films of Chauvel be sustained? Chauvel's production career must be examined with a view to developing a detailed model of how relations of dependency placed him within production, distribution and exhibition circuits. Dependency theory also stresses reciprocal modes of resistance and intervention: Chauvel's strategic self-presentation, his use of notions of independence and their effects, and his interventions in public arenas such as film inquiries and commissions, will be analysed.

But how did an independent filmmaker, doubly marginalised within a production industry already marginalised in relation to established distribution and exhibition circuits, continue to make remarkable feature films, none of which were 'ordinary productions'[30] over a thirty-year period, part of which was characterised by major breakdowns of production in the Australian film industry as a whole? How did Chauvel's independence function in the Australian film industry of the period? With what purposes and with what effects did Chauvel contract relations with production, distribution and exhibition concerns and with state agencies? How did the notion of Chauvel as an 'author' figure within these historical and industrial conditions? In what ways and with what effects was the discourse of nationalist filmmaking deployed by Chauvel?

Nothing less than a properly historical and cultural account of authorship, independence and nationality within the operations of a dependent national cinema is needed. It is worthwhile to begin by looking at the three models of Australian film history, as previously outlined, in relation to Chauvel.

All traditional accounts of Chauvel face a problem of aesthetics, a problem that only certain writings from the theoretical category address productively. Traditional accounts distinguish between those few films and filmmakers that can be regarded highly according to traditional precepts of aesthetic quality, and the rest, which are treated according to slippery varieties of special pleading.

Both compilation films, *The Pictures that Moved* and *The Passionate Industry*, made a 'considerable hero' of Longford and 'strongly elevated his kind of filmmaking'.[31] Longford's works, along with Tal Ordell's *The Kid Stakes* and those few films that are regarded as typifying the bush myth, such as Franklyn Barrett's *The Breaking of the Drought*, are held to stand alone, their aesthetic and cultural value self-evident. Most other films of the first few decades of the Australian cinema are treated as the contingent by-products of a struggling production history or as instances of the nipping-in-the-bud of an early blooming, authentic national cinema. Chauvel is often represented as a promising filmmaker bedevilled by difficulties, both those of his own making and those endemic to film production, distribution and exhibition in Australia in general. Unsurprisingly, then, Chauvel misses out in the pantheon of directorial fame. John Baxter's assessment is harsher than most traditional accounts, but that is because the normative aesthetics of 1960s auteurist criticism are explicitly on show: 'Directness, simplicity, sentiment, a devotion to his homeland: admirable characteristics in a painter or an author, but in a filmmaker too frail to be the basis of a successful career.' 'Financially and artistically naive', says Baxter, Chauvel was never able to make an unflawed film (though *Sons of Matthew* comes close) and was tossed from pillar to post by unfavourable production circumstances and by greedy and unscrupulous distributors and exhibitors. Baxter's judgement damns with faint praise, and calls upon a comparison that was often made of Chauvel, but dismisses its relevance: 'Although lacking De Mille's substantial ability as a director, Chauvel might, with experience and opportunity, have been at least a competitor.'[32]

Auteurist criteria are even more explicit, and unforgiving, in John Hill's account:

> Unfortunately, Chauvel never projected a personal vision of the world in his films. A good piece of characterisation here, a well executed sequence of spectacle there.
>
> Unlike the action films of many Hollywood commercial directors, Chauvel failed to unify all the elements at the filmmaker's disposal to forge a statement on men or their environment.

It is possible that, had there been a healthy industry, Chauvel wouldn't have had to spend nine-tenths of his time being an entrepreneur and producer – as D. H. Lawrence said: 'All the mad struggles with material necessities and conveniences – the inside soul just withers and goes to the outside' – and he could have spent more time as a director. Then perhaps his work may have been more aesthetically satisfying in retrospect.[33]

Having failed the grade as *auteur* director, however, Chauvel is accepted as a more-than-competent craftsman, *a metteur en scene*. He is hailed as an outstanding 'action director', the category into which traditional aesthetics can comfortably place Chauvel's distinctive predilections for location shooting while at the same time implying a limited vision. Traditional historian Eric Reade remarks that Chauvel's first two films, his 'meat-pie westerns', stamped him as 'essentially an outdoor man of action' who would 'remain' that way.[34] However, Chauvel's much vaunted action sequences only become important within traditional history because it lacks an appropriate aesthetic sense of the films. Traditional history reads textual significance as a function of the heroic surmounting of extreme obstacles to production. Much is made, for instance, of the Light Horse charges in *Forty Thousand Horsemen*, the Tobruk battle sequences in *The Rats of Tobruk* or the Aboriginal warfare in *Uncivilised*. But these well-known examples of 'action direction' have no more (or less) importance than one might expect in similar war or adventure films, and are not necessarily well integrated into the narrative. Their textual significance cannot be read off from accounts of production difficulties.

More special pleading is found in traditional accounts when Chauvel is cast as a victim of media imperialism, a picture being painted of the heroic independent battling in the face of indifference and opposition. Anecdotes about Charles and Elsa having to hawk their silent films personally around back-block picture houses, and having to pay exhibitors to take off American programs in their favour, are recycled throughout these accounts. Added to these anecdotes are accounts of Chauvel's independence making him ripe for picking by the industry: 'When Chauvel died in 1959 he was virtually penniless. All the profits of his films had disappeared, mostly into the pockets of distributors who charged ruinous percentages or bought for low prices the world rights to his films at a time when he needed the money badly.'[35]

The extent to which such motifs of 'independence against the industry' are adequate grounds on which to build an account of Chauvel's career need to be examined in detail. As with Chauvel's authorship and independence, so with his nationalism, according to such accounts. A 'fierce' nationalist, 'the true measure of his greatness lies in his refusal to compromise his vision of Australia, and his unswerving dedication to the concept of producing distinctively Australian films for world audiences'.[36] However, it is not a question of whether or not 'compromise' was necessary, for what counted as nationalism (and indeed nationhood) was subject to variation. Both the colonial or post-colonial status of Australia in relation to Britain and the concept of the 'social imaginary' of a national cinema being informed by Hollywood suggest that there are more subtle methods of affirming the distinctiveness and challenge of Chauvel's work than those embodied in the rhetoric of uncompromised nationalism.

Perhaps the most developed traditional assessment of Chauvel is Andrew Pike's 'Early, Commercial and Good Film'.[37] Much of this article is a careful discussion of the significance of Chauvel that avoids the auteurist discourse of Baxter and Hill. One central historiographical assumption is firmly in place, however: a teleological model that attempts to unify the career and explain some of the aesthetic difficulties posed by Chauvel's work by recourse to a biographical growth-to-maturity model. Like Reade, Pike finds the career encapsulated by 1926 and it is then simply a matter of the seed growing into the tree. The most problematic of Chauvel's films, the 1930s *In the Wake of the Bounty*, *Heritage* and *Uncivilised*, can be smoothed over as 'mere preliminaries to the work which Chauvel was to achieve during the war and after'. This 'apprenticeship' model (Chauvel's presumed apprenticeship in the codes of Hollywood classicism and in national representation) can be found throughout traditional accounts of Chauvel.

Transitional history, such as that of Lawson,[38] finds it difficult to place Chauvel with any consistency. Such polemical cultural nationalism typically gives emphasis to Longford or Ordell as vanguard nationalist filmmakers because of their social realism, apparently subverting the mainstream's commitment to imported models of society melodrama or Australianised westerns. If there is one thing Chauvel was not, it was a social realist! Lawson's article contains not one reference to Chauvel.

Three writers have contributed to the development of a theoretical account of Chauvel: Bill Routt, John Tulloch and Bruce Molloy.[39] Routt, the most ambitious of the three, attempts to rehabilitate Chauvel by proposing a governing aesthetic context for his work. Tulloch discusses Chauvel briefly in the context of his general recasting of the silent cinema, while Molloy provides detailed thematic discussion of the films.

In Routt's analyses, Chauvel's work is singled out as 'perhaps the most intensely personal films of the early Australian cinema in the sense that they are instantly and intuitively recognisable as Chauvel's'. They are, notwithstanding what Baxter and Hill say, the work of an *auteur*. He produced a unified body of films defined by systematic recurrences of theme and by consistent stylistic traits. To these latter traits Routt assigns the term 'naive style': a style found in a wide range of cultural forms including art, literature, and the cinema. The naive style arises out of conditions of colonialism; indeed, Routt argues, the best approach to Chauvel's films is as 'parables of colonialism'. He speculates that the absence of mother figures in the films is compensated for by the operations of a higher-level discourse of empire–colony relations coalescing around the figure of the mother country.

The status of the films remains highly controversial; Routt attempts to insert them into an aesthetic heritage – the naive style – within which their strangeness may not be written off merely as badness. They are films that are avowedly and stridently nationalist, yet precisely because of this they irrepressibly register the 'impossible condition' of colonialism:

> The identity of a colony – its cultural form and substance, which is to say, its very self – is wholly the creation of the mother country. To deny that culture would appear to be nothing less than obliteration, suicide. Yet at the same time, a colony knows itself outcast. It has been forbidden to drink the flow of culture at the maternal source. A colony, then, is – and is not. Doubly-bound, the colonial population will fervently protest its loyalty and, with equal ferocity, proclaim its independence. Loyalists will seek to resolve the conflict by eliminating geography and history, ignoring what they know full well, asserting that no hatred stems from the outrage of their rejection. Nationalists, in their turn, will attempt resolution by rejecting the rejector; asserting the chimera of a parthenogenic 'national identity'. The one denies her hatred, the other her love; the one denies her individuality, the other that difference within.[40]

Now the general consensus on Chauvel is that he was the architect of the most avowedly nationalist filmmaking in Australia. We begin to see that this nationalism was subject to historically available discourses, with their thorough and often contradictory mix of ideas of empire, colony and nation, as well as to governing principles of stylistic intelligibility derived from Hollywood classicism. Routt demonstrates the interdependence of these two forces. On the one hand, he shows that what counted as nationhood was a function of empire–colony power relations. On the other, he argues for the unity of Chauvel's output despite, or even because of, the notorious 'badness' of the films: bad scripting, anachronistic acting, poor continuity, and so on. These elements must be seen in the light of the nature of the films boldly essaying the 'impossible condition' of colonialism: no wonder some of them falter under such Promethean ambition!

Fertile as they are, Routt's arguments inadequately account for the historical and industrial nature of Chauvel's films. They need to be understood as *differentiating* themselves from the codes of Hollywood classicism and from the way these codes were followed in most other Australian feature filmmaking of the time. But there was also an attempt to have this difference *accommodated* within standard practices of production, promotion and reception. The differentiation can be plotted at different levels. There is Chauvel's commitment to connecting commercial feature production with a type of documentary impulse: the relation between this impulse and the various narrative and generic patterns particular to each film forms a dominant theme of the book's analyses. With regard to production practice and promotion, Chauvel's unique status and independence within the film industry develops over time and is crucial to the funding and promotion of his films.

The main limitation of Tulloch's account of Chauvel in *Legends* is that it is so brief, and that it is restricted to the late 1920s, the first and least distinctive phase of Chauvel's career. Tulloch finds Chauvel of particular interest in his treatments of individual filmmakers' work in terms of the dynamics of a dependent culture. Chauvel seems to combine local and American strategies and stylistics:

> As a grazier's son with acute business acumen, he realised that films with traditional Australian bush values could appeal for their financing to squatters. But his experience of Hollywood also suggested to him that films with a specific local 'slant' could become American best sellers, hence there should be no contradiction between either funding or making films which were authentically Australian and had an international appeal.[41]

This avenue of assessment is an effective antidote to those who would place local and international options in opposition, and speak of 'compromised' visions. Further, Tulloch flatly contradicts the notion of Chauvel as the financial *naif* and heroic independent: 'If Longford was Australian cinema's great Romantic, Chauvel was its organisation man' (p. 269). It was his business acumen that enabled Chauvel to be the only Australian director of silent films to make a success of sound features. Tulloch also correctly reads Chauvel's evidence at the 1927 Royal Commission into the film industry as moderate and conciliatory, belying the imputation of a fierce nationalist independence from the start of his career.

Molloy's study of the themes of Chauvel's feature films attempts a rigorous application of an early cultural–structuralist method. The central limitation of Molloy's approach is that it is resolutely non-cinematic. Questions of aesthetic 'badness' that need addressing are displaced by his focus on the social–mythological content of the films. Molloy, therefore, can make startlingly traditional statements about Chauvel: 'Chauvel's narrative style is generally straightforward, but some variety is introduced by the use of conventional devices'; 'The mixed narrative structures [of *Wake* and *Rats*, for instance] are the least satisfactory, drawing attention to the mechanics of the narrative and introducing consequent complications'; or '*Despite* the melodramatic excesses and naivete of characterisation, Chauvel's films make him a significant figure in Australian feature production' (emphasis added).[42]

Three phases of Chauvel's career

Whether or not Chauvel was an *auteur* or a romantic seer, a financial *naif* or an organisation man, whether he was a heroic independent or whether he rode on the infrastructural support of established studios and government and distribution backing, is not to be resolved by simply disproving some of the accounts outlined above. It is true, however, that some of these accounts are based on inadequate evidence. However, this chapter is principally interested in *historicising* the terms of this debate. In the following sections of the chapter, the case for Chauvel's authorial and aesthetic status, his independence and nationalism are put forward. First, we should look at the actual history of Chauvel's career.

Much of the debate over Chauvel is cast in ahistorical terms. What passes for history is a growth-to-maturity model of increasing success, confidence or control. This is inadequate. Rather, there were variable *periods* and *forms* of independence; there was an industrial *construction* of a Chauvel 'legend' that had certain effects on the funding, styles and receptions of *some* of his films. He used a striking range of approaches to the question of national representation, and made a variety of negotiations with Hollywood classicism. After all, what could be more apparent than the principle of historical change over the almost forty-year span of Chauvel's career? This is a period that saw film moving from the 'photoplay' to the international art cinema, a period during which Australia changed from a pre-depression British dominion staples-supplier to being presented by Charles and Elsa (in *Australian Walkabout*) to British consumers as an exotic armchair tourist spectacle on television, the modish leisure technology of the 1950s!

The first phase of Chauvel's production career, during the 1920s, was a period of independence because he was a marginal operator in relation to the wider industry. He was an entrepreneurial individualist who gave relatively compliant evidence before the 1927–28 Royal Commission, evidence at odds with the general thrust of the claims of the majority of producers. The second phase, during the years to the end of the Second World War, was characterised by the establishment of a 'biographical legend' of Chauvel, and by concerted attempts by him to form industrial alliances in the areas of both production and distribution, rather than remain independent. This period saw Chauvel taking on the role of lobbyist and public spokesperson for production interests in the industry. The third phase, covering the postwar period to Chauvel's death in 1959, can be defined by a strongly independent stance that was different from the first phase in that the viability of independence was made possible by the achieved status of the biographical legend.

By breaking up Chauvel's career in this way, connections can be made between its aesthetic elements and its industrial elements. While each aspect – Chauvel's films, his industrial career – has properly distinct conditions of existence for analysis, there is a series of parallels between them. Making these connections embraces Bordwell's call for a film history that grasps 'the complex interaction of economic and cultural [as well as stylistic and industrial] factors that define cinema as a social practice'.[43]

The approach taken does not chart a 'growth to maturity'. Emphasis is placed on ruptures and differences between the three phases, while not neglecting influences flowing from one phase to another. Each phase, including industrial, cultural and filmic elements, is treated as a complex whole, organised according to the differing articulations of the biographical legend, Chauvel's independence and nationalism, and film style.

From biography and authorship to the biographical legend

Rather than a conventional biographical approach, the focus here is on the historical construction of the 'biographical legend' of Chauvel. David Bordwell, in his study of Carl-Theodor Dreyer, outlines this approach:

> we can situate a filmmaker's work in a film history by studying the persona created by the artist in his public pronouncements, in his writings, and in his dealings with the film industry ... However subjective, even self-centred, such a legend may appear, that legend has an objective function in a historical situation. The biographical legend may

justify production decisions and even create a spontaneous theory of the artist's practice. More important, the biographical legend is a way in which authorship significantly shapes our perception of the work.[44]

The biographical legend of Chauvel was a historical construct that was deployed, by the filmmaker himself and by promotional practices within the industry, with dramatic effects. Tracing this construct allows the debate on authorship and Chauvel to be recast. It is not necessary to hold to an inflated auteurism, with its romantic notions of individual genius in full control of the generation of film meaning, or to revert to second-order rehabilitations of Chauvel as a heroic independent battler and merely competent action director.

As Bordwell puts it, utilising the concept of the biographical legend is not 'reducible to saying that Dreyer's [or Chauvel's] aesthetic views simply reflected his production circumstances, or that as a young man he blueprinted an aesthetic project and set out to live it'. The *construction* of the legend draws several, not necessarily harmonious, factors into play. For Bordwell, 'there is no simple congruence between legend and films'.[45] The biographical legend of Chauvel negotiates potential incongruences between location shooting and studio work, documentary realism and melodrama, nationalism and beholdenness to 'other' (empire and American) models of style, meaning and industrial power, and between independence and institutional support. There is also the *historical* construction of the legend to account for – its derivativeness in the first phase of Chauvel's career, its emergence and consolidation in the second, and its maturity in the third.

The melodrama–nation link

An account of the melodramatic mode must figure in any assessment of the significance of Chauvel's films. In traditional history and aesthetics, melodrama is regarded as an imported model, obstructing the fulfilment of an authentic Australian cinema. However, there are strong antecedents and parallels, in theatre, literature and vaudeville, for an Australian melodrama in the cinema.[46] But it is not necessary to assert, against the cultural nationalists, that melodrama is a neutral or even a positive vehicle for the articulation of nationality.

What must be questioned first is the traditional conceptual map of early Australian cinema (including Chauvel) that dubs melodrama and genre films as formulaic and American in their inspiration and those that exhibit social realist or documentary elements as more authentically Australian. This tidy architecture can be dismantled by discriminating between melodramatic forms in Australian cinema of the period. Chauvel's films, with the exception of the two 1926 silent films *The Moth of Moonbi* and *Greenhide*, can be characterised as 'high melodrama' in terms of their consistent tone and style, a concept in agreement with Routt's account of the naive style. This differentiates Chauvel's work from most Australian cinema of the period. We can discriminate between *generic* melodrama and the high melodramatic *mode*. The former may well have been constituted through imported models such as the society melodrama of the 1920s (sometimes criticised at the time for just this reason), which persisted into the 1930s in certain productions from the Cinesound and Efftee studios. The latter, at least as articulated in Chauvel, is held to no particular genre, indeed often may subvert generic consistency. The remarkable cases in point are *In the Wake of the Bounty* and *Uncivilised*.

The high melodramatic mode is distinguished from generic melodrama because it risks all, taking great liberties with aesthetic form and audience expectations. There is a tonal consistency in this mode that often creates generic inconsistency because it is trying to take us beyond the constructed, fictional world of the film into realms of 'truth' or 'utopia', appealing to audiences' deepest psychic desires and civic hopes. 'The melodramatic utterance', argues Peter Brooks in his path-breaking study *The Melodramatic Imagination*, 'breaks through everything that constitutes the "reality principle", all its censorships, accommodations, tonings-down . . . Desire triumphs over the world of substitute-formations and detours, it achieves plenitude of meaning.'[47] Brooks regards the high melodramatic mode as a global challenge to both realism and modernism, the dominant modes of aesthetic expression in the twentieth century. It is 'the mode of excess': the 'truths' asserted within the high melodramatic mode are so wide-ranging that the aesthetic form in which they are expressed can hardly support them. Such a mode makes 'large but unsubstantiable claims on meaning'.[48]

The concept of the high melodramatic mode is crucial in understanding Chauvel, being the most appropriate of available forms for the articulation of a 'vision', like that of the descriptive writers, of the identity of Australia and of national development. Chauvel's vision of the nation makes large but unsubstantiable claims on meaning. It bears repeating that there is nothing necessary in this link between melodrama and nation; nothing inherent in the high melodramatic mode that makes it a vehicle of cultural imperialism *or* that points to anything uniquely Australian about it. There is, however, something culturally and historically specific about the *way* it was deployed by Chauvel. While the history of the melodramatic mode is remarkably intertwined with religious, political and other extra-aesthetic factors,[49] it shows no particular fealty to projects of national definition. The following establishes how Chauvel constructed this link. It is not an account of how Chauvel fulfilled some predetermined pattern for himself or for the Australian cinema.

First, Chauvel's linking of melodrama with nation displaces the opposition of form and formula (melodrama) and authentic marks of nationality (social realism). Chauvel's films undoubtedly deploy strong elements of documentary or social realism, in much the same way as the descriptive writers of the period oscillated between reportage and sensationalism, fact and fiction. His passion for, indeed obsession with, location shooting is most evident in this respect. But Chauvel was never a straight documentarist or realist. 'Locationism' is an ugly word, but I can think of no better one to catch Chauvel's intense commitment, despite the massive technical and financial obstacles, to shooting the 'true' country, without implying that it was driven by a coherent documentary aesthetic. The concept of locationism engages with Chauvel's nationalist desire to make 'Australia a film star'[50] and with his independence; no one else risked as much in production as he did. Locationism was also a major means by which he sought to differentiate his work from the dominant regimes of Hollywood classical cinema.

The way in which Chauvel's films were funded and promoted further registers their locationism. Press releases and other promotional statements, read without seeing the films, would lead one to believe that the story elements were immaterial to the films' attractions, spectacle and documentary detail being enough in themselves. And there is the Chauvels' assertion, in their travel book *Walkabout*, that 'through all the years we have spent filming dramatic screen plays in Australia we have always wanted to film our country factually'.[51]

However, the locationist impulse is *not* the generating mechanism of the films themselves. Rather, this impulse is taken up into the melodramatic vision of nation, and it is this that drives the films. It is no wonder that many of Chauvel's films 'break down' in the struggle to produce coherent narrative worlds, for they are called on to carry the heavy weight of harmonising conflicts of sex, race and nation within utopian visions of totality.

Second, the melodrama–nation link was not there from the start. What constitutes the link changes over the decades of Chauvel's production, not least because changes in social, political and economic factors alter what is considered as nationality. If Chauvel is simply *assumed* to be Australia's pre-eminent nationalist filmmaker, the category of nationality remains inert. It is inadequate, and uninteresting, to tie a notion of Australian identity emerging through a process of maturation with Chauvel maturing as an auteur. Various histories – of Chauvel's fortunes within the film industry, of the film industry itself, of the history of the nation – intersect with and cut against such a developmental framework. The pull towards unity within Chauvel's work is a force exerted by the consistent appearance of the high melodramatic mode. However, this destabilises generic and stylistic consistency, and, when considered with variations in national definition, a strong pull towards disunity must also be taken into account.

These are some of the fascinating questions that provoke our interest in Chauvel's project of 'featuring Australia'.

Chapter 3

(1988) Apollonius and Dionysus in the Antipodes

The early Australian cinema up to the 1950s turned often enough to the near Pacific region – the 'South Seas' – to suggest something of a cultural and industrial principle at work. Let us call it 'second order colonialism'. Perhaps most impressively at the start, there was Frank Hurley, whose Antarctic travelogues, *Home of the Blizzard* (1913) and *In the Grip of the Polar Pack Ice* (1917), together with his films and his remarkable composite photography of Great War campaigns, were forerunners to the enormous successes of his Papua Travelogues, *Pearls and Savages* (1922) and *With the Headhunters of Unknown Papua* (1923). Later in the 1920s, Hurley produced and directed his only two feature films, *The Jungle Woman* (1926) and *The Hound of the Deep* (released in Britain as *Pearl of the South Seas*) (1926), as pragmatic spin-offs of his South Pacific 'adventures'. Then there is Charles Chauvel's extraordinary travelogue-drama set in Tahiti and Pitcairn, *In the Wake of the Bounty* (1933), and the series of South Pacific 'location exploitation' features engaged in by the Lee Robinson–Chips Rafferty partnership in the 1950s: *Walk into Paradise* (1956), *The Stowaway* (1958) and *The Restless and the Damned* (1959).

These are the feature highlights; a whole host of documentary, newsreel and travelogue material during the period also bolsters the claim for a recurrence, a principle, at work. This is a principle emanating from the status of Australia as a 'Second World' nation-state, operating as a kind of linkman in a chain of representational command from First World metropolises to the alterity of the Third World, relaying images of the other through delegated authority. Models of the cultural psychology of colonialism and colonisation need to take account of more than the bilateral master–slave dialectic that dominates classic studies like O. Mannoni's *Prospero and Caliban* and Franz Fanon's *The Wretched of the Earth*.[1] Benedict Anderson's analysis of the role of creole populations in the formation of modern 'modular' nationalisms[2] suggests much about the 'linkman' function played by Second World cultural elites in fashioning derivative national identities out of an overdetermined investment in the values of their colonising 'parents'. The dialectic for Second World cultural elites is then complicated by their being both master and slave, colonising with an over-invested fervour, and being simultaneously colonised through such agency.

Nation-states like Australia thus have histories of resistance, hesitance or inability to turn in on themselves to recast their own status as slave *and* master. For it to be otherwise would have meant, on the one hand, a greater distance from colonising parents and a stronger post-colonial 'identity', and, on the other, a very different history of cultural contact with the Indigenous peoples of the continent. Rather than turn in, the dialectics of Second World colonisers–colonised can be acceded to by turning out, to 'near neighbours', where the linkman function can be played out more unequivocally.

But all this homogenises the interplay of Second World cultural elites and their Third World subjects of representation overmuch. Two very similar yet very different figures, and principles, in the early Australian cinema can be used to see how far, and within what parameters, differences can be established. Two figures: Frank Hurley and Charles Chauvel. Two films: *Jungle Woman* and *In the Wake of the Bounty*. Two principles: the Apollonian and the Dionysian.

Both Hurley (1885–1962) and Chauvel (1897–1959) are colossuses of Australian cultural representation, Hurley more so in photography than in the cinema. Both men had long careers. Each was fabled for his perfectionism, Hurley as a photographic technician, Chauvel as a producer–director of epic vision. Both were obsessives, driven to find authentic location material beyond the 'civilised' world. Both turned to the 'South Seas' at significant points in their careers to further this desire: Hurley made repeated journeys to Papua in the early 1920s and Chauvel went to Tahiti and Pitcairn in 1932. Both journeyings were major expeditionary incursions in their own right; Hurley went further up the Fly River and into Lake Murray for longer than any white man had done before. Chauvel, together with his wife, Elsa, and cameraperson Tasman Higgins, were claimed to be the first to bring a camera to Pitcairn Island, the isolated settlement of the descendants of the *Bounty* mutineers.

However, because these two figures are so similar it is imperative that they be distinguished. Consider the melancholy spectacle of the 'witheringly obdurate confidence'[3] of Hurley, the Victorian man – adventurer, explorer, servant and master of the age's new technology, a 'man's man' shunning the company of women, even his wife and daughters, and the consolations of religion, despite the rhetorical displays of 'correct' spiritual sentiment strewn through the voluminous diaries.[4] Marching resolutely from the certainties of Victorianism through the holocaust of the twentieth century (what a trove of experience!), the confidence turns finally to a near autistic asociality at the end. No one was even to know about the heart attack; no one is left even a shard of a message.[5] Hurley, whose brand of Pictorialism, practised with such innovative panache up to the late 1910s, caged himself into such increasingly superseded aesthetics that photojournalism, the documentary movement and 'the human face in photography' simply passed him by. His estimable reputation, fame, success and indefatigable productivity rendered such questions of minor moment.

For Chauvel, the consolidation and rewards of success were to remain an elusive goal throughout his career. Chauvel was 'endowed . . . with Christian principles' which nevertheless we can read only at the level of architectonics in the films.[6] He was a 'perfectionist . . . in the artistry with which he gave skilful emphasis to the beauty of the unadorned form and sanctity of the feminine sex'.[7] (It was a naughty tradition in the family for Elsa and their daughter, Susanne, to give Charles a 'female art' calendar each year.) The unbreakable thirty-year partnership of Charles and Elsa in the Australian film industry was unparalleled, here and elsewhere, and they together suffered the resentment born of 'inflexible social attitudes'.[8] Chauvel didn't hoard human experience in personal diaries, but lavished it on films that spill over with a 'high' melodramatic, Dionysian spirit.

Hurley was the perfect linkman. He was able to be positioned, by powerful brokers like Stuart Doyle, as a convenient foil against nationalist resentment in the production sector on the eve of the Royal Commission inquiring into the film industry in 1927. Moreover, his feature 'adventures' of 1926 were backed by British mogul Sir Oswald Stoll, 'head of easily the largest film company and studio in England', as part of Stoll Picture Productions' policy of farming out a proportion of its output to exotic locales.[9] Neither were these kinds of positionings atypical of the full career-trajectory of Hurley. There is nothing in the Hurley *curriculum vitae* indicating anything so much as moments of reflexive nationalism that would give pause to the smooth passage of his work through its various, and often fulsome, international reception.

Pearls and Savages and the 'ethnographic' work engaged in by Hurley's party in Papua in the early 1920s form a necessary companion study to the later feature projects. Consider the 'cunning' ruses to scare the natives off so that the expedition could espy the Kopivari – the 'Holy of Holies'; and marching through villages 'collecting' items of interest.[10] No wonder the otherwise withering confidence of *Pearls and Savages* sometimes barely manages to edit out a narrative closure of an unintended sort for our obdurate adventurers: look at the last few sequences of the film for the spears being thrown at the expedition's boat!

Jungle Woman is a sort of 'collector's item'. Because a feature, and therefore a character-based drama, was the only adequate response to the problems of circulating Hurley's 'ethnographic' material in the international market, the time-honoured modular plot devices of nineteenth-century stage and early screen melodrama are imported into a film project whose self-understanding is still fundamentally that of 'spectacle documentary'.[11] But this is not how it turns out. Hurley simply didn't have the aesthetic capacity to cope with the, for the time, highly experimental documentary-drama form. Pike and Cooper's words are judicious but apt: 'The film as it exists today certainly has many striking scenic effects and interesting ethnographic details, but the plot is dominant and reveals Hurley's naivety about human relationships.'[12]

Look at the positioning of the 'jungle woman' herself, Hurana, played in black face by a Sydney actress, Grace Savieri. Seemingly imputed a centrality by the title of the film, she occupies such a place only by virtue of a 'non-preferred' reading against the grain.[13] She is a weird composite character who performs all the functions of the most positive female 'type' of the early Australian cinema – the bush woman/squatter's daughter – and more. She is 'a captive maid, who by her superior intelligence has gained ascendency over the Chief', as one of the film's intertitles informs. Thus coded as sur-native, but also non-white, she enables the narrative to perform all its moves. She overcomes the 'stone age' superstitions of the Chief about 'white man's magic' medicine (the captive Martin South's quinine), thus saving the white man's life. She aids his escape, feeds him from nature's bounty, the cow tree, as they journey through the jungle to the white outpost of Bunda Bunda, and is fatally bitten by a snake as she tries to turn it aside from him.

For all this, Hurana is mercilessly punished by the discourse of the film. Martin South's love is Eleanor, who waits out the narrative at Bunda Bunda 'beseiged' by South's blackguard companion in gold fever, Stephen Mardyke. The film has two chilling scenes where Hurana's love for South is peremptorily repudiated. Hurley accommodates here the political dubiety of 'mixing races'[14] with great alacrity. After his capture, South 'awakens to a consciousness of his terrible predicament': in his mind's eye the solicitous Hurana is 'replaced' by the dreamy Eleanor. The moment doesn't last, and he is shattered. In a later, parallel, scene, the set-up is Hurana gazing at the white man as he gazes at his photograph of Eleanor. Compare Chauvel's *Uncivilised* (1936), which has a very similar narrative structure but very different discursive logic capped by a 'symbolic' interracial marriage.

A closer analysis of surface similarities also reveals striking differences between Hurley's South Seas and Chauvel's Tahiti in *In the Wake of the Bounty*. The tale of the mutiny on the *Bounty* has attracted repeated retellings as, the foreword to Chauvel's film tells us, 'the most tragic and strange sea story of all time'. An extensive literature has been produced which often divides on the question of the determinative causes of the mutiny. Chauvel claimed, in the 'novelisation' of the film, that he had done a good deal of background research for the film which led him to 'place the softness of Tahiti and its women first among the elements which caused the mutiny'.[15] The implications of this for the film are intriguing. For as Chauvel reasons:

> Many leaves from the story of the *Bounty* had been allowed to fall by the wayside. Lieutenant Bligh had never drawn the veil unreservedly from the picture of his six months' dalliance at Tahiti, nor had any of his mutineer prisoners. Bligh certainly blamed the women of

Tahiti, but he gave no suggestion of any moral lapses on the part of his men – this perhaps would have reflected upon the discipline of his command. Certainly his mutineers never blamed the women of Tahiti – there would have been short measure for any sailor of Britain who blamed the lure of native women for a mutiny at sea. The sailors blamed the tyranny of Bligh, and so Tahiti's loose leaf, if ever written, was allowed to flutter from its place in history and drift away upon a lazy tropic tide . . . the terrible tragedy of the *Bounty* caused a veil to be drawn over six months of highly spiced and colorful adventure – covering a great midsummer night's dream which in its fullness can never be told.[16]

This tale, then, is an explicit provocation, a narrative desiring to 'tempt' the reader into an unholy, transgressive position. It is tempting in itself, and not entirely inappropriate, to read the foregoing passage symptomatically, with its ironic reciprocal reinforcements of silence, and its slippages across leaves falling, veils being drawn and withdrawn, 'Tahiti's loose leaf' and so on. What is undeniable is that Chauvel at the time was offering a provocation in the form of his prioritisation of causes and in his explicit project to 'draw back the veil', leading as it did to his first of a number of transgressions of Australian film censorship codes. 'Charles was determined', his wife wrote disarmingly, 'to make this point clear and to leave no stone unturned in its direction.'[17] The extent of the provocation can be traced by comparing *In the Wake of the Bounty* with the 1935 MGM/Frank Lloyd *Mutiny on the Bounty* (with Clark Gable and Charles Laughton). This film centres much more extensively on the brutality of Bligh than on sexual transgression (which is not unexpected, as Laughton won an Academy Award for his role as Bligh).

In the Wake of the Bounty is an extremely peculiar stylistic amalgam of documentary and dramatised sequences. Its diegesis is split into several planes with, at times, awfully disjunctive relations among them: the time of the mutiny (1789), the retelling of it in

England by Michael, the 'blind prophet', who survived the mutiny (1810), the immediate aftermath in Tahiti and Pitcairn and on the *Bounty*, and present-day Tahiti and Pitcairn (1932). For all this 'surface' disjunction, however, the film follows its own discursive logic quite rigorously. As Bill Routt puts it, 'it is not a story or a documentary but a moral tract'.[18]

Chauvel, then, sets up a 'provocation': a scenario of a utopian heart of darkness or dystopian Kipling tale. The closest the film approaches the sexual–racial heart of darkness is in the documentary sequences at Tahiti. These begin with a travelogue-style narration which, though spoken by the blind prophet Michael in 1810, are emphatically in the contemporary (1932) documentary visual style of later segments of the film. Into these documentary sequences are then inserted the spectral presences of the *Bounty* sailors, character-constructs from the dramatic diegeses of the film. These characters cavort with 'licentious', half-naked Tahitian women, whose dress and disposition could have permissible 'reality' only within the diegesis of documentary. Then follows a long rapidly edited sequence of dance and desire without narration (in a text so strongly 'led' by voice-over narration, this absence is in itself significant), where the camera is for once mute witness to the intrinsically overdetermined nature of the spectacle.

This is the first of two condensed nodes of discourse in the film, in which drama and documentary levels are collapsed, generating the film's sense of high-melodramatic 'truth'. This is the axis of 'transgression'. The second, the axis of 'expiation and atonement', as we will see, centres on the last sequence of the film, the death of David Young's baby. In the first nodal point of high-melodramatic discourse, documentary intervenes in what has hitherto in the film been a predominantly dramatic filmic register (spartan sets, static camera or ponderous camera movements, 'melodramatic' gestural performance and line delivery, diegetic character as narrator). In the second, drama intervenes in a hitherto predominantly documentary register (location shooting, *mise en scène* of Edenic nature, several travelling camera shots, social actors 'performing' themselves rather than dramatic characters, no sync sound dialogue, non-participant narrator). The construction of both modal points transgresses the conventions of the different diegetic 'worlds' of the film, setting up complex regimes of viewing which can only be negotiated by their being read in the light of the overall discursive logic of the film. This discursive trajectory is the classic high-melodramatic movement from the moral vertigo of transgression of sexual, racial and vocational ('short measure for any sailor of Britain') boundaries to the equally vertiginous exhilaration of atonement for the sins of the past generations.

We can begin to see, then, how *In the Wake of the Bounty* can engage in a reflexive analysis of second-order colonialism. The film's narrative universe has nothing explicitly to do with Australia, except in the foreword's passing reference to Bligh 'afterwards' becoming the Governor of New South Wales and the reference to Cook, earlier the cartographer of the eastern coast of Australia, being right in his description of Tahiti as 'this strange paradise beneath the sun'. Indeed, *In the Wake of the Bounty* is alone among Chauvel's films in having nothing, at the level of narrative, character or setting, to do with Australia. However, this is far from being the case at the level of discourse. The *Bounty* mutiny takes its place within the genre of legends and salutary tales of British colonialism. It occurred at around the time and place of the founding acts of British colonialism in Australia. *In the Wake of the Bounty* is centrally concerned with the dialectic of metropolis–colony relations; indeed, it is the most radical of Chauvel's films in taking this dialectic to its logical conclusions. The mutiny and its aftermath read in the film as a salutary tale within the historical discourse of colonialism. Rather than being pro- or anti-colonialist, it essays the 'impossible condition' of the colony, and carries this in Chauvel's most rarified, 'theological' example of the high-melodramatic mode.

Its moral–biblical trajectory is one of 'transgression will out', which structures its discourse on metropolis–colony relations, itself summarisable in these terms: the attempt to completely sever the tie with the mother country in order to establish an autonomous society in 'utopia' will result in dystopic distortions and an over-compensatory reinvestment in the values of the mother country. How does this 'moral tract' structure further elements of the film?

The pressure generated by the dialectics of utopia–dystopia and of colonial overcompensation tend to produce the diegetic 'fractures' for which *In the Wake of the Bounty* is notorious. Throughout the film the narration oscillates obsessively between extolling the paradisal nature of Tahiti, Pitcairn and the South Seas generally and simultaneously decrying its effect on the sailors. This is not only the case with the 'blind prophet' Michael's melodramatically gestural narration, whose radical ambivalence is at least partly motivated by his having been one of the survivors of the mutiny to have returned to the 'mother country'. It is also there in the 'contemporary' travelogue-style narration of the second half of the film, which combines visual panoramas of verdant utopias with narration that alludes to forests which 'echo to the maddening dance of primitives' and to 'the blasphemy of ruthless pirates'. Tahiti is summed up as a place where 'passionate pleasure and scheming commerce mix in a melting pot of colour and creed'. Over a quiet, observational shot of a descendant of Fletcher Christian, we are reminded that he is hoeing in the very place where Christian was killed in the bloodbath that followed the escape of the mutineers to Pitcairn Island! A sequence demonstrating the physical health of young Pitcairners is radically undercut by the narrator's remark that considering there had been 160 years of inbreeding, their 'physique and mental capabilities surprise one'.

All of this is not mere mordant objectification of a truly exotic microsociety, however. There is much to suggest the Chauvels' abiding fascination and, somehow, identification with the Pitcairners. They inscribe themselves energetically within the diegesis of the film, becoming almost a sub-plot unto themselves as they bear the brunt of the difficult landing on the island (this sequence takes on powerful meaning in the light of the final sequence of the film), assist in the community's daily chores, and engage in various sightseeing tours.[19]

The film's final scene secures the movement of its discursive trajectory. We cut abruptly from the long contemporary travelogue to a barely motivated dramatised scene: one of the tiny and isolated Pitcairn community's babies is dying. There is a cut to another set, a passing British steamer's radio room, where two contemporary seamen converse, one of whom reminisces that he should have been a doctor. They take the radio calls of the Pitcairners' 'spiritual' leader, Edgar Christian, but disregard them, saying that 'the old man wouldn't venture near that looney lot'. They exchange pleasantries, one colloquially calling the other 'old man'. Edgar, knowing he has finally lost radio contact with the unresponsive British ship, commiserates with the father of the baby, also calling him 'old man'. The parents pray that their baby's death may be seen as atonement for the island's past. The film ends over waves crashing threateningly in Pitcairn's rocky harbour. Despite a massive reinvestment in the values of the metropolis – revivalist religion, grooms at marriage ceremonies resplendent in British naval costumes, a thoroughly Europeanised social order – the lines of communication with the mother country/the 'old man' have been definitively severed, and severed by the 'parent'.

It can be seen, then, that, in terms of libidinal investments, a capacity for the complex aesthetics of documentary-drama, and a reflexive stance towards second-order colonialism, our Antipodean Apollonius and Dionysus are two very different cases in point in any essaying of the Australian cinema's appropriation of the South Pacific.

Chapter 4

(1985) Hollywood genres, Australian movies

Debate on Australian feature-filmmaking in the 1970s and 1980s was organised around the opposition of culture/industry. This applied on the legislative front, in discussions of funding policy and in public relations as much as in reviewing and criticism. In its crudest form, this opposition was posed as a stultifying and conceptually impoverishing either/or argument: either culturally specific films, dealing in recognisable Australian realisms, which authenticate and affirm Australian concerns, and succeed or fail in overseas markets on the strength of those concerns, or else internationalised films, geared to a culturally undifferentiated market.

Roughly analogous to this opposition was another, that between art cinema and overtly commercial filmmaking. In this related form, 'Australian' film was yoked to the prevailing regimes of art cinema. It was held to be deserving of government subsidy because it contributed to national self-definition and thus should not stand or fall by market imperatives alone. Textually, it was positioned as distinct from Hollywood, according *mise en scène* priority over Hollywood's overdetermined, vitalist narrative thrust and closure. Instead, it invited pleasure in the epiphanic moment of the reverently registered gesture, intonation, accent, slang, landscape, decor or attitude that betokened Australian-ness. These were quiet films. On the other hand, overtly commercial practice either irreverently ransacked the images of Australia in order to highlight its brashest excesses and/or demonstrated little concern for serious national self-definition; the point was to justify filmmaking in Australia principally in terms of a healthy bank balance.

However, there are clear signs in many Australian features of the 1980s that the filmmakers are unwilling to be held to these oppositions. This is emphatically not to say that such films as *Starstruck*, *Mad Max* and *Mad Max 2*, *Far East*, *The Man from Snowy River* and *Phar Lap* have hit on the 'correct formula' for filmmaking in Australia, or have 'resolved' the problems arising from the oppositions between culture and industry. These oppositions arise from the application of differing criteria for success, relevance or potential audience and are thus not amenable to solutions simply at the textual level. A survey in terms of promotion, distribution and reception would reveal differing degrees of success according to a variety of criteria. My primary purpose here is to show that the paradigmatic opposition of cultural precision vis-a-vis commercial proposition, between which feature-filmmaking oscillated for most of the 1970s, has been broken down and remodelled in a variety of innovative ways.

The Man from Snowy River and *Phar Lap*, to take the most highly visible instances first, assemble a wide range of generic motifs, pre-established forms of *mise en scène*, and stock characterisations that are drawn in a relatively undifferentiated fashion from their sources. Both narratives are organised around what has become a stock motif, drawn from the *Bildungsroman*, the adolescent's entry into adulthood. This motivates the strong, even fetishistic, attachment of both narratives to the spectacle of 'horseplay', which form of motivation and spectacle could be said to be the Australian counterpoint to recordbreaking Hollywood spectacles of adolescent science fiction: the *Star Wars* cycle, *E.T. The Extra-Terrestrial*, and so on. This motif also assists the simplified negotiation of sexual difference in both films, in much the same way as Hollywood science fiction.

However, *The Man from Snowy River* and *Phar Lap* can by no means be situated in the 'trans-Pacific' space occupied by films like *Patrick*, *Roadgames* or *Race for the Yankee Zephyr*. But for crucial developments in the marketing and international visibility of Australian features, they could be mistaken for latecomers to the dominant genre of the period or nostalgia film, the Australian art cinema of the 1970s. They both trade on treasured pieces of the national heritage: the durable Banjo Paterson ballad and the story of Australia's greatest horse. They reactivate the stock responses organised around the period films of the 1970s: the reverently registered *mise en scène* of a richly textured past. The point about these films is not to *decide* on what side of the old opposition they might finally be situated but to note the ease with which they move across and around the divide.

Controversy always surrounds foreigners starring in Australian feature films in order to improve international marketability. However, a reversal of this movement is suggested by the trend of Australian actors emerging as figures of international appeal. One quite audacious deployment of this trend is the insertion of Bryan Brown and Helen Morse into the positions of classical Hollywood stars in John Duigan's *hommage* to *Casablanca*, *Far East*. While *Snowy River* and *Phar Lap* may in part attempt to counterpoint 'new' Hollywood's adolescent appeal, *Far East* takes on the weighty heritage and cultish contemporary circulation and rememorisation of the golden age. Similarly, *Mad Max* and *Mad Max 2 (The Road Warrior)* appropriate the Hollywood genre film, specifically the road movie. Judging from the *Mad Max* films' marketing successes, it is an extremely successful appropriation. A lot of critical effort has been spent in excoriating these films' violence, nihilism and lack of cultural specificity. This criticism neglects their relations with similarly spurned Australian road movies, like *Stone* and *Pure Shit*. More significantly, however, such criticism misses the point about generic convention: road movies *are* violent and nihilistic, and generally foreground Promethean individualism over cultural placement. However, there is no need to stress the (relatively weak) point that the *Mad Max* films have their precedents in the Australian film tradition; it is more important to see that their complete mastery of the genre – their sheer technical virtuosity and aggressively decadent vitalism – outdoes Hollywood on the grounds it knows best. This kind of 'transcendence' of the genre opens a range of possible further generic transformations, like those worked by the 'Italian' western on another thoroughly American genre. Such a cinematic coup must widen the potential resources of Australian feature production.

A similar claim should be made for *Starstruck*, and its relation to the musical genre. I want to pursue the way in which *Starstruck* 'Australianises' the musical in some detail, because, if my theme is a degree of reconciliation of past oppositions, then the musical may well be the pre-eminent genre through which reconciliation is proposed.

Gestures of reconciliation are offered throughout *Starstruck*, particularly in the unashamedly utopian finale in which, in a series of tight parallel cuts, the 'contemporary' world of Americanised showbiz and the 'traditional' domain of residual American culture are brought together under the aegis of the triumphant musical *tour de force* of Jackie and the Wombats. This utopian moment is strongly overdetermined by its taking place on New Year's Eve: the ritual time out of time of promise and hope, carried in the film by the luminous burst of fireworks over the Opera House. The integrative moment, so appropriate to musical comedy, may be decisively contrasted with the disintegrative use of the same ritual moment, New Year's Eve, in the last sequences of *Heatwave*.

Starstruck's reconciliatory moves go further, in its loving incorporation and transcendence of the Australian-ness of the ocker comedies of the early 1970s like *The Adventures of Barry McKenzie*, *Alvin Purple*, *Stork* and *Petersen*. *Starstruck*'s Pearl, Nan, Reg, Lou, Hazza, Mrs Booth and the ocker culture of the Harbour View Hotel are not really deployed to scandalise delicate bourgeois sensibilities, but rather celebrated as a kind of cultural residuum. They are neither *the* typical Australian profile nor, more importantly, are they presented as culturally dominant. Bazza, Alvin, Stork and Petersen were representations of an anxious and thus bellicose anti-culture (which is not necessarily a dismissal, simply an historical placement). The narratives of their films charted the jocular terrorism of official culture by anti-culture; they could hardly move towards a moment of utopian integration such as that in *Starstruck*. If one wishes to reassess the lost opportunity for cultural self-inspection signalled by the critical rejection of the ocker comedies, the starting point might well be *Starstruck*. The film offers an outrageous master-sign for such a reassessment: the sexualisation of the kangaroo! For the 'Temper' production number at the *New Faces* try-out at the Lizard Lounge, Jackie introduces herself with a strip out of an outsized, stylised kangaroo suit.

The representation of Australia has been organised around a series of powerful bursts of utopian mythologising, like the 'Advance Australia' campaign and innumerable instances of media advertising. What is significant about *Starstruck*, in this refurbishing of national consensus, is that the musical is probably the most appropriate cinematic genre in which such utopianism may surface.[1] Richard Dyer argues with regard to the central category of the musical, entertainment:

> Entertainment does not... present models of utopian worlds... Rather the utopianism is contained in the feelings it embodies. It presents, head-on as it were, what utopia would feel like rather than how it would be organised. It thus works at the level of sensibility, by which I mean an effective code that is characteristic of, and largely specific to, a given mode of cultural production.[2]

The musical is exemplary entertainment in these terms because music, non-representationally, generates the emotional temperature of the communication.

It would be misleading, however, to homogenise the musical genre, and so render criticism as little more than a matter of (musical) taste and sensibility. As Dyer remarks, 'sensibility' is itself coded, and culturally specific. *Starstruck* has provoked extravagant responses among critics and various sectors of general audiences; these responses arise because the film secures a particular set of cultural and textual positions from which the unstructured utopian affirmations are 'felt'.

Rick Altman points out that the etymology of the word 'entertainment' carries two senses (*entretenir*, to maintain, support, converse with; *diverter*, to distract), which are usually opposed rather than seen as dialectically interrelated:

> Entertainment is either a highly developed form created by past-masters in the art of dialogue, geniuses at sensing the mood of an audience, or it is a drug which lulls the masses to sleep, bribes them with pleasurable dreams, and thus distracts them from the stern tasks that are their true destiny.[3]

Criticism of *Starstruck* has tended to minimise the significance of its critical postures and, focusing primarily on its qualities as *divertissement*, it has either hailed or dismissed the film, according to taste. The question, then, is to examine how *Starstruck* lies at the intersection of diversion and discourse.[4]

Starstruck is indeed replete with 'empty' utopianism, which is simply to say that it avowedly grafts itself onto Hollywood traditions of the musical. The bookended theme song, 'Starstruck', demands 'Be what you like/like what you be/It's no dream . . . Chase my dreams of fantasise or bust/You won't find me inside my cloud of dust/Be my hero, be my star . . . Who do you want to be/What do you want from me/When are you going to see/That I've got a right to dream'. The film is papered wall-to-wall with Hollywood models. Jackie inserts herself audaciously into the role: 'Well it's sticky in the jungle/Can't hide from the heat/jungle drums are playing/A jungle beat/Well those Hollywood hearts/Watch them a-flutter/You can't make a star of a girl gorilla . . . Queen Marlene she's the star of the screen /Is this the way that it's meant for me . . .' ('Monkey in Me'). Angus, the Mickey Rooney-like, exorbitantly hopeful *Wunderkind*, speaks the film's schematic utopianism: 'You start out wanting a VW, you end up with a VW. You start out wanting a Jag, you get a Jag.' And again, when it appears that Jackie has lost her chance for fame and love and the pub will be lost:

JACKIE: But what will we do?
ANGUS: We rehearse the band. We find an image. We crack the Opera House. We save the pub.

Such are the trajectories and desires of utopia. However, all is not simply Hollywood *hommage* and adolescent triumphalism. The terms in which the film deflects these elements towards Australianisation have already been suggested. This amounts to Dyer's codification of entertainment within culturally specific interests. The difficulty and potential significance of this achievement – that is, if the precedent constituted by *Starstruck is* followed up in subsequent Australian filmmaking – may be gauged by comparing the complete aberrance and cultural non-specificity of Powell with Pressburger's attempts at the musical in British cinema, *Tales of Hoffman* and *Red Shoes*.

There is further work on the musical genre in *Starstruck*. Within a genre 'so sexist . . . that it is rarely even mentioned' in discussions of representations of women in Hollywood,[5] *Starstruck* celebrates a resilient matriarchal order. The film constitutes an audacious, utopian displacement of the dominant (patriarchal order) by the residual (Pearl and Nan's ocker matriarchy) and the emergent (Jackie's unstructured feminism and Angus's polymorphous, pre-Oedipal vitalism), to use Raymond Williams's characterisation of coexisting cultural forces.[6] The offhanded violence done to patriarchal icons almost rivals that done routinely to women in classical Hollywood: Reg's comatose career throughout the film; Lou, whose significance is assessed wonderfully by scriptwriter Stephen MacLean: 'I can only think that Lou was a good root and Pearl likes a good root'; and the 'Tough' production number's camp parody of Australian masculinism. And our voyeuristic interest in Jackie, invited through Robbie's attraction to her at the Lizard Lounge, is comically revoked by her 'undressing' Robbie as she robs him of the sheets in bed and by her high-wire costume's pastiche of bondage and sexual fulsomeness.

Dyer reserves the clearest utopian tendency in the musical genre for those films that 'try to dissolve the distinction between narrative and numbers, thus implying that the world of narrative is also (already) utopian'.[7] Certainly, the dominant global movement of *Starstruck* is towards reconciliation of narrative and number, wherein life aspires to the condition of music. This aspiration is established early in the film in the 'morning-after-the-night-before' sequences. The scripting, editing, camerawork and choreography of the routine around Mrs Booth's cats in the kitchen and Jackie's return (Nan: 'You must be good and tired.' Jackie: 'No, just tired.') are as exhilarating as any formal production number. The overall narrative movement of the film is from disparity of narrative and number to reconciliation of them in the final integrative movements of the New Year's Eve finale. The wholly different contexts of two performances of the 'Starstruck' number exemplify this movement. The first takes place in Angus's schoolroom daydreams, the second cannot be contained within even the commodious formal utopia of the Opera House.

Part 2 Australian television

The television mini-series as a genre is probably the most ambitious form of television; in its achieved forms, it is also one of the most socially and historically engaged. The mini-series shows what the medium is capable of at the quality end of the spectrum, and places in relief the realities and constraints of television production today. If, as suggested in the previous Part, the neglected cinema before the revival was a limit case for cultural recovery, then this Part's account of the historical mini-series is a test case for some of the greatest achievements of Australian television.

As a study of the capability of the medium, Chapter 5, 'Style, form and history in Australian mini-series', sets out benchmarks for what might constitute levels of achievement in the historical mini-series format by establishing 'qualitative criteria for discriminating amongst mini-series in terms of their use of the format and their approach to historical reconstruction'. In doing this, it seeks to make the bases for such judgement explicit and therefore contestable.

The Kennedy–Miller company is of immense importance to the film and television landscape in Australia. The company is one of the great stayers, and leaders, on the scene, making films from the 1970s with the *Mad Max* trilogy and then some of the best mini-series of the 1980s. Chapter 6, 'Kennedy–Miller: "House style" in Australian television', a detailed study of the company's output in this period, is a telephile's engaged analysis of what made its television the most exciting of the 1980s.

Still going strong, Kennedy–Miller is responsible for most Australian-based blockbusters of the past decades: *Babe* (1995), *Babe: Pig in the City* (1998) and *Happy Feet* (2006) were all major feature-film successes. These films, and others, have done much to keep the industry on its feet through some very hard times in the 1990s and 2000s. (George Miller also made the American movies *The Witches of Eastwick* (1986) and *Lorenzo's Oil* (1992), and the 1996 documentary *40,000 Years of Dreaming: A Century of Australian Cinema* financed by the British Film Institute.) But the telling point is that Kennedy–Miller has not produced for Australian television since the early 1990s.

In many ways, industrially, historical mini-series are the 'jewels in the crown' of Australian TV,[1] but they are jewels frozen in time. The conditions that gave rise to them from the late 1970s to the early 1990s were: very generous tax deductions for investors, a very different network environment in which the perennially lowest rating network, Ten, was looking to brand itself with up-market caché in the context of a decade of the flourishing of cultural nationalism (and was headed in the early days of this period by Rupert Murdoch), and a financing regime that allowed producers to finance most, if not all, high-budget productions in the local market. These factors together allowed for an unprecedented run of high-budget productions, intensely engaging with the national narrative in epic aesthetic formats. This is summed up in the Kennedy–Miller essay in this way: 'the mini-series gives us back an Australian "history" and "culture" embedded in a masterful play within the "imported" genre conventions that have *become* part of that history and culture.'

All of these conditions no longer obtain. Historical mini-series are a laboratory case of what broadcast television no longer is. This can be briefly illustrated by looking at two 'mini-series' screened in 2007, *Curtin* and *Bastard Boys*.[2] 'Mini-series' is in quotation marks because *Curtin* is a telemovie, a single-episode production, not a mini-series, which already signals that cost is one of the major inhibitors of contemporary historical reconstruction.

The first thing to note is that both of these productions and indeed most attempts at historical drama in the last several years have been undertaken by the ABC rather than the commercial networks. No longer is there the ambition of the commercials to mark out such territory.

Curtin (like *The Last Bastion*, discussed in Chapter 5) takes an iconic moment in Australian history – the imminent threat to Australia's borders in 1942 and the decisions by Prime Minister Curtin to bring Australian troops home from the Middle East to defend the country after the fall of Singapore and to align the country's interest with the US defence strategy. It has all the set and costume design hallmarks of the mini-series, but is excessively constrained in its depiction of these momentous events, no doubt due to funding constraints. Rather than the epic sweep and multiperspectivism of the best of the 1980s series, it is reduced to a chamber drama with no shift to world events via documentary footage. It shares with the classic 'AFC genre' films of the 1970s the propensity to end without narrative resolution. Curtin, at his most self-reflective and self-doubting, simply 'fades out' at the end, in the time-honoured traditions of Australian anti-heroism.

Bastard Boys, a two-episode mini-series, is altogether more ambitious and risk-taking. It dramatises the 1998 dispute between the Maritime Union of Australia and Patrick Stevedores and paints a broad picture of what was the most tumultuous workplace dispute in all the Howard years. It takes risks in looking to engage the distracted viewer of contemporary television by ramping up the severe language and the melodramatic characterisation – the excessively white and black portraits painted of the union leadership (particularly the character of Greg Combet) and Patrick's leadership (in the black hat, Chris Corrigan). However, there is little of the classic Kennedy–Miller signature multiperspectivalism and little of the way in which recent political events were transformed into a dramatic structure in, for example, *The Dismissal*. There is creative hesitancy, always closely tied to budget stringency but also a function of the challenges of historical reconstruction. As Chris Scanlon points out, 'trying to portray the complexities of recent political history on a tiny canvas: not quite drama, not quite documentary, it never manages to free itself sufficiently from the events of 1998 to offer a deeper reflection on the implications of those tumultuous events on the country'.[3]

Chapter 7, 'Australian television in world markets' (written with Liz Jacka), also analyses a situation that no longer obtains. It traces the conditions for the growth of Australian television exports up to the mid-1990s, featuring the careers of some of the more successful exports (*Neighbours*, *Paradise Beach*, *The Flying Doctors* and the international television service Australia Television) in case studies. The international television market has changed substantially in the decade since the mid-1990s, with major import substitution in Europe and Asia, increased trade in formats rather than completed product, and international players investing much earlier in the production cycle, including establishing offices in Australia.

But one thing doesn't change: *Neighbours* is still on the box in Britain!

Chapter 5

(1993) Style, form and history in Australian mini-series*

In retrospect, the program that is generally regarded as the first Australian historical mini-series, *Against the Wind*, can be seen to have pioneered many of the protocols of production and reception that have characterised this distinctive television drama format. Produced in 1978 for the Seven Network at the considerable cost, for the time, of $76,000 per episode, the program consisted of thirteen one-hour episodes and dealt, with critical historiographical insight, with the first decades of colonisation in Australia. *Against the Wind*, with its large number of episodes and its discrete as well as continuous episodic structure, tended to resemble earlier Australian historical serials (such as the thirteen-episode *Luke's Kingdom*, 1974–75) more than the mini-series proper. However, its epic historical thematics and narrative coverage, its widely discussed revisionist account of the historical record on early convictism, its promotion and reception as history as well as drama, and its huge critical and ratings

---

* Dates for mini-series discussed are dates of first broadcast in the major metropolitan areas; in some cases these differ from year of production.

success all foreshadow the contours of the historical mini-series phenomenon of the 1980s.

And quite a phenomenon it became. From 1980 to mid-1986, fifty mini-series were made in Australia, and the bicentennial year saw the release of another considerable group (*Captain James Cook, Melba, True Believers, Dirtwater Dynasty, The Alien Years* and *All the Way*) together with the recycling of several series. The mini-series boom was very much an outgrowth of the 10BA tax legislation; its inauguration in 1980, and the diminution of its benefits and effective replacement by 1988, neatly bound the 'high' period of mini-series production.[1] These close links indicate something of the complex of institutional preconditions and contexts for the prioritising of the mini-series at the high-budget end of film and television financing in the 1980s in Australia.[2] These favourable conditions gave us such memorable critical and ratings successes as *A Town Like Alice* (1981), *1915* (1982), *The Dismissal, Waterfront* and *Power Without Glory* (1983), *The Last Bastion, Bodyline* and *Eureka Stockade* (1984), *Anzacs, The Dunera Boys* and *The Cowra Breakout* (1985), *A Fortunate Life* and *The Lancaster Miller Affair* (1986), and *Vietnam* (1987).

However, it is not the purpose here to analyse these preconditions and contexts, nor to survey in broad strokes this plethora of mini-series. Rather, the purpose is to be both more abstract and more particular than either of these approaches would determine. The essay addresses the distinctiveness of the mini-series as a televisual format and indicates some of the innovations and challenges that Australian historical mini-series present in both their representations of national history and in their expansion of the 'horizons of possibility' of televisual form. Such an approach attempts to construct a stylistic and generic map of the Australian mini-series, demonstrating continuities and variations within the format.

A hybrid form

The mini-series is a quite recent addition to the established array of television formats – news, current affairs, light entertainment, series and serial drama, documentary, sport and so on. It is a veritable hybrid, split between the series and serial drama formats, and between documentary and dramatic modes. It can be defined as a limited-run program of more than two parts and less than the thirteen-part season or half-season block associated with continuing serial or series programming, with episodes that are not narratively autonomous (as they are in the series format). Thus, strictly speaking, the term 'mini-series' is a misnomer. However, it is closer to the series format in so far as it moves to conclusive narrative resolution across a limited number of episodes, unlike the serial, with its indefinitely (and what seems at times, infinitely) deferred denouements. Its hybridisation of documentary and dramatic modes creates real definitional problems, and perturbs many viewers and commentators because of the ethical, legal and political imponderables raised by its taste for 'impersonating' history, but it excites just as much rapturous response for the risks and challenges it takes as it 'inscribes the document into experience'.[3]

The mini-series' hybrid status, as might be expected, poses further problems for general theories of televisual form. Commentators have thus sought family resemblances between cinematic forms and modes of promotion and the mini-series. While there are intriguing connections, the dramaturgical structures deployed in mini-series defy easy assimilation to a cinematic model. Finally, the approaches to issues and events taken up in the most interesting examples of the format move easily around traditional categories usually held to divide televisual material into entertainment and information/education. These questions are looked at more closely now.

Quality television

Taking perhaps the most evident aspect first, the Australian historical mini-series is 'quality', 'event' television. Its status is analogous to that of the art cinema in relation to mainstream commercial cinema, albeit without the financial and promotional marginalisation typically experienced by art cinema. Historical mini-series are produced on regularly record-breaking budgets for television, are accompanied by major promotional campaigns, often as flag-carriers leading into new ratings periods, and in turn attract lavish spin-off campaigns and critical and ratings successes, all of which contribute to their status as 'exceptional' television.

The mini-series' placement as quality television registers at several interrelated levels. At an institutional level, it can be traced to the need for the major US commercial networks to inaugurate and market their own genre of up-market material in order to counteract the allegiances public television, cable and subscription services were soliciting from the demographically sensitive market sectors with high disposable incomes. It is evidenced by the diverse and high-profile circulation of the mini-series as event in contiguous formats – from glossy presentations on production history (Brian Carroll's *The Making of A Fortunate Life*), novelisations (Sue MacKinnon's *Waterfront*), reprints of journalistic accounts (Paul Kelly's *The Unmaking of Gough*, reprinted as *The Dismissal* on the release of the mini-series by the same name), coffee-table records of the series (Kristin Williamson's *The Last Bastion*), through to voluminous numbers of letters to the editor, historical reminiscence by actual protagonists, lavish and detailed critical reviews by more usually dyspeptic newspaper critics, and many educational packages produced for secondary students of history, media and social studies.

Further, it is on display in the textual forms and protocols of production of the mini-series. With their high production values – a fastidious attention to historical verisimilitude, epic shooting schedules, the use of film rather than videotape as shooting stock, the highly publicised use of theatrical workshopping techniques to prepare actors exhaustively for historical impersonation – mini-series bear direct comparison with other established zones of quality such as the BBC and ABC classic serials (*The Windsors, The Sullivans*) or the Australian period film of the mid- to late 1970s (*The Getting of Wisdom, The Irishman*). The way this textual and production rhetoric of quality marks out a difference for the mini-series now requires further analysis in terms of its modes of historical representation, its patterns of dramaturgical and narrative structure, and its inflection of the hybrid form of documentary-drama.

Historical representation

Consider the relation of historical mini-series like *The Last Bastion, The Dismissal, The Cowra Breakout* or *Vietnam* to other forms of Australian historical drama, such as the period film – *The Getting of Wisdom, The Irishman, The Mango Tree*, and so on – and television series like *Rush, The Sullivans* and *Carson's Law*. These texts typically centre around fictional characters who achieve a form of 'everyman' status such that they can be considered representative of a nation and its experiences (in youth, in war, in depression). Thus *The Sullivans* presents a 'typical' wartime Australian family. Crucially, these texts operate to set predominantly fictional narratives and characters' lives against the backdrop of historical events: wars, depressions. Tom Ryan notes of period film protagonists, however, that they are people who do not influence the course of history to any extent: they are victims of, rather than participants in, historical events.[4] They achieve representative status precisely because of their historical anonymity.

In contrast, the historical mini-series often deals directly with actual historical events – the Eureka Stockade, the First and

Second World Wars, the dismissal of the Whitlam government, the Kelly story, the Castle Hill rebellion – and offers accounts of those events. Moreover, it often deals with 'large' historical figures – Menzies, Curtin, Churchill, Roosevelt (*The Last Bastion*), Lalor (*Eureka Stockade*), Kelly (*The Last Outlaw*), Bradman, Jardine (*Bodyline*), still-familiar politicians (*The Dismissal*), Melba (*Melba*), Kingsford Smith (*A Thousand Skies*). Rather than being victims of history, or in some cases actually attempting to evade historical change, these characters tend to be represented as the *makers* of history, determining and directly influencing the course of events. In centring such figures and constructing accounts of the events in which they participated, the historical mini-series attempts to accede to history in direct rather than mediated terms, that is, as merely the backdrop for a narrative. In doing so, it operates in different conceptual terms from the period film. For in so far as the protagonist of the period film achieves a sort of everyman status, the genre itself operates in a literary or mythical rather than a historical register. This point is underscored when one considers the reliance on literary adaptation in the period film – for example, *Picnic at Hanging Rock, The Getting of Wisdom, My Brilliant Career, We of the Never Never* – and the lack of it in the most pertinent instances of the historical mini-series. This, in turn, invites a rather different position for the viewer of the mini-series: as knowledgeable citizen rather than distracted consumer.

The period film tends also to reconstruct the past in nostalgic terms. It presents the past as a lost, desirable time, as a golden age of lost ways and values. In contrast, the historical mini-series' representation of the past is not so much nostalgic as it is critical and interventionary. While the period film trades on this mythic representation of a national past, the historical mini-series frequently recreates Australia's past in less nostalgic terms. Thus it criticises the Australian's naivety (rather than innocence) in *The Last Bastion* and *The Dismissal* and presents lazy, prejudiced Australian soldiers as prison guards in *The Cowra Breakout*. *A Fortunate*

Life is primarily an account of a young man's ability to survive a neglected childhood rather than an affectionate reminiscence of a difficult past.

Many mini-series, particularly those produced by the Kennedy–Miller organisation, also promote a more radical 'multiperspectivism', one that effectively displaces the unreflective chauvinism to which so much recent Australian media is prey. In doing so, these mini-series produce remarkably innovative *elliptical* approaches to major historical events in the nation's history. Thus almost half of *The Cowra Breakout* is spent on the Japanese side, encouraging empathy with their point of view. The Japanese scenes contain Japanese dialogue and English subtitles, an extremely unusual departure from the conditions of intelligibility of commercial television. Similarly, *Bodyline*, while more conventionally reverting to a 'little Aussie battler' mode in its later stages, constructs much of its account with reference to the point of view of Jardine (captain of the MCC tour in 1932–33 and a convenient Lucifer in Australian sports hagiographies), Edith (Jardine's English sweetheart) and Fender (friend of Jardine and gentleman cricketer). *The Dismissal* multiplies perspectives and points of narratorial authority with dizzying speed. *Vietnam*, like *The Cowra Breakout*, insists on Vietnamese perspectives and shows them to be as fraught with division as Australian positions with regard to the war and the personal tensions it provoked.

Further, it is arguable that these mini-series take seriously the radical historiographical dictum that 'the past is only interesting politically because of something which touches us in the present'.[5] Thus, *The Last Bastion* mounts a case, *inter alia*, for a greater multilateralism in Australian foreign policy at a time (1984) when the ANZUS alliance was in crisis over New Zealand's refusal to allow US nuclear warships into its harbours and the United States' consequent withdrawal from bilateral defence arrangements. This much is explicitly claimed for the series by one of its producers and scriptwriter, David Williamson, in an interview in the documentary *The*

Making of The Last Bastion. Similarly, it is clear that both *The Cowra Breakout* and *Vietnam* are major documents contributing to setting the emergent discourse of multiculturalism on the national agenda. *The Dismissal* was deemed by the Ten Network to be a sufficient potential intervention in early 1980s politics to delay its broadcast twice until after the March 1983 federal election. It was held to be a unique, and uniquely courageous, staging so close to the event of the most destabilising contravention of constitutional convention in Australian, and probably Westminster, political history.

Dramaturgy and narrative

The historical mini-series presents us with innovative narrative and dramaturgical models when compared with established television formats. All mini-series present themselves with a rhetoric of epic structure, virtually all operate on the model of the nineteenth-century *Bildungsroman*, and several of the best engage with formative historical events in a documentary-drama mode. What are the salient implications to be drawn from these shared formal characteristics?

Epic structure means extreme etiolation of narrative trajectory. A good deal of the criticism that mini-series attract focuses on this point: skeletal narratives padded out to fit predetermined program durations. However, if we consider both the usual length of the mini-series – eight to ten hours of viewing time – and the propensity for historical mini-series to rework events whose narrative consequences are already widely known, its dramaturgical cues for sustaining viewers' interest must lie outside narrative enigma. The commodious temporal format typically allows for a displacement of *event* by *causation* and *consequence*: the events inscribed in titles such as *The Dismissal*, *Bodyline* and *The Cowra Breakout* occur well into the second half of the respective series; in the case of *The Dismissal*, *The Last Bastion* and *Vietnam*, there is a pointed following-through of the political, social and public policy issues that are consequent on the events that are the series' *raison d'etre*. In this sense, the historical mini-series offers an unparalleled upgrading of the terms within which historical information and argument are mediated through mainstream television. Consider, by comparison, that television's representations of history trade on either a comforting nostalgia or a superficial nominalism: on the one hand, history as a lost Eden of traditional values (*The Sullivans*) or as a pure spectacle of the 'otherness' of a national past (*This Fabulous Century*); on the other, history as merely an indefinitely prolonged series of discrete phenomena (news and current affairs).

The pull, then, of narrative enigma is displaced in the historical mini-series by the fact that its plot and resolution have gained social currency before the text is screened. The series' prologue might announce its resolution (the early narration of *The Dismissal*), the narrative may be familiar as social knowledge or as part of a canon of well-known literary texts (*Bodyline, The Dismissal, Eureka Stockade, The Challenge, A Town Like Alice*). Regardless, the circulation of publicity around the screening of a mini-series guarantees such prior knowledge. As a consequence, a different viewing position is invited. The central place conventionally occupied by suspense in televisual drama is replaced by an emphasis on what John Caughie has called the 'documentary look': the terms in which the viewer is situated in relation to the text's careful reconstruction of the past. The ambience of this re-creation can become a central focus of the historical mini-series. This is not to suggest that there are never suspense structures. The known nature of the outcome of the plot, however, alters the function of suspense. One experiences a sense of pathos and tragedy in *The Dismissal* because of the knowledge that Whitlam will be sacked. Similarly, we attend to the *mode* of debate about Japanese honour in the Cowra internment camp *because* its consequences are 'foregiven'.

Much of this 'foregiven' status of the mini-series text has been ascribed by some critics to an all-pervading 'recognition-effect' that secures a safely confirming viewing position.[6] This criticism, however, overlooks or elides crucial aspects of audience composition and response. Not all audiences recognise the historical material with the facility and smugness implied by such criticism. On the contrary, for younger audiences, the historical mini-series may be an unparalleled means by which the document is inscribed into experience, if the number of educational packages produced to accompany mini-series into the classroom is any guide. Second, far from being lulled, many viewers regard mini-series as significant – verifiable or falsifiable historical arguments, if the amount and nature of public correspondence generated around them is taken into account. Third, such a criticism smacks of a governing aesthetics of suspicion: the pleasure taken in the recognition-effect need not necessarily be ideologically complicit in principle.

Perhaps the most crucial narratorial and dramaturgical modality of the historical mini-series, however, is its multiperspectivism – the way in which the epic length and structure both necessitate and make possible a multiplication of authorising perspectives within a sprawling narrative field characterised by the *Bildungsroman* format. Albert Moran puts it this way:

> Structurally, such narratives tend to sprawl. Although the focus is on one or two individuals, nevertheless, as part of an epic sweep, there is often a variety of stories and the accumulation of much social material, the latter often characterised by a painstaking accuracy of detail. The historical credentials of the form are often doubly secured; the elongated time scheme, as well as the extended social and even geographic dimensions and the narrative trajectory of the central figures, is frequently intermeshed with the narrative of more public events. Such narratives often require a 'slowing-down' of the main story. With the accumulation of parallel plots, tangential episodes, multiple themes and so on, the main narrative is frequently displaced. In the end such a narrative may accumulate so much diverse material that it is difficult to bring it to a close. Endings are often not so much a

climax as a 'point of let-up' where certain resolutions are achieved and the story is over.[7]

In the most interesting examples, there is a foregrounded battle for enunciative authority where narrative order is put under considerable stress by contending claims on the historical record. The entrusting of narrative authority on the English side for most of the first half of *Bodyline* was certainly a controversial displacement of enshrined Australian chauvinism. *The Dismissal*'s radically complex mode of narration disseminates narrative authority across time and political combatants. Commentators have variously equated the line the program takes with that of Fraser, Kerr or a left-Labor position of 'maintaining the rage'. Whatever else such differing readings suggest, they attest to the innovative multiperspectivism that certain historical mini-series produce.

Documentary-drama: A stylistic and historical continuum

A third general issue of the nature of the historical mini-series as a textual system concerns the vexed question of documentary-drama. The BBC's banning of Peter Watkins's *The War Game* and the diplomatic crisis between Britain and Saudi Arabia over *The Death of a Princess* are two of the more explosive events which attest to the legal and political as well as textual volatility of the form.[8] This volatility should caution against attempts to define the format; rather, it is more constructive to consider documentary-drama in the historical mini-series on a continuum between two sets of limiting markers. Towards the 'conservative' limit, one might situate mini-series like *1915*, which presents itself as a straight literary adaptation, is structured around fictional characters against a backdrop of historical events, and which attempts little, if any, textual work integrating archival material into the dramatic reconstruction. Towards the 'innovative' limit might be programs like *The Dismissal* and *Vietnam*, which work from original screenplays and make complex use of mixtures of fictional and historical protagonists and archival and reconstructed diegetic material. Somewhere between the two are situated mini-series like *Power Without Glory*, derived from an innovative *roman à clef*, *Anzacs*, *The Last Outlaw* and *Against the Wind*, historical mini-series with original scripts written by experts on their respective subjects which attempt some measure of historical revisionism but which are essentially 'straight' historical dramas; or *The Last Bastion* and *Bodyline*, with their original scripts, mainly historical protagonists and set-piece mixtures of archive and drama.

Let us consider in some detail this question of a stylistic and representational continuum comprehending a broad range of approaches to televisual form and to history in Australian mini-series. There are, of course, many methods of constructing critical parameters for the sixty or so series – more than 400 television hours! – under consideration. A starting point could be their consistent and undoubted importance as rating successes, and the implications of this for the reinvention of indigenous, serious drama with commercial potential could be pursued.[9] The industrial emergence and fortunes of the format might be the focus.[10] Alternatively, period or source groupings in the mini-series might be followed, producing an account such as the following:

- Literary adaptations: *1915, A Fortunate Life, Water Under the Bridge, For the Term of His Natural Life, A Town Like Alice, Robbery Under Arms, Lucinda Brayford*
- Non-historical: *Return to Eden*
- Contemporary history: *The Dismissal, The Challenge, Tracy, Vietnam, Sword of Honour, All the Way, Shout!*
- Early history: *The Timeless Land, Captain James Cook, Against the Wind, The Last Outlaw, For the Term of His Natural Life, Eureka Stockade, Robbery Under Arms*

- Early twentieth-century history: *Anzacs, 1915, A Fortunate Life, Melba, The Alien Years*
- Mid-century: *The Weekly's War, Nancy Wake, The Lancaster-Miller Affair, The Petrov Affair, True Believers, The Last Bastion, The Cowra Breakout, Bodyline, Dunera Boys, A Town like Alice*
- Generational sweep: *Dirtwater Dynasty, Women of the Sun*.

Rather than pursue these kinds of groupings, however, a stylistic and representational continuum would attempt to establish qualitative criteria for discriminating between mini-series in terms of their use of the format and their approach to historical reconstruction. Employing the criteria introduced above, this would involve setting 'conservative' and 'innovative' markers on two axes, the stylistic and the historical.

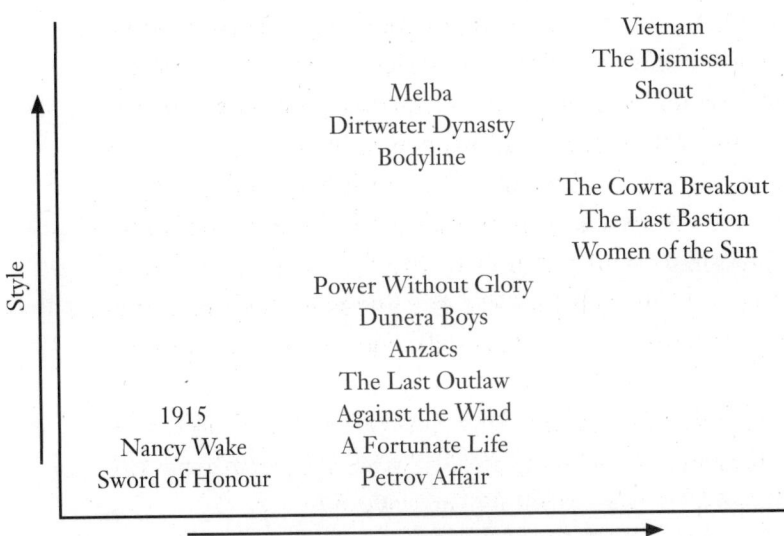

A grid like this, gross as it is, can act as a heuristic device to suggest some fruitful means of categorisation, enabling us to specify the stylistic and representational parameters of Australian mini-series. Let us plot, then, some of the points on this grid.

The Last Bastion

The Last Bastion (1984) is significant for its uncompromising focus on the historical moment of Australia's greatest danger during the Second World War. It is one of only two mini-series (*The Dismissal* is the other significant example) to suppress romance as a major dramaturgical motor and concentrate throughout on political–diplomatic–military vectors in order to structure the drama of the series. It is thus peopled entirely by large historical figures in what are at times complex narrative interactions, which are nevertheless rendered as classically dramatic. This mini-series marks the only contribution to the format by the pre-eminent scriptwriter David Williamson (who was also co-producer). In contrast, *The Petrov Affair* (1987) attempts a reconstruction of a similarly complex historical moment, but fails to develop a coherent dramatic field. Like *Against the Wind* (1978) and *The Last Outlaw* (1981), *The Last Bastion*'s principals claim to have done original research on their subject that will 'substantially rewrit[e] Australian history'.[11]

As we have seen, *The Last Bastion* also makes a strong political argument against Australian diplomatic and military dependency, and by its resilient focus on the drama of diplomatic manoeuvres against the backdrop of a nationalist reading of Australia's marginal international status it takes a reasoned stand against the moralist doxa of both conservative populism and *gauchiste* purism that parliamentary politics and allied diplomacy is a corrupt and corrupting game. Throughout *The Last Bastion*, the effect and affect of political rhetoric is centred and successfully dramatised, as it is in few other mini-series, *The Dismissal* and *Vietnam* excepted. This is a considerable achievement in itself.

One of the most intriguing issues a series like *The Last Bastion* raises is that it arrives at a classical Whitlamite position of greater diplomatic and military independence for Australia by a route that runs counter to the way the same position is argued by contemporary Left historians. Michael Dunn, for instance, in the tradition of the antinationalist Left historiography of Humphrey

McQueen, puts Curtin in the position of having merely shifted dependencies from Britain to America.[12] It suggests much about the commercial and dramaturgical imperatives of research and scripting for television mini-series that Curtin is produced as a Whitlamite *avant la lettre* in *The Last Bastion*. But it also suggests something of the import of such television work that it is ordering 'popular memories' to provide antecedents and traditions for what is still today (within political agenda-setting) considered aberrant and utopian.[13]

The Petrov Affair and *The Dismissal*

Compare *The Petrov Affair*, on the one hand, and *The Dismissal* (1983), on the other, with *The Last Bastion*. The latter series, by the insistence of its achieved political and diplomatic focus, creates a kind of correlative formal interest when considered against dominant character structures of television drama. *The Petrov Affair*, by comparison, is an 'incoherent' text at the level of both political–historical argument and dramatic structure. Drew Cottle, in his discussion of this series, needn't have worried so much over the pernicious New Right ventriloquism of the series, because it has failed to find a line – dramatic as much as political – through the dense weave of issues surrounding the Petrov affair.[14] Nevertheless, the series is an interesting failure because it suggests something of the difficulties posed by the hybrid form of the mini-series. In this case, the genre recipe of the spy thriller and the complexities of political and popular address around an excessively localised moment in Australian history don't play off each other productively.

The Dismissal, by contrast, succeeds spectacularly in finding a dramatic style appropriate to an equally complex and divisive political moment, the sacking of the Whitlam government. This is the mode of reconstructed Greek tragedy: an audacious hyper-dramatisation that grasps the literal import of the cliche 'political theatre', attempting as it does to perform the psychic–social ritual of turning solipsistic left-wing melancholy into a more productive work of 'national mourning'.[15] It is within this global purpose that the radical stylistic gestures of *The Dismissal* – the overwrought omniscience of narratorial voice, the dramaturgical and character architecture of classical Greek tragedy, the quasi-Method actors' preparation and physiognomic and gestural impersonation – should be understood. *The Dismissal*, as its producer and scriptwriter Terry Hayes has noted, 'changed the landscape of Australian television'.[16]

Melba and *Shout!*

Another obvious pairing of mini-series is that of *Melba* (1988) and *Shout! The Story of Johnny O'Keefe* (1986). What a strange text *Melba* is, exemplifying as it does so many of the stylistic imponderables of the mini-series format. It has all the hallmarks of the conservative spirit of reconstruction: period costume, chamber drama, and a straight biographic focus cutting against any claims to multiperspectivism. On the other hand, this describes only half the program time; after the first episode, the rest is given over to enormous chunks of Linda Cropper deftly mouthing a veritable *catalogue raisonné* of Melba's operatic career. Like the expansive periods of subtitled Japanese and Vietnamese in *Cowra Breakout* and *Vietnam*, the mere fact that commercial network television took to its bosom such 'marginal' interests – opera, multiculturalism – is cause to suggest stylistic departures of some moment.

Look also at the demands that the dramaturgy of *Melba* places on audiences: its ponderous pacing and movement (or, rather, lack of it), its mostly unrelieved reliance on a talking heads/chamber drama format, and the evaporation of narrative tension or enigma through excessive signposting. The success of *Melba* must point to the successful marketing of mini-series as addressing the heightened civic consciousness of audiences, as providing informative 'history lessons'. This form of address legitimises a divergent (reflective, conscientious?) mode of dramaturgy within the regimes of commercial television and therefore creates a space, however underdeveloped it is in many mini-series, for such strangenesses as, here, the oracularity of opera repeatedly suspending an already extremely leisurely narrative movement.

Interestingly, though, the address to a heightened national consciousness in *Melba* can be regarded as very much balanced against the more recent industrial imperatives to sell high-budgeted mini-series in overseas markets. *Melba*'s investment prospectus claims that the series 'will be an international series which combines a major title, momentous events and international locations'.[17] As can be seen from this series, as well as such examples as *The Last Frontier* (1987), *Nancy Wake* (1987) and *Dirtwater Dynasty* (1988), these industrial vectors have decided effects on choices of location, generic convention and cast.

The same could not be said for *Shout!*. One of the most tightly narrativised mini-series (written by Robert Caswell), it also has a highly complex form of local address and a powerful approach to the relation of archive and drama. Historian Ray Evans's fine analysis of this series dwells on some of the problems posed by its compelling attempt to represent the dialectics of cultural dependency in an import culture such as Australia's.[18] The historian will still find much that falls short of the full amplitude of considered analytical research in even the most outstanding television drama, but that should not divert our attention from the achievements of such television drama, of which *Shout* is indisputably an example.

For a mini-series, *Shout!* has a frenetic, almost hysterical, narrative pacing and a central characterisation, Terry Serio as The Wild One himself, who stands alone among principal characters in mini-series as a whirlwind presence (Nicole Kidman's performance as Megan Goddard in *Vietnam* comes to mind as similar). The opening sequence sets this tone: the oneiric camera movement through an empty Sydney Stadium, into the past, into the big production theme number 'Shout', and then out again, in slow motion, to a surreal gesture of childhood psychodrama, with little Johnny O'Keefe screaming to get his own way with his mother, and teacher Brother Marzorini ominously laying down The Law of the Father. The dense circumambient aurality, the oneirics, the performer as ritual sacrifice – it all recalls Martin Scorsese's *Raging Bull*, and not simply because it is set in a converted boxing ring.

The dream theme is doubly appropriate, because it is the dream of movement within the fixed rules of exchange in a culturally dependent nation that is the narrative crux of *Shout!*. 1954: Johnny courts Maryanne at the flicks; they watch a Cinesound Review item that tells them that Australian car manufacturing can't at the moment be as good as overseas models – 'in the meantime, we can always dream'. Lee Gordon, displaced American, has a dream of 'world-class entertainment for Australia'. 1956: Johnny and Maryanne kiss at a shopfront display of televisions as Shirley Strickland and Betty Cuthbert win gold at the Melbourne Olympics, giving Johnny the opportunity to demand recognition that Australians can be as good as anyone in the world.

But *Shout!* is minimally chauvinistic in its cultural politics. If anything, as Evans points out, it accords too great a role to the enabling status of Lee Gordon, and its strict bio-pic parameters move the focus away from developments parallel to that of O'Keefe in Australian rock. Nevertheless, it 'performs' the dialectics of exchange in an import culture brilliantly and, on the way, provides – as does *Melba* – an extraordinary repertoire of the aural and visual archive running, in *Shout!*, from the 1950s to the 'psychedelic' 1970s.

Sword of Honour and *Vietnam*

Finally, consider another comparison between two mini-series with similar thematic foci, *Sword of Honour* (1986) and *Vietnam* (1987). Both deal with the effects of the Vietnam War on several members of a family; both cover similar time-frames – the mid-1960s to 1972 (in the case of *Vietnam*) or 1975 (in the case of *Sword of Honour*). Both map generational difference and conflict on to national conflict; both deal with the intensified intra-generational conflict posed by war service on the one hand and the counter-cultural peace movement on the other; both have major reconciliatory finales. However, the manifest differences between the two can serve as a telling demonstration of the kinds of issues that are central to an appreciation of style and representation in Australian mini-series.

These two series belong towards opposite ends of the stylistic and historical continuum mentioned earlier. *Sword of Honour* is a straight character drama that does little with the capacious narrative potential of the mini-series format except fulfill its worst-case scenario: slackness of narrative movement unrelieved by anything else punctuating or layering the plot at the level of archival inscription, the insertion of large historical figures, or even a heartfelt chauvinistic nationalism. Gestures towards some of these bottom-line elements help to salvage bits of otherwise equally awful series such as *All the Way* (1988), *The Challenge* (1986) or *Captain James Cook* (1988). Even in its central theme – the fortunes of an extended family group over an extended time span – *Sword of Honour* manages little, because the characters undergo little fundamental reorientation, as *Vietnam*'s central quartet of characters do. Perhaps the only moment of layering or arresting intensity in the eight hours is in the third hour, when Tony is taken to Frank's private altar to military glory, mateship and death. *Sword* might have elegant symmetries of character construction, as Ina Bertrand's analysis of this and other treatments of Vietnam in recent film and television posits, but they never move off the analyst's page.[19]

Vietnam, by contrast, has all the hallmarks of an omega point in Australian mini-series production. It has invented a dramaturgy of the archive, going further than any other series not only in archival inscription but in integrating that into a complex, multiperspectival dramatic structure. Each pivotal character – Douglas, Evelyn,

Phil and Megan – has his or her own narrative trajectory, which interweaves with other pivotal trajectories as well as providing the focus for a series of relatively autonomous subsidiary narrative worlds. Historical movement – eight years from November 1964 to December 1972 – also means the slow accretion or layering of perspectives such that when the family finally re-forms at the end, we have learned to think of them historically. To think of the central characters historically is to decentre them in purely characterological terms. They gradually assume the status of markers of sectoral divisions within a historically delineated population, itself undergoing irreversible sea-change. Their tentative reconciliation at the end is strongly overdetermined by its taking place on the night of Whitlam's 1972 electoral triumph. This propitiatory utopianism is probably the most breathtaking example of the mini-series best-case scenario – the successful mapping of the personal on to the public and vice versa. The narrative architectonics are constantly enlivened by a prodigiously pleasureful amount of archival quotation, aural as much as visual, which can be read both for its own sake – the texture and pathos of instant recognition and impossible difference – and in terms of its layering of narrative. *Vietnam* can lay claim to constitute a remarkable *Gesamtkunstwerk* of Australian television.[20]

Conclusion

Consideration of the general characteristics of the Australian mini-series in this discussion has prevented extensive analysis of more than a few important examples, but it has suggested that such work is valuable: the mini-series offers a rich field for investigating the potential for innovation in contemporary television. The format, and the uses to which it has been put in certain series at the 'innovative' end of a continuum, might suggest a greater range of possibilities for broadcast television than general accounts of it and of its differences from cinema have suggested. Further, the mini-series has arguably given local and international audiences many memorable representations of major determinants of Australian history.

Chapter 6

(1988) Kennedy–Miller: 'House style' in Australian television

Kennedy–Miller Productions became regarded, during the 1980s, as the most dynamic 'boutique' production house in Australian film and television. Examining its mini-series output within the frame of a production house case study, as is done here, enables several constitutive features of the contemporary industry to be embraced, while focusing most particularly on the textual and cultural features of a remarkable body of work: *Mad Max* (1979), *Mad Max 2/The Road Warrior* (1981), *The Dismissal* (1983), *Bodyline* (1984), *The Cowra Breakout* (1985), *Mad Max Beyond Thunderdome* (1985), *Vietnam* (1987), *Dirtwater Dynasty* (1988), *Sportz Crazy* (1988), *The Clean Machine* (1988) and *The Riddle of the Stinson* (1988). (This latter year also brought *Fragments of War: The Story of Damien Parer* and *Dead Calm*.) To these may be added the intriguing 'side' issues of George Miller 'moonlighting' on *The Twilight Zone* (1983) for Stephen Spielberg, the arrangement for Kennedy–Miller to work on much of the post-production of the big Warner's film *The Witches of Eastwick* (1987) as part of the deal for Miller to direct, and the company acting as executive producer of John Duigan's 'personal' project, *The Year My Voice Broke* (1987).

House style

The 'production house case study' has had a venerable, if intermittent, tradition. At its best, it has sought to place a context-sensitive focus on the distinctive relations of production, output and vision of a 'creative ensemble' during a particular historical moment within a wider industrial field, usually of mainstream entertainment. Film critics and historians have spoken at length of the preferred genre specialties, financial standings and ideological predilections of principal personnel of the Hollywood majors during the period of the established studio system and assimilated these to a weak sense of 'house style'.[1] However, the focus of such attempts is too broad when considered against smaller-scale framings of the 'creative ensemble' carving out a negotiated difference within mainstream entertainment industries. Early examples of such an approach to analysis of media industries – Hugh Fordin's study of the Freed Unit at MGM, David Pirie's *A Heritage of Horror* on Hammer in England[2] – were intent on celebrating intensive and successful genre production in continuity with the global thrust of their respective – Hollywood, British – film industries.

Perhaps the crucial advance in the production house case study method was provided by Charles Barr's and John Ellis's work, and debate, on Ealing Studios.[3] In these important studies, the question of Ealing establishing a negotiated difference within the context of the wider national industrial context was pursued. The distinctive relations of production set up by particular personnel were considered as determining in some way the style and recurrent concerns of the film product of the studio. Additionally, the distinctiveness of Ealing was posited, at least in part, as consisting in its project of national definition – the 'projection of England'. Since these studies, research into 'contexts of creativity' has been continued by the Leicester group, among others, and full-blown production house studies, such as those on Euston Films and MTM, have appeared. Elements of the house study approach in the Australian context can be found in Albert Moran's monograph on *Bellamy* and his general history of Australian drama production, *Images and Industry*.[4]

What are the defining marks of the industrial position and 'house style' of Kennedy–Miller? One immediate observation would be that a governing assumption of most production house studies is a measurable, significant and widely perceived difference holding between the company style and product under examination and the wider industry context and its implied norms. In the context of Australian filmmaking, the longevity of Kennedy–Miller (the present company was formed after the first *Mad Max* film, but the initial Byron Kennedy–George Miller partnership had been in operation since the mid-1970s) certainly establishes a difference in terms of the typical company structure attending feature production. In the context of independent television production, it is not so much longevity that is pertinent but that Kennedy–Miller lays claim to being the most significant and successful producer across the boundaries of film and television.

There have been a few earlier instances of 'small packagers' (as Kennedy–Miller would be designated within the topography of Australian television) moving between film and television. What distinguishes Kennedy–Miller within this history are (1) its consistently high success rates, (2) the comparable levels of critical and commercial success both film and television projects have enjoyed, and (3) the extent to which production and textual style have crisscrossed the 'divide', informing each other.

But, first, what is the nature of the company's 'creative ensemble'? Perhaps most importantly, the Kennedy–Miller 'discourse' embodies an explicitly anti-auteurist stance and an advancement of the notion of 'corporate authorship'. This may not appear particularly distinctive within television production, but for a company that 'made its name' in film and maintains international circulation principally on that initial reputation it is significant. This is the reason advanced by George Miller, among others in the ensemble, for maintaining a distance from otherwise favourable conditions for film production in Hollywood. A hierarchical division of labour is to be resisted – thus one of the attractions of television, where a more formed tradition of collaboration exists. The longevity of Kennedy–Miller, one of the few 'real' independent production companies in Australian film and television, according to Hayes, has allowed a tradition of collaboration to develop momentum over the decade.

There is to be no 'rote' television, organised around 'industry standard' distinctions. Many writers of script material, with the major exception of Hayes, are directors as well in the Kennedy–Miller ensemble: Chris Noonan, John Duigan, Phil Noyce, John Power, Michael Jenkins, Denny Lawrence, Lex Marinos. Producers and co-producers might also write or direct: Hayes, Miller. Ensemble members who enter further down the line, as researcher, line producer or co-writer, might 'move up' or multi-task as scriptwriter, creative producer or production manager: Francine Finnane, Margaret Kelly, Barbara Gibbs. Carl Schultz, feature director, became 'comprehensive' working on *The Dismissal* and *Bodyline*, according to Hayes. George Ogilvie, theatre director, has spoken of the way in which the 'collaborative' atmosphere of Kennedy–Miller smoothed his 'phenomenal mid-life turnaround' to television and film direction: 'the medium of film has brought him closer to the possibility of true collaboration than he'd ever experienced in theatre'.[5] That Ogilvie co-directed *Mad Max Beyond Thunderdome* with Miller is a 'fair indication of the brashly unorthodox methodology that his [Miller's] company is now famous for'.[6] A similarly fair indication of the collaborative atmosphere would be that those who allegedly can't work within the ensemble frame, such as Ron Blair on *The Dismissal* and Robert Caswell on *Bodyline*, have been fired. Such incidents and others have led to the Screen Writers' Guild 'warning' its members about Kennedy–Miller's contractual conditions and accreditation.

This repertoire or ensemble model, when successful, can also act as a power base, enabling the Kennedy–Miller principals to distance themselves from industry parameters in various ways, while at the same time providing a kind of umbrella organisation for patronage of various kinds. Terry Hayes maintains a distance from the Screen Producers' Association, and delivers himself of recipes for industry reorganisation which basically promote the Kennedy–Miller model as the model for survival into the 1990s: the AFC standing back from policy formulation and providing seed money only – 'bureaucrats' shouldn't intervene; let the industry renew itself through 'quality' television rather than throwing public money at high-risk feature production; the emphasis should be on developing scripting talent – there are only three or four 'good' scriptwriters in Australia and Kennedy–Miller has used the talents of all but one of them, David Williamson. The Kennedy–Miller 'powerbase' also enables Miller's international reputation as auteur director *not* to lead to either/or choices of where to pursue a career, as such reputations have for other Australian 'pantheon' directors.[7] *The Twilight Zone* and *Witches of Eastwick* did not pose major shifts of trajectory; Miller was able to engage in these American projects without 'breaking stride' with Kennedy–Miller production plans.

As patron, the company principals pride themselves on having provided an umbrella for the transition to television of a number of the country's foremost directorial talents in film and theatre – Phillip Noyce, John Duigan, Ken Cameron, George Ogilvie. There has been general 'service' to the industry, in the screen acting and writing workshops sponsored by the company. Providing the umbrella for Duigan's 'personal' project, *The Year My Voice Broke*, was especially pleasing, and showed the reach of the Kennedy–Miller 'bloodline'.

An important symbol in the formation of the Kennedy–Miller signature was the widely reported and celebrated importation of theatrical workshopping techniques into preparation for mini-series and, later, feature films. This contributed a great deal to the 'circulation' of Kennedy–Miller television drama as 'making character exploration an art form', which, intriguingly, sits cheek by jowl with characterisations of Kennedy–Miller film work as cartoon-strip genre exploitation having, in Phillip Adams's inimitable words, 'all the moral uplift of *Mein Kampf*'.[8] The management of contradictions in the signature will be discussed later, but note here the difference for television practices (and, indeed, most film practices) implied in the full-blown Stanislavskian Actors' Studio rhetoric employed to describe Kennedy–Miller workshopping by its initiator, George Ogilvie:

> You're creating a world together. I discovered that a director can actually leave an actor alone with their role – as long as you develop a world in which that actor can live. I'm reacting against . . . the director . . . making the actor do what he wants him or her to do, rather than bringing out what the actor knows is inside. Instead of just admiring an actor's performance, I want to be absorbed into the world they inhabit. Too often, I find I'm just watching performances, and they stand out because the world in which they live is inadequate.[9]

Hayes similarly describes the Kennedy–Miller workshopping enterprise as a search for 'organic realism' and part of his, Byron Kennedy's and George Miller's 'curiosity' that led to various 'inquiries' – into the institution of Hollywood immediately after the first *Mad Max*, into 'pure acting' with *The Dismissal*, into repertoire collaboration: 'we've got to get on the same train if we're all going to end up at the same destination'. Of course, the actual process of workshopping has included writers, directors and technical crew as well as actors, and can be seen in quite practical terms as a creative form of personnel management on large, unwieldy epic projects. Whatever, this innovation stamped the Kennedy–Miller signature indelibly on Australian television in 1982, at the point of the mini-series upsurge. There have been attempts at imitation, and other directors had used it previously, notably Stephen Wallace in *Captives of Care*. It was used by Equity and some actors to demand a general upgrading of conditions in Australian television, but no one else has applied it on the scale of Kennedy–Miller.

Another distinctive industrial aspect of the signature is the 'monogamous affair' the Ten Network has enjoyed with the company as purchasers and broadcasters of all Kennedy–Miller television product in Australia, which is paralleled by a similar relationship with Warners for the second and third *Mad Max* films, *The Witches of Eastwick* and *Dead Calm*. Ten took up *The Dismissal* despite misgivings about its 'difficult' subject matter and has since been able to build its reputation for 'quality' drama on the shoulders of Kennedy–Miller. This in turn has advantages for Kennedy–Miller in that it has accrued a 'big residue of bargaining power' with the network, according to Hayes. As mini-series budgets move near the $800,000 to $1,000,000 per hour mark, Hayes argues that Kennedy–Miller is virtually unique in being able to extract comparable network presales.[10] Thus it is in the relatively luxurious position of being able to meet the present imperative towards co-production and internationalisation on its own terms. For instance, although *Dirtwater Dynasty* has many of the marks of the international trend in current mini-series, it has been able to resist 'overseas casting pressure', unlike *The Last Frontier*.

Of course, none of these marks of distinctiveness make much sense without some accounting for the accrued textual signature and success of Kennedy–Miller material. There have been no 'failures'; each individual film or mini-series has made a marked contribution, whether in financial terms, in international visibility, in stylistic innovation, or in terms of agenda-setting national representation, and often several of these at once. The company has been 'incredibly successful'[11] and stands second to none in Australian film and television, except perhaps when considered against the optimum financial records of the Hogan/Cornell *Crocodile Dundee* films.

The Kennedy–Miller principals see themselves fundamentally as 'storytellers'; all the categories reflective of an industrial division of labour should be dissolved into this one overarching concept. Storytelling implies a desire and an ability to tap the collective unconscious. Miller and Hayes learned from encounters with Joseph Campbell, one-time Jung editor and author of *Hero with a Thousand Faces*, that:

> the function of storytellers [is] very basic . . . that stories are shared by different cultures throughout all time and space, and that through that process we are given access to the totality of human experience. You and I as individuals are not likely to share all the experiences available to humankind but somehow myths distil experience and put us in touch with what is eternal in man.[12]

These are the sorts of claims that might not seem out of place in the discourse of the Promethean auteur, but when they are situated as central to a film and television company's 'house style', and when a series of stylistic, thematic and organisational implications flow from them, grounds for a distinctiveness must arise. Such claims certainly resonate strongly with the bardic or social-ritual function identified below as characteristic of Kennedy–Miller mini-series. They also are consistent with much of the critical effort expended on articulating the particular power, success and influence of the *Mad Max* films.[13] Certainly they are cited by Miller as the reason for the strongly cross-cultural attraction of the films: 'those of us who did *Mad Max I* were the unwitting servants of the collective unconscious',[14] breaking ground for Australian film in places as diverse as Japan, France and southern United States. Thus, there is no final difference for Kennedy–Miller between storytelling in an explicitly national frame and a 'universalist' tapping of the roots of collective experience.

This might also suggest a way in which 'inconsistencies' in appraisal of the Kennedy–Miller signature – *Mein Kampf* over humanist character study – are managed. The signature intersects with different institutional spaces – over time, from 1979 to the present [1988], in terms of funding strategies, across the parameters of film and television – by experimenting with 'storytelling' in different formats. It further indicates certain interconnected weaknesses and strengths of Kennedy–Miller rhetoric.

On the one hand, there is Hayes's argument that the 'message' of the mini-series can be summed up as 'don't trust the bastards', 'those in power will always let you down'. Such a conservative populist reading of the storytelling imperative doesn't do justice to Kennedy–Miller's institutional dramas, *The Dismissal* and *The Clean Machine* in particular, but also *Vietnam*. On the other hand, there is the storytelling imperative turned to quite radical ends, with Hayes's insistence that the story field of a mini-series must have contemporary resonance in the social field of audiences. On this basis, Hayes regards many of the choices made by Australian mini-series producers to be flawed, to lack 'resonance'. And, of course, such radical recasting of history sends the professional historian, self-appointed keeper of the public past, into apoplectic overreaction.[15]

Further pursuing the Kennedy–Miller signature, we might note the productive blurring of any final distinctions between film and television personnel and the consistent predilection for original scripting over literary adaptation. But, finally, consider the signature as a product of a *male* ensemble. There is no doubt that a rough homology exists between the mostly male constitution of the Kennedy–Miller creative ensemble and the types of material worked on. As Margaret Kelly, creative producer on *The Cowra Breakout*, notes, 'They are boys, and they're interested in boys' subjects'. But Kelly also points out that it was her reaction that probably short-circuited a mooted project that 'involved only women'.[16] The ensemble approach has additionally given certain women possibilities of 'organic' movement through the creative hierarchy; as we have seen, the best examples would be Margaret

Kelly, Barbara Gibbs and Francine Finnane. And the 'prestige' signature has showcased the talents of emerging performers such as Nicole Kidman in serious dramatic roles that were hitherto unforthcoming. Certainly one of the most ingenious roles, Edith Clarke in *Bodyline*, and some of the more memorable performances and roles in Kennedy–Miller material have been women's: Tina Turner 'in all her black Americanness'[17] in *Beyond Thunderdome*, Nicole Kidman in *Vietnam*, Victoria Longley in *Dirtwater Dynasty*. And the roles accorded Longley in this series precipitated an innovative 'feminisation' of the epic mode, the central dramaturgical motor of the mini-series format.

The mini-series

General issues relating to the mini-series as a distinctive form of Australian television drama form a kind of analytical 'hinterland' to the readings of Kennedy–Miller series that are offered here and that have been developed elsewhere.[18]

The Dismissal has accrued a legendary status. If the first *Mad Max* threw the possibilities of genre reworkings in the Australian cinema into high relief, *The Dismissal* 'changed the landscape of Australian television'[19] such that it can be used as a benchmark of innovative possibilities forgone in the present climate of imperatives towards internationalisation.[20] Despite the major successes of the first two *Mad Max* films, Kennedy–Miller's concept for 'the first television program in the world which has dared to deal with politicians still in power'[21] had real difficulty being sold. Finally, the original *Mad Max* connection – Greg Coote, who, along with Graham Burke, was one of the instigators of the Roadshow distribution deal in 1979, was by 1982 at Ten in Sydney – came through with a presale for the series, despite pessimism about its ratings chances. It just seemed so 'ABC'! Treated like a hot potato by the network – rescheduled twice in the midst of early election fever in late 1982 to early 1983 – it was broadcast at an inauspicious time in the wake of the 'saturation politics' of the March 1983 elections. Despite all this, episodes peaked in the 40s in some markets, it averaged 38 in Sydney and had an all-cities average of 32 – a major success. Also, it may be that *The Dismissal* 'changed the landscape', but its *sui generis* focus on contemporary politics has remained just that – largely untouched by subsequent mini-series.

None of this, however, can detract from *The Dismissal*'s unparalleled *experimentation* in televisual form and historical representation. Like many ground-breaking texts and styles in the revival period (the 'ocker' film, *Mad Max* and other exploitation genre reworkings, to name the most outstanding), this series has not received adequate considered appraisal, beyond, that is, its plethora of journalistic kudos. An 'aesthetics of suspicion', which now appears overwrought and precious, governed much response from textual critics.[22] In effect, if not in intent, this kind of analysis ironically comes to resemble the textually illiterate dismissals of mini-series' work of popular-dramatic historical representation by too many historians. To avoid the tedium of raking over old coals, it is worth reframing the question of *The Dismissal* as 'experimental project'.

First, *The Dismissal* experiments in the transposition of cinematic to televisual form. George Miller has spoken of the difficulties a cinematising mentality has in dealing with the delegative, 'objectifying' propensities of television, the fact that camera movement and framing, tense choices and spectacle have to be rethought for a 'medium of lazy filmmaking'.[23] *The Dismissal* may be thought of as the Kennedy–Miller series that pushes the format as far towards a cinematic model as possible, which is not surprising, given that it was the initial television project, and followed on the heels of two films lauded for their 'cinematicity'. *Bodyline* and, to a greater extent, *Cowra Breakout* embrace the format and push its propensities in more 'medium-specific' directions. *Vietnam* and *Dirtwater Dynasty*, in very different ways, establish 'recombinant' – televisual and cinematic – forms.

The overwrought and highly insistent narration of *The Dismissal* can be seen as a 'cinematising' device, 'bridging the gap' between television drama and audience. Interestingly, Miller cites *Rebecca* as a model for constructive use of narration, and certainly the noir-like tone of determinist fatality pervading *The Dismissal* is set up by this means. The narration plays a very complex role in mediating past for present: it 'corrects' statements, intervenes in and reframes open-ended dramatic situations within the temporal diegesis, 'reminds' the audience of matters that occurred between 1975 and 1983, and provides sweepingly global moral and ideological frames for the events. Jodi Brooks, in 'Dismissing', enters into detailed discussion of the complex variations of tense, 'degrees' of omniscience, and narrative function performed by the narration. She also invokes different models for such insistent narratorial intervention: Japanese Kabuki, Greek choric 'ventriloquism', the modernist novel. In her deft hands, *The Dismissal* could start to become, in Barthes's terms, a scriptable text – an amazing experiment in televisual form and modes of historical inscription that opens up a veritable world of possibilities. However, it all has to be finally sheeted home to an aesthetics of suspicion and the allocation of political brownie points:

> *The Dismissal* flaunts itself. It is an unashamed spectacle offering security – the thrill of anticipation in the security of retrospection, and mastery – an incorporative voice-over claiming not only temporal control but also spatial control, a religiosity which transcends any recreation of a political event.[24]

But 'religiosity' gives it away. The high commitment of the Kennedy–Miller 'creative ensemble' to what Fiske and Hartley call the 'bardic' function of television[25] comes up against a poststructuralist suspicion of any gesture of 'incorporation'. But such suspicion is an *a priori* refusal of the self-understanding of most, if not all, broadcast television, and not only that (extremely large) proportion of it that deserves the utmost refusal. It all depends on what constructed community one is 'incorporated' into.

All Kennedy–Miller mini-series invoke this bardic function, proclaim their status as 'social text' through their transparent use of history for the present, albeit with differing results. But the bard or the Kabuki 'shouters' or the Greek choric voices know their place. To be able to comment, they must adopt a position somewhere to the side. The bardic, or ritual, function of these television 'histories' implies no one political or ideological position, but *a* multiplication and historicisation of them. Their *politique* is the more indirect one of actively inviting differing responses, while at the same time reopening 'old' discourses buried by the amnesia of a 'managed' history and 'equalising' more marginalised discourses.

The Dismissal is the most explicitly 'experimental' of the Kennedy–Miller series in its adoption of the bardic function. It invents a dramatic style appropriate to a complex and divisive political moment – the sacking of the Whitlam government – and to a perceived work of 'national *mourning*' yet to be undertaken:

> But I want to tell you about our country and about something that happened then that nearly tore it apart. This isn't going to be easy – it's still there, in our memory. For many Australians, bitterness is never very far away, but maybe now we can understand, and to understand is to forgive. (Part 1)

Understanding *The Dismissal* as heightened social ritual also 'explains' why it puts itself forward, and is used, as a form of public Rorschach test – why commentators have variously identified it as privileging a left Labor stance of 'maintaining the rage', as identifying Fraser with the narration's omniscience, or of 'saving' Kerr by limning his tawdry role in terms of a grandiloquent Hamlet. The work of mourning implies no 'symbolic' unanimity, but an engendering of a process.

The cinematising tendency of *The Dismissal* contributes here as well. For a mini-series, it has a very strong narrative tempo controlled by the inexorability of its timeline and continual movements of retrospectivity and prospectivity at the level of narration. The actual diegetic spaces employed for the most part throughout the series are a succession of parliamentary offices, corridors and backrooms. But these minimal televisual spaces are layered with a dense cinematic texture, a heightened interpenetration of what John Caughie calls the 'dramatic' and 'documentary looks'.[26] Throughout, the documentary look – composed of date and place titles, narration, newspaper headlines, reconstructed television interviews, implied actuality footage (such as the Kerr 'boyhood' in Part 5) and actual archival material (such as Whitlam's 'Kerr's cur' speech in Part 6) – resonates. As well, the dramatic look dynamises the 'chamber drama' of endless political plotting and counterplotting. *Mad Max* stylistics ricochet around the cramped rooms – rapid track-ins, oversized close-ups of the faces of the principals, *leitmotifs* of angle and framing such as shooting Fraser and Whitlam constantly from beneath, montage and *verite* sequences. The visual and aural texture of *The Dismissal* owes much to this unprecedented interpenetration of documentary and dramatic modes.

Bodyline was spectacularly successful. It is the highest rating Kennedy–Miller mini-series, averaging 47 over its four nights in Melbourne and 37 nationally on initial broadcast. It is also, and probably not coincidentally, the Kennedy–Miller series that can be marked out most clearly as invoking a populist mode of address around a topic – the 'bodyline' cricket test series between Australia and England in 1932–33 when, as the program publicity put it, 'England declared war on Australia' – more encrusted in chauvinistic legend than any other Kennedy–Miller mini-series treatment.

Seemingly acknowledging the rather intractably spotless image of Don Bradman in national folklore, the Kennedy–Miller ensemble sought for other trajectories and dramatic loci to structure their first 'long' mini-series, effectively decentring the individual 'hero'. The result is a remarkably elliptical approach to the moment announced by the series' title: the bodyline tests. Indeed, less than 10 per cent of series time is spent on the cricket field, and more than half the narrative has elapsed before the actual bodyline series commences. Very few Australian mini-series play this loose with their historical anchorages.

As was remarked often in the publicity buildup to the series, the cricket action sequences might occupy only a fraction of screen time but they are the material that will attract the most attention. 'The whole enterprise is a challenging one ... because nobody before has tried to dramatise action on a cricket field, much less bodyline action.'[27] Or, the wider question of the dramatic representation of sport as a mythological locus of Australian culture is invoked:

> The real importance *of Bodyline* is that it breaks new, or almost new, ground. It is remarkable that in a country where so many of our heroes over the years have been sportsmen there have been so few attempts to dramatise their deeds. If *Bodyline* succeeds, it may be the start of a new tradition.[28]

It is here that *Bodyline* maintains the Kennedy–Miller 'bloodline' of stylistic innovation. The cricket action sequences once again 'invent' a documentary-drama style where none like it existed. They are truly strange. On the one hand, great effort was expended, in research, costuming and the training of actors, and set and location design, to 'document', to 'recreate' the historical texture, and similar effort went into publicising it. On the other hand, there is a studied 'unreality', a surreal metaphorisation on the dramatic plane that sent the 'purists' into a frenzy.[29]

There is a gesture towards the Packerisation of televised cricket, particularly in the construction of a sonic field and the use of individualising cutaways in these sequences. But the 'intricate patchwork'[30] of sound, camera movement and angle, slow and fast motion and analytical editing has its own 'cinematic' integrity and intensity rivalling the boxing set pieces of *Raging Bull*, all stitched together around the marvellously explicit documentary anachronism of Norman May calling the games. The 'unreality' of these sequences derives not only from the unavoidable amateurishness of the cricketing talents of the actors but, at a higher level, the supplanting of the technique of cricket by the technique of cinema as spectacle. This is part of the series' strategy to displace the pedantry of 'tens of thousands of cricket experts out there waiting to pounce on the most trivial error'[31] and to secure for itself a broadly based audience and a reviewers' rhetoric of cinematic pleasure: 'cheeks blowing, then to his feet pounding towards the wicket, boots thumping on the turf like the sound of a heartbeat through a stethoscope'.[32]

Bodyline also works to secure such an audience through its approach to narrative structure and narration. When these elements are taken together with the foregoing, we can begin to see the logic of the public circulation of a series like *Bodyline* as 'simply not cricket. It breaks almost all the rules that govern commercially-produced television drama in Australia'.[33] There is the 'daring move'[34] of a female narrator – Jardine's sweetheart, Edith Clarke – who, as one of the several diegetic 'delegates' of audience sectors, 'knows nothing' about cricket but articulates its 'anthropological' significance. She is, after all, an Egyptologist! From her long prologue, here is the quintessential Kennedy-Miller opening gambit:

> It's a time that's gone now. Fading from our memory, it will soon survive only in the tales we tell our children. But what a time it was – a time of Empire . . . never before or since has any country embraced a craze the way that Britain embraced their Empire . . . To understand, you have to go back . . .

This is probably all the more significant as Edith is a 'composite' character, created specifically to perform this function. Cooper, the sports journalist who also performs a sort of delegated narratorial role in the body of the series, is another 'composite'. 'While important to the integral story, neither is central to the historical plot', says the publicity.[35] Thus, the multiperspectivist narrative structure of this 'sprawler' shifts focus across several characters, historical and fictional – Edith, Jardine, Fender, Bradman, Bradman's sweetheart and then wife, Jessie, the journalist Cooper, the respective national boards of management, the barracker.

Most particularly, though, the centre of the narrative is Jardine and this constitutes the central displacement and dramaturgical ambiguity for the Kennedy–Miller 'signature' within the protocols of Australian mini-series. Is *Bodyline*'s focus on Jardine and the texture of Empire values to be read in the Kennedy–Miller tradition of 'making character exploration an art form'[36] or as a reductive chauvinistic appeal to the 'C'mon Aussie set'?[37] In one sense, of course, it is both, and this is what probably allows *Bodyline* its status as the most 'popular' of the Kennedy–Miller mini-series. But it does point to an aspect of its structure that is at once its boldest innovation and its main frailty. The expansive exploration of the background and motivations of Jardine (who is constructed on the model of narrative 'enigma') decisively displaces nationalist parochialism, but it unbalances dramatic symmetry, as there is no comparable Australian characterisation (it is the Australian test 'ensemble', rather than Bradman alone, who are characterised). It is not until *The Cowra Breakout* that the elegant symmetries of 'character exploration as an art form' are achieved.

The Cowra Breakout has the lowest ratings figures of the Kennedy–Miller series – an all-cities average of 25 – and it is not hard to see why. It is that unusual occurrence for Kennedy–Miller – a critical success with average ratings. It goes further than any Australian mini-series in that format's 'natural', but rarely fully exploited, direction – commercial network 'art' television.

It embodies dramatic protocols that push commercial network television to its limits – hence audience bemusement reflected in its ratings. It is perhaps one of the purest examples of the mini-series format in terms of style, dramatic structure and social-ritual function.

Consider first the nature of *The Cowra Breakout* as 'social text' and its relation to dramatic structure. On the face of it, the Cowra 'incident' is an unusually marginal event or issue when compared with the kinds of thematic substance typically associated with the mini-series as epic sprawler. Onto this slim historical base, however, a veritable world of contemporary concerns has been mapped. The mini-series as social text always generates a myriad of caveats about historical anachronisms, about 'getting the record wrong'. But *The Cowra Breakout is* one long anachronism. Bearing a close resemblance to art cinema (*Merry Christmas Mr Lawrence*, for example) it is a full-blown discourse on multiculturalism that generates two classic art cinema characterisations – the symmetrically constructed Australian and Japanese leads Stan Davidson and Junji Hayashi. The elegantly reciprocal and interdependent humanist journeys of these two characters are both inconceivable then and absolutely necessary now. This gives the series a powerful Janus-faced dual focus: traditional costume drama and the realities of war, and multiculturalist art television and 'Family of Man' character study. And this is very much reflected in the bifurcated reception of *The Cowra Breakout*. On the one hand, it was the series 'the RSL loves to hate' and much ink was spilled on the 'strains on credulity' of the narrative structure engendered by the need to produce its Romeo and Juliet 'greatest love out of greatest hate' theme.[38] On the other, it was lauded as a humanist document transcending empirical detail and certainly any such straining.[39]

There is a thorough stylistic outworking of *The Cowra Breakout*'s humanist theme of reciprocity. Fully one-third of screen time is occupied with subtitled dialogue engaged in by an ensemble of Japanese actors headed by six flown in from Japan for the series;

this alone pushes *The Cowra Breakout* to the limits of commercial network television. There is a full embracing of the languidness built into the *politique* of the format; like *Bodyline*, the event that gives the series its title occurs at the latest possible moment. Indeed, the whole stylistic and thematic mode of the series is given in microcosm in the first episode, in the extraordinary *temps suspendu* set pieces in New Guinea, and the rest is a slow outworking of this narrative kernel.

The first episode plunges us into two long scenes of guerilla warfare. In the second, almost nothing happens for three sequence blocks – about twenty-five minutes of story time. Altogether, the New Guinea sequences constitute about ninety minutes of the most innovative use of the slowness of the format seen in an Australian mini-series. The extent of the parallels between Stan and Junji are laid out here: the soldier's religion – Australian Catholicism and mateship, Japanese bushido, 'the way of the soldier is death', Stanley the altar boy and Junji's altar at which he prays. Both Japanese shave, as did Stan and Mick. We see letter-writing, the start of the motif of Junji's diary which will last to the end of the series. Just as Stan loses his faith as a result of the horror at the mission station, so bushido is brought into question by the act and consequences of being captured.

The parallelisms and reciprocations are rigorously followed. The codes of honour lead Stan to become a soldier-pacifist, to deny his affection for Sally in honour of the memory of Mick, and even to forgive the cowardly Lieutenant MacDonald, who will 'suffer enough'. For his part, Junji must bow to the wishes of the captives' vote to attempt a suicidal breakout. Each personal but interdependent trajectory moves the series inexorably away from 'mere colour and movement' into thorough psychological interiorisation. When the big breakout comes, Stan and Junji are classic art cinema protagonists, helpless spectators undone by self-knowledge but vindicated by the series' time-fracturing 'humanist ideologies':

Let it be said that setting a rattling good pace is not the major preoccupation of either cast or crew. The aim is to meticulously and slowly layer image upon image, incident upon incident and character upon character to state again and again that war brutalises, maims and kills not just people, but the cherished beliefs and illusions which form the bedrock of societies.[40]

Vietnam and *Dirtwater Dynasty* can be seen as a kind of synthesis of Kennedy–Miller's cinematising strategies and its embrace of the mini-series format, though in different ways. *Vietnam* is the most achieved Australian mini-series. It rated in the mid-30s in Sydney and rather lower elsewhere, resisting the trend downward in mini-series ratings in the mid-1980s. It offers an unparalleled upgrading of both the cinematising tendency and the embrace of the format.

Vietnam's multifaceted work of archival inscription produces an extraordinarily textured visual and sonic *mise en scène*. Most uses of archival material in mini-series merely work to secure the 'recognition-effect', to authorise the fiction or, to put it another way, to break down what the aesthetician Edward Bullough called the 'psychical distance' between textual field and audience.[41] *Vietnam*, however, dramatises and reworks archival material extensively and in several ways, shifting the usual relation of one to the other.

First, there are extended, inter-sequential integrations of archive and drama/characterisation. Consider the start of the second episode, which moves from archival footage of an Easybeats concert to Megan and her girlfriends trying to 'crack it' as groupies after the show, after which the signifier 'Easybeats' is loosed from its diegetic moorings as 'Sorry' plays over Megan's flight in her father's car to Serge in Sydney. Drama comments on the archive and archive comments on drama, as, for instance, Menzies' American firepower speech is spoken over Phil's training in the philosophy of absolute reciprocity in war, or as Lyndon Johnson's speech in Australia provides the aural cue for the extended sequence of Le's rape by the American platoon. Evelyn and Megan are stitched into the archival footage of one of the most momentous anti-war marches, on 30 June 1971, and this is in turn redramatised by Phil taking mugshots, ASIO-style, singling out his mother and sister from the demonstrators. Bill Peach and Paul Murphy play themselves as major figures in the 'original' highpoint of investigative journalism in Australia, *This Day Tonight*, when Serge, playing out the famous appearance of draft resister Michael Matteson, provocatively debates Attorney-General Ivor Greenwood on the program. Reading the plethora of paradigmatic music of the period is more than a matter of mere texture, of nostalgic recognition-effects: it cues the tone of many scenes and, sometimes, editing patterns; it *structures* desire – of characters and spectator alike. In episode three, an American soldier sings 'Light My Fire', tells Phil the story of his singing the song to block out the cries of his wounded buddy, and then delivers the line as sexual invitation as he walks away with a Vietnamese prostitute.

Second, there is a further level of inscription of the archive: the archive as characterisation and drama. Evelyn instances her nascent personal coming of age by 'quoting' the highly pertinent, for late 1966, rhetoric of cultural nationalism to no less a future champion of it than an attentive John Gorton, and Ainsley Gotto. Australian Minister of Defence Shane Paltridge has to stop munching his way through a thick sandwich as notorious footage of the massacre of the innocents, the meat in the sandwich, is screened for him as part of their Saigon briefing in January 1965, referencing the unforgettable Damien Parer rushes sequence in *Newsfront*. Veronica Lang, as Evelyn Goddard, replays her role from the film version of *Don's Party*, right down to dress-style and gesture. Graeme Blundell (Miles Hagger) plays a composite of actual-historical and fictional-historical figures. He is 'Bruce Petty' and Megan's seduction of him is played out in the manner of an *Alvin Purple* scenario with the ages reversed! In a marvellous cameo, 'Diamond Jim' McLelland plays himself as the historical figure of fifteen years past. And Laurie and Le watch Marbuk take Jedda to his own people on the frail raft, from *Jedda*, on television in their Marrickville home: both couples – the wounded warrior and the frightened refugee – social outcasts for crossing barriers.

Then there is the far greater complexity of structure that epitomises the dramatic possibilities of multiperspectivism characteristic of the format. The Goddard family provides four pivotal characters – Douglas, Evelyn, Phil and Megan – and each has his or her own narrative trajectory, which interweaves with other 'pivotal' trajectories as well as providing the focus for a series of relatively autonomous subsidiary narrative worlds.

The dramaturgical model on which *Vietnam* is based is one of *structural homology* between what John Ellis in *Visible Fictions* described as the basic syntagmatic units of television programming, the sequence and the series.[42] Almost all sequences in the series play out a kernel of contending scenes, characters and perspectives: the generation gap, old teenagers/young teenagers, Canberra/Sydney, Australia/Vietnam, political process/family process, the resettlement village/the rest of Vietnam, Laurie and Le's home/the rest of Sydney, and, subtending them all, the multiple perspectives offered by archive and dramatic mixes. These emerge, through accretion and repetition, as the series-long ingredients of dramatic and narrative tension. (The exceptions to this pattern are the breathtaking *temps suspendu* set-pieces that have become another part of the Kennedy–Miller signature.) Each sequence is marked off by the motif of the freeze frame and the slow fade of colour – *this* program passing into history. Dramaturgical symmetries abound: Laurie escapes an explosion, then cops one; Le is raped by American soldiers, then emotionally raped by Phil; Pascoe lectures on the absolute reciprocity of war, then embodies it; American soldiers rape Le and kill her father, the NLF murder Lien's brother, the South Vietnamese Regulars 'torture' Truong Long. Intermittently across the ten hours, the narrative re-centres around the trajectories of the central characters: Evelyn masters her 'hysterical' language (a trope for both her learning Italian and escaping the humiliations of her marriage) and Megan masters her sexual conduct, while Phil practises his photographic 'career'.

Historical movement from 1964 to 1972 across fifty sequences means character change determined by that which is going on in the world. This is the opposite of dominant television dramaturgy in its series and serial formats: 'everything happens, nothing changes'.[43] The central characters gradually assume the status of markers of sectoral divisions within an historically delineated population itself undergoing irreversible sea-change.

Dirtwater Dynasty synthesises the cinematising tendency and the mini-series format in a different way. Terry Hayes signals this difference in speaking, in a publicity-conscious fashion, of the origins of *Dirtwater Dynasty* lying in the decision:

> to devote ourselves to much more traditional storytelling: taking Kennedy–Miller back to its roots, as it were, doing the sort of thing that had generated *Mad Max*, and taking a fictional story that was big and broad and trying to do it in a really intense narrative fashion.[44]

A corollary of this is a strategic stance of clearing the decks for a different approach to the dramaturgical motor of the mini-series, toward a less 'pompous' one, one frankly imitative of classical narrative cinema:

> Take most of them [Australian mini-series] – including some of our stuff – and they don't have narrative pace ... They tend to rely on the fact that, just because it is Australian, you can afford to be a bit indulgent. If *Dirtwater Dynasty* rates, it will show that what the audiences out there are looking for is that real locomotive drive which, frankly, is the thing that made all the great Hollywood films.[45]

Hayes further compares *Dirtwater Dynasty* to *Lace*, which was fictional rather than referential, a feverish melodramatic pacing, dynastic, and also American. This is not surprising in one sense, given that Australian mini-series have been characterised by an almost uniform anchoring in history, at least as a pretext – the only true exception being *Return to Eden*. But Hayes's remarks should also be seen in the broader industrial context that might group *Dirtwater Dynasty* with such Australian series as *The Last Frontier*, *Melba* and *Nancy Wake*. As mini-series budgets reach big-feature costs, and in the current climate of co-production imperatives and major changes to the industrial infrastructure of Australian film and television, the inevitable logic of internationalisation asserts itself. Following the strategies of feature-filmmaking, *The Last Frontier* imports Linda Evans and structures itself as a 'transposed' Western, and *Melba* and *Nancy Wake* seek figures and stories with European resonances and shoot in predominantly European locations.

How does *Dirtwater Dynasty* compare? It demonstrates the 'modular' nature of contemporary nationalist representation, its syncretism and portability.[46] There has always been the stylistic option of the transposed Western in Australian filmmaking, of exotic locations in 'the last frontier', and at this level *Dirtwater Dynasty* is no different. But this kind of 'positive unoriginality', to use Meaghan Morris's words, is invested with the rhetoric of an import culture's 'takeover fantasy'[47] at the level of style. This is what distinguishes *Dirtwater Dynasty* within the current group of 'internationalist' mini-series and secures for it a comparable place as the *Mad Max* films within the Kennedy–Miller signature.

Hayes's concern to reinvest the mini-series format with an analogue of cinematic pacing seems to have been picked up 'well' by the critics:

> in rapid succession murder, rape, incest, insanity, drought, bushfire, war, greed, patriotism, history, nudity, gold, God, racism and retribution, all at a pace that beats Donald Campbell's land speed record at Lake Eyre.[48]

But despite such marvellous recommendations, there is a limit to the analogy. *Dirtwater Dynasty* generates its 'pace' out of an enormous succession of events and a proliferation of central characters as Richard Eastwick's dynasty unfolds, not out of any consistent cinematisation of space, time and character along the model, say, that we have seen at work in *The Dismissal*. Nevertheless, there are significant ways in which *Dirtwater Dynasty* fulfils the role Hayes calls on it to play.

First, *Dirtwater Dynasty* is not simply a succession of dynastic fortunes on the model of a television series or serial – a 'Dynasty down under'. It sustains a consistent narrative logic that Hayes sums up as the Biblical maxim 'What shall it profiteth a man . . .?' That is why the conclusion has the force of cinematic closure typically absent from most historical mini-series. Eastwick's relentless drive to found a dynasty founders on the fact that the very last in a long line of progeny, who have otherwise succumbed to the historical forces of the twentieth century, is a nun, committed to celibacy and poverty! 'The bastard finally got me!' chuckles Richard, the octogenarian tycoon.

Notwithstanding the linearity and symmetry of this overarching narrative logic focused on the central character, the multiperspectivist sprawl more typical of the mini-series format is still evident. There are a whole series of subtexts, some more organic than others, that complicate any simple ascription to *Dirtwater Dynasty* of a nonspecific international exportability and align this 'fictional' series with the social-ritual space of national representation seen in the earlier Kennedy–Miller material: 'I think it's a rather good Bicenntennial subject, really. It deals with all those issues that made this country great – greed, racism, hatred and, above all, a sense of humour.'[49]

It is based loosely on the empires founded by cattle kings like Sidney Kidman; in *Dirtwater Dynasty* these empires take on Third Reichian overtones with Eastwick's dream that his should last five hundred years! The dispossessive nature of this empire-building is dwelt on. Eastwick's long battle with his similarly ambitious neighbour, Hasky Tarbox, leads to the enduring bitterness of the latter's daughter Emma, who is able to stall Eastwick's final land grab out of revenge. Emma has other reasons. She has also been deprived of her only love – Eastwick's first son, David – in the 1914–18 war, and of their child, aborted on the only decision that Eastwick and Hasky Tarbox can make in concert. There is also an Aboriginal subtext which turns on brutal dispossession and rape, but then 'returns' with the calm survivalism in the performances of Kristina Nehm and Ernie Dingo and the identification with that world of Lonely Logan (Bruce Spence). All the while, Eastwick is being dispossessed of his various children by war, abduction and the generation gap.

But perhaps the major subtext resides in the way women intersect with and 'exceed' Eastwick's world of empire-building. This subtext turns principally on the extraordinary three-part performance of Victoria Longley, as first wife, then daughter, then grand-daughter, of Hugo Weaving's Richard Eastwick. This does more than simply create a gender 'balance' in major roles; it tips the balance decisively in favour of women's intergenerational pathos, adaptability and survival across the catastrophic course of twentieth-century history. This is achieved in the melodramatically conceived performance gesture of the characters played by Longley being ever younger as Weaving grows ever more Tiresias-like, seeing all, but increasingly impotent to change the course of history; wanting to die but unable to, because unfulfilled. The 'character' of women, condensed in Longley's performance, rises like a phoenix from the ashes of monomaniacal empire-building and, as we have seen, has the last say.

This suggests a second major way in which *Dirtwater Dynasty* creates an analogue of cinematic experience: how 'seriously' can we take this melodramatic 'apotheosis of kitsch'?[50] How seriously can we take a black-hatted villain named Hasky Tarbox, an abject deflowered virgin (however black) named Esmerelda, Bruce

Spence as an outback 'wisdom of the ages', and Harold Hopkins adding incest to injury as a sweaty-palmed preacher – *à la* Robert Mitchum in *The Night of the Hunter*?

> This is the land of my childhood, the oldest land on earth, the place of endless summer and soaring skies. This is Australia, the outback, a harsh and unforgiving land. I can look back on it now across the track of eighty years and still remember what it was like standing on the very edge of a new frontier. Nature seemed much grander then. The stars were closer, the sun was hotter, the rivers wider. And in my mind's eye I can see all of us moving through the landscape like a strange tribe . . .

Perhaps Josh McCall's opening oration, 'quoting' *Jedda*, has been bicentennialised once too often. And perhaps the splurge of film quotation, starting with *Citizen Kane* and moving through the *Days of Hope* social realism of our eponymous hero gaining a name in the gritty Midlands to a compendium of Western iconography and Australian period films, moves *Dirtwater Dynasty* too far into the space of the hyper-real. Among commentators, only Phillip Adams picked up on the overreaching tonal gymnastics of the series, in a damning review which manages to mention just about everything that makes *Dirtwater Dynasty* intriguing.

The 'largest' quotation is that of the 'melodramatic imagination', a process which encourages belief even as it brackets it within a pleasureful tissue of quotation. And the quoted traditions are what sustain the belief. This dialectic is what allows a 'serious' reading – of the 'social imaginary' of Australia inscribed within an archaeology of the Western, of a 'feminisation' of the epic mode – to exist rightfully beside the pleasure taken in the hyper-real.

We can see, then, why *Dirtwater Dynasty* occupies a place in the Kennedy–Miller output similar to that of the *Mad Max* films. Like them, the mini-series gives us back an Australian 'history' and 'culture' embedded in a masterful play within the 'imported' genre conventions that have *become* part of that history and culture. As Tom O'Regan puts it, apropos another Kennedy–Miller series, the social text of such mini-series involves the need:

> to state the terms and outlines of that history ... in order to obtain the same sense of epic sweep, the same projections of figures onto the stage of history that Hollywood output is routinely able to assume without such elaboration.[51]

Chapter 7

(1996) Australian television in world markets
(with Liz Jacka)

Australian television programs have begun to be a quite visible presence on the stage of world television. The success of *Neighbours* and *Home and Away* in Britain are the most dramatic sign of the export successes of Australian television, but there are few territories in the world now that do not contain Australian material as part of their program mix. Following the initial acceptance of Australian cinema as an art house favourite in the 1970s, the next decade saw a large number of prestige Australian mini-series on screens in continental Europe, Britain, New Zealand and, to a much lesser extent, North America. Since the mid-1980s, Australian serials and series have also become standard fare in many of these territories and Australia is well represented worldwide in genres like children's drama, documentary, science and technology programs, comedy and nature programs.

The general forces that have fostered increased globalisation and peripheral nations' television export have specific inflections in the case of Australia. Indeed, Australia may be understood as a limit case insofar as it shares some characteristics that have produced the metropolitan (US and UK) dominance of television trade – the English language and high levels of commercialisation – while also sharing characteristics of other peripheral nations, such as being a substantial net importer of films and television. This 'in-between' status arises from its Anglo-Celt white settler-dominion history which places it between 'core' and 'peripheral' countries in the world system.

Australian production costs are relatively low compared with other English-language production markets, particularly the United States. Because Australia's population (and therefore production) base is small, the industry has to be efficient to survive. Its relative efficiency is largely a function of sophisticated technical and creative resources. However, its domestic market is small relative to the amount of television material produced, and this, combined with the rising cost of all forms of television, but particularly high-end drama, necessitates the search for external financing and markets. The subsidy, investment and regulation infrastructure in Australia for film and television has contributed over the years to the diverse portfolio of formats and genres produced domestically, allowing the production industry and the viewing public to retain their own voice despite the small population base. Australia's high level of commercialisation from the inception of its television system (which has meant the development of one of the largest advertising bases per capita in the world), in tension with its small market, has also meant that the production industry had to develop relatively cheap production protocols for a variety of long-form and one-shot drama.

It is significant that this predominantly anglophone country is an English-language production centre. This is becoming increasingly important, because the more internationalised television becomes, the more crucial the language of production becomes. An English-language production centre automatically lowers its product cost and potentially increases its markets. Australia is not limited to export within its geolinguistic community or region. Its biggest aggregate market is Europe (including

Britain, it totals 40 per cent of total export trade), whereas the anglophone North American market is resistant to Australian (as well as most other foreign) imports. Language is neither the major enhancer nor the inhibiter of export success in these territories. While it is probably a support for the 'geolinguistic hypothesis' that Australia clearly enjoys a certain comparative advantage by producing in English and being primarily an anglophone culture, several factors parallel to the 'geolinguistic hypothesis' are relevant to Australia: opportunities for export to rapidly expanding and commercialising territories (Europe in the 1980s and early 1990s; Asia in the 1990s) and export to cultural as much as linguistic 'common markets' (the UK and New Zealand). A further point concerns the hybridity or recombinant nature of the Australian television system. Having been largely modelled on and influenced by high levels of imports from the two premier television centres, the United States and the United Kingdom, it has internalised best practice in both commercial and public service practices.

The Australian face of international television

It is possible to argue that '[w]hen Australia became modern, it ceased to be interesting' – interesting, that is, to an international cultural intelligentsia and anthropological audience.[1] Equally, it is arguable that the country has attracted international interest again at present due in no small part to its audiovisual output. What made the country interesting in the nineteenth century was the radically pre-modern cultural difference of its Indigenous peoples set against a transplanted white settler colonial culture. What has produced interest again is its emerging profile as a postcolonial and multicultural society – a postmodern 'recombinant' culture – well suited to playing a role in global cultural exchange.

This view is put strongly by Andrew Milner, who argues that social and cultural modernity was only ever partially realised in Australia:

> Thus Australia has been catapulted towards post-industrialism at a speed possible only in a society that had never fully industrialised; towards consumerism in a fashion barely imaginable in historically less affluent societies; towards an aesthetic populism unresisted by any indigenous experience of a seriously adversarial high culture; towards an integration into multinational late capitalism easily facilitated by longstanding pre-existing patterns of economic dependence, towards a sense of 'being 'after', and of being post-European, entirely apposite to a colony of European settlement suddenly set adrift, in intellectually and imaginatively uncharted Asian waters, by the precipitous decline of a distant Empire.[2]

Athough it underlines reasons why Australian popular culture has a certain dynamism within globalising and postmodern cultural exchange, this view is a partial and rhetorical account. There remain strong modernist institutions and structures, of which the public broadcasting sector is a major contributor, as well as a strong, if constantly deprecated, reliance on a central state as well as a ramified series of local and regional structures that arose out of the prototypically modernist project of nation-building. John Caughie's comments on the way postmodernist trends overlay rather than eclipse modernist traditions in British broadcasting are even more appropriate for Australia, because it has had an embedded commercial ethos for longer than Britain, so the 'overlay' process has been a less traumatic one:

> British television, and much European television, is still rooted in modernity, the concept and practice of public-service broadcasting, part of an unbroken tradition of 'good works' dating from the administration of capitalism in the latter part of the nineteenth century.

While that tradition is clearly under threat from the readministration of capitalism and the redistribution of power in global markets, nevertheless the scenario of magical transformation – the marvellous vanishing act of deregulation: now you see 'quality', now you don't – in both its optimistic and its pessimistic variants seems naive.[3]

Australia's central public broadcaster, the ABC, exemplifies this combination in its performance of its charter functions as a modernist nation-building instrument, while also enthusiastically exploiting commercial and corporate opportunities in new markets (its satellite venture in Asia, ATV) and new media (pay TV). Australian historical mini-series of the 1980s (some of them exported widely) are also prime examples of this combination. Extremely popular commercial successes, screening almost exclusively on commercial networks in Australia, they were nevertheless imbued with the modernist educational public service ethos of reconstructing popular memory about major defining moments of the nation's history.

International exposure of Australian television product and representative figures span the modernist/postmodernist spectrum. Those stellar few who enjoy mogul status in world television include pre-eminently Rupert Murdoch, since 1985 an American citizen but whose Australian patrimony and business roots are the subject of considerable review as commentators and antagonists alike seek to chart the causes and effects of his success as 'ringmaster of the information circus'.[4] Supposedly 'Australian' traditions of sharp practice and derring-do, anti-establishment commitments and brash populist beliefs are held to contribute to his interventions in British television and press, the establishment and hard-won success of BSkyB and the continuation of that sucess with the takeover of Star TV and his lead in the major expansion and commercialisation of television in Asia, eastern Europe and India. His mastery of populist press traditions are credited with underscoring the invention of tabloid television: 'Tabloid television, as the term is generally understood, was born in the United

States. But before anyone cries Yankee cultural imperialism, they should consider this: if the Americans nurtured the genre, Australians fathered it.'[5]

The Australian system seems to have bred a talent for successful low-budget commercial television and has attracted a reputation, for better or worse, throughout the world for it. Australian producers, like some Latin American and Egyptian companies, have churned out a considerable body of soap-opera hours which occupy considerable space in terrestrial and satellite schedules. In many situations, this means being able to substitute for and possibly even compete with US program offers. This attracts criticism from countries that perceive themselves to be threatened by the Trojan horses of US culture. In New Zealand, the view is put that 'Australian programmes are merely American programmes once-removed ... as a consequence of the internationalisation of television, Australian television networks had readily adopted formats and styles "born in the USA". Such formats and styles have now been passed on to New Zealand, in the form of Australian-made programmes or as local adaptations of Grundy productions'.[6] When a study showed Australia to be a significant supplier of light entertainment into Europe, this was seen as setting an unfortunate precedent for the further development of a local production industry: 'The question is whether the European programme industry has to follow the Australian recipe: imitation of American TV formulas, thus stimulating the globalisation and homogenisation of the international TV market.'[7]

At the other end of the spectrum, producers of quality drama in the British tradition have enjoyed a royal road to the BBC and the ITV, and have established long-term co-production and co-venture arrangements with such central public services based on the highest quality values of television practice. Australian producers can 'play at being American' – the two-edged sword of the postcolonial condition, playing a game of reverse imperialism, but within the rules of subordination – without reserve. They can equally strongly eschew that path. The first model is exemplified by the advocates of increased offshore production in Australia, or by those productions, like *Paradise Beach*, made primarily for the US market. The second finds no better exemplar than the Kennedy–Miller company, whose outstanding historical mini-series of the 1980s were found too 'parochial' by many international buyers, who expressed bewilderment that a company with a world reputation for feature-film successes (such as the *Mad Max* films) should evince no interest in 'modifying' their television output for the international market. In some cases, as with the Village Roadshow/Warner Roadshow group, these two traditions can even exist under the same corporate umbrella (for example, with Village Roadshow producing *Paradise Beach* and Roadshow Coote and Carroll producing *Brides of Christ*).

The Australian system has neither the depth of public service ethos and product of the UK system nor the universalist appeal and range of talent of the US system, but its recombination of both systems affords it certain strengths beyond that seen in similarly medium or small sized, peripherally placed industries. This doesn't guarantee export success, but it does suggest the variety of models available to Australia producers.

International 'careers' of Australian programs

We now turn to some brief case studies that assess individual programs' success or failure in a variety of territories. Long-form series drama (*Neighbours*, *Paradise Beach*, *The Flying Doctors*) is emphasised, as it is the hardest to succeed in because it involves an extended exposure to detailed cultural representations and involves strong, ongoing involvement with character and situation. But Australia's only international television service (Australia Television) is also discussed, for it raises different cross-cultural and industry issues.

Cultural neighbours?

Arguably the most outstanding example of Australian series export is the *Neighbours* 'phenomenon' in Britain, running from 1986 to the present day. Australian drama has been seen on British television screens for many years, including, since the late 1970s, serial drama such as *A Country Practice, The Sullivans, The Flying Doctors, Richmond Hill* and *Prisoner: Cell Block H*. *Neighbours* began on BBC 1 in October 1986, stripped in the early afternoon from Monday to Friday. Its unanticipated success led to the day's episode being re-screened in the early evening, allowing it to capture a far greater proportion of young viewers and leading to runaway popularity. By 1988 it had become the most popular children's and young adults' program on British television and it has remained in the ten most-watched programs in Britain for several years. In an effort to counter it, the ITV network from 1990 similarly strip-scheduled *Home and Away* to immediately follow *Neighbours* in the early evening. By early 1989, no less than fifteen hours a week of Australian soap opera was scheduled on British television, an amount far greater than the five hours of US drama, and greater even than the ten hours of local long-form drama.[8]

This provided a platform for a number of Australian programs, produced a wide range of social responses, and helped foster the development of new and more organic co-production arrangements between the British and Australian industries. By 1994 there were signs that the 'Australian cycle' had waned somewhat, with the ratings for *Neighbours* slipping and with a greater degree of industry resistance to foreign programs dominating key parts of the schedules. However, the United Kingdom remains by far the most significant export market for the Australian television industry.

Much effort has been expended to explain the factors underlying this success. It was clear from journalistic commentary that the most public and popularised mode of explanation for the success of soaps like *Neighbours* and *Home and Away* in Britain rested on speculations about the mythological content and serial format of the programs. The soaps are seen as filling a need in the public imagination once occupied by medieval morality plays and preaching, as providing models of behaviour directly relevant to their particular audiences. The serial format allows the consequences of such behaviour to be followed and also allows for varying means, times and degrees of involvement and several points of association with and 'reading' of character.

A viewer survey also provided interesting conclusions relevant to the question of consumption of non-domestic material. There was some evidence bearing out one of the *East of Dallas* team's dictums[9] that a moderate foreignness (or what one British critic called the soaps' 'slight foreignness')[10] engendered more involvement and enjoyment among some viewers. This idea is expanded by that critic in these terms: 'characters outside our class system . . . can speak to us more freely than any well-defined character in an English soap, whose very definition would risk provoking all the class antagonisms which are so easily aroused here'. The 'morality tale' element put forward by critics for the appeal of soaps needs to be framed within this sense of slight foreignness. That is, the exotic or foreign elements – that 'Australians get into each other's lives and homes more than British people do', that there is a pleasing degree of 'old-fashioned' verbal cliché in the scripting, that overall the most widely noticed characteristic is an inference about life in Australia (that social interaction is more fluid) – carry with them a sense of attractive difference which is read in the act of viewing as a commentary on British life.

Textual and audience-reception examinations of the success of Australian television in Britain can only be partial explanations, however. What they miss is a sense of the 'sharp end' of the social intertext created around Australian soaps, any ideological evaluation of their impact in the industrial circumstances of British television in the late 1980s. A case can be made for *Neighbours*, and at least some of the other high-rating Australian drama, fitting all too well into the dual trajectories of deregulation and re-regulation of British television in the late 1980s. On the one hand, it was cheaply and readily available soap that answered a need for the BBC to respond, in an increasingly constrained financial environment, to attacks on its elitism and the challenges of the new commercialism. On the other, it was clean, morally unproblematic soap, well suited to the moral re-regulation that proceeded apace with structural deregulation and the skew towards commercialism.

Often, the press rated the appeal of *Neighbours* against the 'bad' models of soap: 'not high life like *Dallas*, not low life like *Eastenders*, just everyday life'.[11] The 'moral crusade' which elements of the press mounted around their constructed opposition between *Neighbours* and *Eastenders* demonstrates the degree to which Silj's 'sedimentation of other social practices'[12] peculiar to a host country can dramatically affect the reception of popular imported television material. The most intriguing aspects of audience response to *Neighbours* may lie in the fantasy projections the soap fortuitously generates in a particular host society with historically close ties to Australia.

These aspects of the social intertext of *Neighbours* were complemented by program scheduling. Both industry commentators[13] and some journalists regard such factors as a necessary and even partially sufficient recipe for success. Kate Bowles[14] argues against the 'common mythology' that 'open plan housing, beautiful people and hot weather' in *Neighbours* and *Home and Away* are the key ingredients. It was their placement in the schedules – the late afternoons as well as, with *Neighbours*, the early afternoons – that laid the basis for their fantasmic Australianness to become a featured factor. Indeed, it was supremely good timing that *Neighbours* became the first such program to be stripped across the weekdays in Britain; the leading edge of a scheduling revolution within the commercialisation that both BBC and ITV have pursued strongly since the mid-1980s. (The second program to be similarly stripped was *Home and Away*.)

'Playing at being American': *Paradise Beach*

A contrasting case, this time of failure in the United States, was *Paradise Beach*. This relatively short-lived serial screened in 1993–94 on the Australian Nine Network and in several major markets through a similar time period. It represents a good example of the contemporary term 'playing at being American'. The production and marketing strategy for *Paradise Beach* was unique in contemporary Australian serial television, in that, while it was unequivocally an Australian production (both for regulatory purposes and for maximising opportunities for local success), it was aimed primarily at the US market and other markets (being presold to BSkyB satellite television in Britain, South America and parts of Europe, mostly sight unseen, a testament to the distribution profile of the participants in the venture).[15] It appeared to bring together an exceptionally strong production, distribution and exhibition alliance. *Paradise Beach* was co-produced by Village Roadshow Productions, with its studio complex at the Gold Coast offering complete production facilities, the Nine Network (the strongest rating network needing successful local drama and an equity partner in the Warner Roadshow Movieworld Studios), and New World International/Genesis, a large US distribution company specialising in mostly US soap opera for the US syndication and international markets (*Baywatch*, *Santa Barbara*, *The Bold and the Beautiful*).

Paradise Beach was virtually simultaneously launched in Australia and the United States, and followed soon after in other territories. It was heavily promoted in Australia, filling an early evening slot, and received its highest exposure at premiere, but dropped quickly in the ratings. In the United States, it was cleared by Genesis/New World for 85 per cent of the syndication market in a test campaign during the northern summer of 1993, an unprecedented exposure for a foreign-made serial. Paralleling the theme of the program ('It's where teenagers from everywhere converge to cut loose, find the perfect wave, and fall hopelessly in love'), it was aimed at its target teen audience at the end of school for the academic year. However, it did not survive the summer, being pulled from US schedules before it had run the length of its test campaign.

Why did *Paradise Beach* fail? From a purely financial perspective, it didn't fail. The experienced partners knew the program was an experiment and structured its costs so that it was virtually certain of returning modest profits even if it failed to secure ongoing screen-time in the way it ultimately did. However, as a strategy that could be built on by further Australian, or for that matter any foreign (English language), serial production aiming for long-term acceptance in the US market, it was a signal failure. This may be in part due to the very factor that guaranteed its bottom-line security – its extreme low-budget, instrumental production protocols. This approach to production virtually guaranteed an exceedingly negative critical reception in Australia, as well as elsewhere.[16] This cannot be discounted as a factor in the fate of the program locally (and even more so overseas), especially when serial programming needs to build its audience by word of mouth and peer influence.

In some ways, the unprecedentedly hostile critical reaction was misplaced, as the cost structure and schedule slots (both locally and overseas) for *Paradise Beach* suggest the pertinent comparisons should be with daytime soap operas, as Schembri and Malone[17] have argued. However, such a reaction was to some extent invited by Village raising high expectations for the product: it was to be a cross between *Baywatch*, *Beverly Hills 90210* and local product like *Neighbours* (all of them prime time, higher budget and/or established long-term successes). Given the traditions of high-quality *prime time* serial drama produced in Australia and the relative lack of profile daytime and access prime time traditions of soap opera, together with these invited comparisons, *Paradise Beach* was an easy, if probably misplaced, target.

Other, middle-range factors also intervened against the serial. The US market for pre-prime time soaps had declined considerably. The marketplace had become so fragmented and the average attention span so short that there hadn't been a successful new launch of a soap opera for many years in the United States. Currently, no strip soap in the United States runs after 3 pm. As well, a crucial ancillary marketing outlet, the soap opera press (including the three main magazines, *Soap Opera Weekly*, *Soap Opera Digest* and *Soap Opera*, along with teen magazines like *Sixteen*, *Tiger Beat* and *Sassy*), did not promote the program. Again, decisions on the 'rightness', the cultural relevance, of *Paradise Beach* probably defeated the expectation that the specialist press would jump at the opportunity to get behind one of the very few new soaps aimed at teenagers in several years.

The program, by positioning itself so closely to successful teenage prime-time soaps, placed enormous pressure on itself to capture the very short life-span of teenage argot and fashion. The program's US distributors believed that the only way such difficulties could have been overcome would have been for US scriptwriters to have been imported to oversee and generate storylines and dialogue.[18] Such importation, of course, would have defeated the objective of qualifying *Paradise Beach* for the Australian drama quota.

The distributors' comments on writing and technical style also went to fundamental issues of televisual culture. On the one hand, the storyliners tend to 'burn through story' much quicker than in US soaps. Events and emotional reactions that could be milked far more are tossed off in off-camera asides, for example. Like much Australian audiovisual culture, the program consistently de-dramatised action. Dramatic angles and opportunities occur off camera for cultural reasons as much as to avoid expensive effects or complicated set-ups. Therefore, narrative pacing was unfamiliar; the storylining was too fast (the slowness of US soaps is so that audiences can miss episodes and not miss the story), and the emotional temperature was too low.

What the ultimate failure of *Paradise Beach* suggests is that, at least in terms of acceptance of foreign long-form drama in US broadcast television, the English language is not necessarily an advantage (Spanish language soaps have more success in cable). The point of comparison will always be to US broadcast television material, which, in the soap format, is a virtual absolute benchmark for audience acceptance. The Australian long-form successes in the United States have not been live-action adult or teen drama. Rather, they have been sci-tech (*Beyond 2000*) and children's animation (*Blinky Bill*); the first was a format *Beyond 2000* built up as an exploitable international format; the other was a tried and tested children's formula from a highly credentialled Yoram Gross Studios. This underscores the virtual impossibility of seeing foreign long-form drama on US broadcast television. Soap opera, more than any other format, must be allowed to build an audience through stable scheduling and committed marketing, for their 'dispersed narrative structure and incremental characterisation make of them an acquired taste',[19] all the more so when they are foreign.

Social values in a serious culture: *The Flying Doctors* in The Netherlands

A case very different from the commercialising United Kingdom and the supremely commercial United States is provided by the success of *The Flying Doctors* in The Netherlands, the only country in Europe, besides the United Kingdom, where Australian programs have established themselves as part of mainstream popular culture. *The Flying Doctors* began in 1987. For the seven years up to 1993 when the program was cancelled in Australia, it formed the backbone of the public channel VARA's Saturday night schedule, where it regularly won the 8 pm or 8.30 pm timeslot. Because of its popularity with Dutch audiences, VARA began repeats of the program from the opening episode at 6.30 pm. In 1992 it was voted the most popular imported program by the Dutch public.

A number of factors in Dutch television and society combine to account for the success of this Australian series, but perhaps the most important is the unique nature of Holland's public service tradition and the way in which *The Flying Doctors* harmonises with it. The Netherlands had an exclusively public service television system until the advent of private broadcaster RTL4 in 1989. However, its model of public service is quite unlike any other in the world, being based not on 'internal diversity' but on 'external diversity'.[20] This comes about because the bodies responsible for broadcasting are not the actual broadcasters (transmitters of programs) but organisations that are offshoots of the so-called 'pillars' of Dutch social institutions. Each pillar had its own broadcasting organisation and was given air-time on the state-run channel in proportion to the size of its membership. The traditional broadcasting organisations were VARA (socialists), KRO (Catholics), NCRV (Protestant), VPRO (liberal Protestants) and AVRO. The idea was that diversity would be ensured by virtue of each of these organisations choosing programming material that reflected their various ideological positions.

Athough the system was never controlled centrally as in other comparable countries, a Reithian philosophy did to a considerable extent permeate all the broadcasting organisations, notably VARA, the socialist grouping, where a philosophy developed that attempted to wed popularity and progressiveness.[21] VARA is the main purchaser of Australian material in The Netherlands and this broadcasting philosophy animates the taste regime through which its acquisitions staff choose programs, including Australian programs. VARA's Head of Acquisitions regards the BBC as the quality benchmark, and prefers, for instance, *Law and Order* over *LA Law* among US programming 'because it has more of a documentary flavour'.[22] *The Flying Doctors* fulfilled the conditions of being both sufficiently progressive, in VARA's sense of the term (which can be read as pro-social and -communal values, but without the elitism often attributed to classical Reithianism), and popular in the sense that it had a very large and very devoted following among audiences. While the stability of this unique system of institutionalised ideological pluralism has been radically challenged by the rapid success of the new commercial broadcasters like RTL4, VARA has maintained a residual commitment to a form of progressiveness that can be imputed to series like *Flying Doctors*.

The reasons why Australian productions such as *The Flying Doctors* have made more of an impact in The Netherlands than in other European countries such as France, Germany and Italy include the fact that the Dutch are very used to seeing programs in English and programs from the United Kingdom. In Holland, unlike in France, Germany and Italy, programs are subtitled rather than dubbed. Dutch audiences speak English in very large numbers, and they are used to British styles of comedy and drama. Being a small to medium size country, Holland has a somewhat higher level of imported content than the larger European countries, and it has had a higher level of British imports than other countries. So, there is a propensity to be open to British programming, and to the extent that Australian drama styles and British drama styles are similar, and more similar to each other than to American styles, then there is a particular preparedness in Dutch audiences for Australian drama.

However, the 'exoticism' of the Australian outback in *The Flying Doctors* also appeals, in common with other countries where *The Flying Doctors* has done well. It is also a relatively 'safe' program concept, with whatever progressiveness that can be imputed to the program found in the 'warmth' of its portrayal of social solidarity and communitarian values of 'helping people' in a crisis. This entails a contrast with US programming which, according to a senior Dutch public service executive, dwells on racial and social conflict which 'wouldn't wash with the Dutch audience'.[23] And a leading Dutch independent producer accounted for *The Flying Doctors*' popularity in the following terms: 'It's about helping people. We love hospital series. But there is also something Australian about *The Flying Doctors* that appeals. It is very down to earth – that basic earthiness. It shows good people, a healthy people, and an attractive Australian way of life.'[24]

Like most successful domestic serials around the world, but unusually for an imported program, *The Flying Doctors* has spawned its own fan club in the country. The club's magazine contains episode summaries, photos of personalities and places from the show, *Flying Doctor* quizzes and even copies of letters between Dutch fans and the actual Flying Doctor Service operating out of Broken Hill to which fans send donations of money. The show has also spawned a series of novelisations of *Flying Doctor* episodes, which are jointly published by the Australian production company Crawfords and VARA. These publications appear in both hard and soft cover, with lavish colour illustrations of the stars of the show, at popular magazine outlets.

While much of this literature concerns the traditional preoccupations of soap opera fans everywhere, other themes that recur in these magazines and books are pleasure in the sense of community that viewers perceive at Cooper's Crossing and respect for the devotion to duty in the face of danger and hardship that is part of the image of the Flying Doctor Service in Australia. It would be easy to draw the conclusion that the program represents wish fulfilment about values lost in modern urban living, but this alone does not account for why *The Flying Doctors* has done better in the Netherlands than in any other export market. The answer may well lie in the way it fulfils the particular set of broadcasting values of 'progressiveness and popularity' which have dominated the Dutch system until recently.

An ersatz Asian nation? The ABC in Asia
While Australia has a long tradition of broadcasting within the regions of Asia and the Pacific through the shortwave radio service Radio Australia, the most significant additional development in Australian public broadcasting within the region since the establishment of Radio Australia more than fifty years ago is the

Australian Broadcasting Corporation's Australia Television (ATV), launched in February 1993. In the 1990s, Australian public debate and public policy are undergoing rapid, perhaps fundamental, paradigm shifts in its current 'Asianisation' push. Australia's new regional television initiative is overtly driven by diplomatic and trade imperatives. Six out of the ten largest markets for Australian trade are in the regions of Asia, while Australian trade with Japan is now equivalent to the whole volume of trade with the European Union. These trends are set to consolidate strongly in the years ahead.

Australia Television was initiated with a direct government allocation, with a significant portion of its running costs over time expected to be met from corporate sponsorship. It is a single channel television service carried on Indonesia's Palapa B2P satellite. Expansion plans include transmitting on China's Apstar satellites (while contining to transmit on Palapa), effectively giving the service the ability to be received throughout Asia, North Africa, the Middle East and parts of Europe and Russia. It broadcasts from early morning to late evening across four time zones, and schedules mostly selected ABC domestic programs, including children's, language education, drama, documentary, arts and comedy.

The flagship program of the service, and the only major program made specifically for the service is the nightly ATV News bulletin. There are significant correlations between Australian government policies towards the region and the overall stance of the news. While there may be direct instances of state and internal ABC pressure on ATV journalists and problematic policies of pre- or self-censorship through detailed editorial notions of not offending cultural sensitivities in the region, the stance of ATV News is one that seeks to strategically advance Australia's own national development needs to integrate itself diplomatically (in both senses) in the region.

The diplomatic 'mission' of ATV News is also influenced by the fact that, at least in the medium term, the audience for Australia

Television will be almost entirely elites of various countries with which Australia seeks enhanced trading, educational, cultural and political ties, in particular Indonesia, Singapore, Taiwan, Hong Kong and Malaysia, English-speaking elites for whom positive international presentations of national and regional issues may be of special importance (a fact that is highlighted strongly in the service's promotional publicity). This is a posture that could be called 'reverse orientalism'. Edward Said[25] has shown the degree to which the West constructed a myth of non-Western peoples as the threatening 'other' on the basis of oppositions like rational versus irrational and developed versus undeveloped. Reverse orientalism overcompensates for this history, creating a perhaps premature identification with Asia by Australian Westerners.

Interestingly, Australia is represented in ATV News as being *already* an Asian country. Stories that acknowledge it as a country just beginning to come to terms with the rights of its Indigenous population, and as one that is still perceived in Asia in terms of the history of its operation of the White Australia Policy, are mostly absent. Australia, rather, is already multicultural, willing to assimilate with other cultures, and has religious and racial tolerance. ATV regularly features stories that represent Australia politically as a nation sharing the same interests and goals as its Asian neighbours, particularly the development and health of ASEAN. While 'Asianisation' may well be an important public policy question for us, it is hardly reflected in Asian nations' and people's perceptions of Australia, as any sample of Asian media coverage will indicate. ATV News works to qualify these perceptions, in particular through stories about successful emigration from the region to Australia.

The tensions faced by ATV News, and the service generally, include that, while it is one among several of the signals that could be construed by Asian opinion-formers as 'subverting' their national goals in the region, its rationale for Australia is precisely one of 'national development' as part of Asia. And its ability in the longer term to deliver on a key part of its mission – to 'naturalise' the Australian perspective as regional in its significance – will ultimately depend on establishing the credibility of its journalistic credentials. These credentials will have to be fashioned in a context of a sponsored service whose longer-term financial health will depend increasingly on attracting corporate support both in Australia and in the countries receiving the signal. The ABC's marketing document for the service, 'Beaming Across Asia', talks of an audience comprising 'the growing business and government elite in a region providing dynamic export opportunities for Australia'. This projected audience provides more than an attraction for potential sponsors to access an influential market segment; it also nominates those elites that are in a position to influence Australia's integration into the region.

On the evidence of its early period of operation, the service exhibits aspects of development journalism, but Western-style development journalism, a style characterised by a posture of reverse orientalism. This is not necessarily a result of state direction, but arises from shared intent between media and government elites. By its nature, the service will attempt to provide a broader perspective than that which may be deemed appropriate for domestic consumption. This is appropriate and welcome, for Australian media have traditionally focused on European (especially British) and American models, styles and content. However, the challenges it poses for journalists in a volatile cross-cultural mediascape will be significant. Means must be found to allow both Australia's economic aspirations in the region and its traditions of independent journalism to flourish. If the service can address the considerable cross-cultural challenges it faces, particularly the widespread perception in many Asian countries that Australia remains a racist Western country, it has the potential in time to become an important ongoing voice projecting Australia's place in the region.

Conclusion: Benefits and drawbacks of internationalisation

Australia is a small but significant international trader of television programming and an even smaller player in transborder satellite television. However, it exerts a presence on the world's film and television screens that is disproportionate to its population base, geographical position and size of its domestic market. The underlying reasons for this have been outlined in the early part of this chapter. What are some of the effects of increased internationalisation on the domestic policy and industrial landscape?

It is important not to exaggerate the export record and potential of the industry. By world standards the industry is of small-to-medium size and its export record slight in comparison with other Australian service industry exports. For example, education services netted Australia A$1 billion in 1992, compared with an estimated A$65 million for total audiovisual forms (film, television and video). A government report[26] says that in all audiovisual (which, for example, includes music industry inputs), export is only 4 per cent of total revenue. But these data need major refinement. Until 1994, there had been no specific data collection for audiovisual, and the methods by which the available figures have been captured – as part of an overall industry survey – severely underestimate the export dollars being earned from export. They do not take account of the presence of foreign companies' investments in Australian programs, which accounted in 1992–93 for the largest single source of investment in Australian audiovisual product.[27] Nor do they factor in revenues from offshore production, which have put audiovisual in a leading bracket of export-oriented industries in Queensland, nor the earnings of Australian companies producing programs outside Australia (which would exclude the majority of Grundys material), nor the developments in new media products which are being increasingly exported.[28] With these lacunae in mind, many industry representatives have claimed, with justification, that the figures should be closer to $200 million (more than treble the official figures).

Apart from the bald figures, it is undeniable that audiovisual product is the most visible in any export portfolio, and accrues to the country a considerable yet resolutely intangible symbolic profile internationally. *Return to Eden* has been the single most quoted source of positive understanding of Australia in Indonesia.[29] A 1991 study of provincial French adolescents' perceptions of Australia[30] showed that the prime source for general information about Australia was film and television, and that teen music and *Neighbours* personalities Kylie Minogue and Jason Donovan far outscored all other mentioned Australian figures. As Ian Craven argues, *Neighbours* may be regarded as playing a constructive role in internationalising perspectives on suburban rather than bush modalities of Australian life.[31] The Australian Tourist Commission in 1991 studied the impact of soap operas running in Europe for ways to broaden and renovate predominant images of Australia as an outback adventure location. It found significant preferences among Germans for meeting small-town locals (influenced by *A Country Practice* or *The Flying Doctors*), or Italians liking beaches (*Home and Away*).[32]

An increasing international orientation has led the industry and commentators to question whether the 1990s has borne tidings of the 'end of the national project' in higher-budget drama. Graeme Turner has argued that signs in the policy, criticism and production climate indicate that decision makers, cultural intellectuals and industry personnel all now doubt the contemporary viability of cultural nationalism – which served as the intellectual glue holding together state support for, and audience response to, the industry – as a binding rhetoric and policy frame.[33] For Tom O'Regan, the industry's financial troubles of the late 1980s meant that a country 'capable of producing not simply more, but better quality, television, well placed to manage *on its own terms* the popular audience oriented "internationalisation" taking place in the more profitable parts of the international television system' had missed the boat.[34]

However, it is possible to see a greater international orientation, combined with social policies of multiculturalism, recasting traditional cultural nationalism but by no means abandoning it. Asian-related stories as backdrops for Western characters (*A Long Way From Home: Barlow and Chambers* 1988, *Bangkok Hilton* 1989), or the much-worn route of importing an American star to bolster potential sales for an Australian-based story (*The Last Frontier* 1986), and in the 1990s some major television events such as *The Leaving of Liverpool* (1992) and *The Magistrate* (1989), have shown the degree to which international co-production can advance an organic and critically revisionist, yet popular, sense of a multicultural contemporary Australia.

However, overall, it is clear that the programs that travel best, and that have the best potential for export, are not necessarily the most innovative or most searching of Australian society. Saying this only confirms the truism that television is fundamentally a local medium. Humour, and thus comedy formats, most drama, relying as it does on some unavoidable specificities of character and place, and of course the vast bulk of news and current affairs, remain stubbornly resistant to broad-based exploitation in a multiplicity of markets. What international acceptance such formats do find cannot be predicted with any degree of prior accuracy (and thus are resistant to broad policy and strategic settings).

The international marketplace of discrete program trade is, unavoidably, a levelling arena, while transborder television has before it the considerable challenge of creatively overcoming 'cultural screens' as a central aspect of scheduling and marketing. It is in the areas of sport, nature documentary/natural history, some children's programming, and magazine-style science and sci-tech, that global television seeks sufficient purchase in universal thematics (the 'neutral' common values, settings and aspirations Roland Barthes[35] analysed in his 'Family of Man' essay) to offset the discount of cultural screens. It is in these formats, along with those serial drama forms that have established long-term acceptance internationally – what could be called 'volume television' – that the bulk of Australian trade is accomplished.

While Australian television program makers have engaged in significant export achievement in the 1990s, there are dangers in turning such activity over to a policy-led export drive, as current signs in the Australian policy environment indicate. Creative Nation, the government's cultural policy, emphasises industry and specifically export as one of its main elements. The Commonwealth government's Department of Industry has focused on audiovisual as a potential growth area for export, and the broadcast regulator, the ABA, is emphasising the challenge of 'borderless markets' in its consideration of changes to local content regulation.

Australian broadcasting policy, particularly in the area of providing a regulated 'safety net' for local television production, has been based explicitly on the central *cultural* rationale to ensure that Australians see themselves, their lives and society, reflected on their screens in reasonable amounts, and that this reflection take account of the pluralistic nature of the society. An *industry* policy of enhancing export will not necessarily match with this, or rather is not designed to do the same job. The current emphasis on industry policy has the potential to eclipse the original reasons for having a cultural policy for broadcasting.

Strong arguments have been mounted, both within the country and internationally, that Australia should change its currently strong local television regulation to a more Canadian-style system because of the industry growth that would flow from offshore production being able to count within the local quota. There are, indeed, powerful reasons to underpin these developments with unequivocally supportive industry policies and initiatives, but these should not be confused with, or allowed to eclipse, a cultural policy for broadcasting. There are also inbuilt limits to growth of the industry, at least in the areas of traditional program production;

in general, it needs to have secured a local network licence before or while it seeks overseas markets. If the only objective was industry growth (irrespective of whether increased program production found an audience here) then the argument for loosening content regulation would be hard to resist.

Ultimately the arguments for audiovisual export will continue to be the same as arguments for support for audiovisual domestically – cultural first and then economic. This view found support from no less than the prime minister, Paul Keating, in 1992 when he suggested that cultural industries had a role to play in Australia's economic recovery, not just because they could contribute to wealth directly but because they could help to foster a 'sense of national purpose and national cohesion' that could give Australians the spirit to overcome their economic problems.

Part 3 Diasporas and media use

This part of the book moves from the critic-as-fan or cine- or telephile and cultural historian to observer of contemporary cultures, and from mainstream screen culture to decidedly marginal culture. But the attention to so-called 'diasporic' culture (the cultural activity of those who have been dispersed from their homelands by war or ethnic violence, or economic migrants looking for betterment in rich countries, or globally dispersed students and workforces) is by no means marginal in the academic literature. Indeed, my work on diasporic cultures in Australia developed in the context of a burgeoning interest in tracing how globalisation-at-the-margins worked. This field of research and studies is dynamic internationally as well as locally. It is the place where, currently, cultural studies and media studies are most open to cross-disciplinary intersections with anthropology, political science, demography and geography.[1] This 'inter-discipline', with its nuanced attention to structures of feeling, identity and community dynamics, can lend qualitative depth and texture to the oftentimes bald data-driven approaches to multicultures seen in the social science disciplines.

There are interesting links between these essays and the rest of the book. The essays continue to connect the yin and yang of cultural and media studies – close attention to the textual expressions of culture, but also how they are embedded in their social and industrial conditions of production and reception. And the study of the organisation of diasporic cultures is often the story of small business cultures. Chapter 8, 'Theorising the diasporic audience', sets out in short form the challenges that the dynamics of these cultures pose to dominant theories in cultural, media and communications studies. Notions of hybridity (lying as they do from the abjection of in-between-ness to a sophisticated cosmopolitanism), the progressive text, the public sphere and our reflex anti-commercialism all come in for reassessment.

But studies of diasporic cultures also have something to teach about the limits of policy, and thus anticipate the latter parts of the book. They point to the prevalence and necessity of 'grey' markets for culture and information, which arise out of a direct demand unserviced by broadcast and in most cases cable television and other established national and international provision. They illustrate dynamics of international circulation of creative content below the radar of cultural and communications policy, and tell a complicating story about the limits of the modernist dream of a common (broadcast and other) culture. These essays are very much in the cultural studies tradition of analysing 'the whole way of life of a social group as it is structured by representation and by power'.[2]

Chapter 8

(2002) Theorising the diasporic audience

The dynamics of 'diasporic' video, television, cinema, music and Internet use – where peoples displaced from their homelands by migration, refugee status or business and economic imperatives employ media to negotiate new cultural identities – offer challenges for how public media and public culture generally are thought about in our times. *Floating Lives: The Media and Asian Diasporas*[1] examined dynamics that are industrial (the pathways by which these media travel to their multifarious destinations), textual and audience-related (types of diasporic style and practice where popular culture debates and moral panics are played out in culturally divergent circumstances among communities marked by internal difference and external 'othering'). It mapped the mediascapes of Asian diasporic communities against the background of the theoretical and policy territory of understanding media use in contemporary, culturally plural societies. This chapter will interrogate further the nature of the public 'sphericules' formed around diasporic media.

The public sphere, in its classic sense advanced in the work of Jürgen Habermas,[2] is a space of open debate standing over and against the state as a special subset of civil society in which the logic of 'democratic equivalence' is cultivated. The concept has regularly been used in the fields of media, cultural and communications studies to theorise the media's articulation between the state and civil society. Indeed, Nicholas Garnham claimed in the mid-1990s that the public sphere had replaced the concept of hegemony as the central motivating idea in media and cultural studies.[3] This is certainly an overstatement, but it is equally certain that, almost forty years since Jürgen Habermas first published his public sphere argument, and almost thirty years since it was first published in outline form in English, the debate over how progressive elements of civil societies are constructed and how media support, inhibit or indeed are coterminous with such self-determining public communication continues strongly.

The debate is marked out, on the one hand, by those for whom the contemporary Western public sphere has been tarnished or even fatally compromised by the encroachment of commercial media and communications,[4] and, on the other, by those for whom the media have become the main, if not the only, vehicle for whatever can be held to exist of the public sphere in such societies. Such 'media-centric' theorists within these fields can hold that the media actually *envelop* the public sphere. For John Hartley:

> The 'mediasphere' is the whole universe of media . . . in all languages in all countries. It therefore completely encloses and contains as a differentiated part of itself the (Habermasian) public sphere (or the many pubic spheres), and it is itself contained by the much larger semiosphere . . . which is the whole universe of sense-making by whatever means, including speech . . . [It] is clear that television is a crucial site of the mediasphere and a crucial mediator between general cultural sense-making systems (the semiosphere) and specialist components of social sense-making like the public sphere. Hence the public sphere can be rethought not as a category binarily contrasted with its implied opposite, the private sphere, but as a 'Russian doll'

enclosed within a larger mediasphere, itself enclosed within the semiosphere. And within 'the' public sphere, there may equally be found, Russian-doll style, further counter-cultural, oppositional or minoritarian public spheres.[5]

Hartley's topography has the virtue of clarity, scope and heuristic utility, even while it remains provocatively media-centric. This is mostly due to Hartley's commitment to the strictly textual provenance of public communication, and to his interest in Lotman's notion of the semiosphere, more so than Habermas's modernist understanding of the public sphere standing outside of and even over and against its 'mediatisation'.

Complicating this topography, it could be suggested that minoritarian public spheres of the type constituted by diasporic communities are rarely subsets of classic nationally bound public spheres, but are nonetheless vibrant, globalised but very specific spaces of self- and community-making and identity.[6] Hartley is right, however, in his iconoclastic insistence that the commercial realm must be factored into the debate more centrally and positively than it has been to date. There is typically no involvement or very marginal involvement of the public sector courted for diasporic media, in part because the intellectual property and copyright status of much of it is dubious.

Another neglected aspect of the public sphere debate is one developed by Jim McGuigan:[7] the 'affective' as much as 'effective' dimension of public communication, which allows for an adequate grasp of entertainment in a debate dominated by ratiocinative and informational activity. McGuigan speaks of a 'rather softer' conception of the public sphere than is found in the work of Habermas and others, and develops these ideas around the significance of affective popular politics expressed through media mobilisation of Western responses to poverty and aid campaigns. Underdeveloped, though – and tantalisingly so – is the role played by the entertainment content of the media in the formation and reproduction of public communication.[8] This is the domain on which such strongly opposed writers as McGuigan and Hartley might begin to at least share an object of study.

Todd Gitlin has posed the question of whether we can continue to speak of the ideal of *the* public sphere/culture as an increasingly complex, polyethnic, communications-saturated series of societies develops around the world.[9] Rather, what might be emerging are numerous public 'sphericules'. Gitlin asks: 'Does it not look as though the public sphere, in falling, has shattered into a scatter of globules, like mercury?'[10] Gitlin's answer is the deeply pessimistic one of seeing the future as the irretrievable loss of elements of a modernist public commonality.

The spatial metaphor of fragmentation, dissolution and of the centre not holding assumes there is a singular nation-state to anchor it. Thinking of public sphericules as constituted beyond the singular nation-state, as 'global narrowcasting of polity and culture', assists in restoring these sphericules to a place of undeniable importance for contemporary, culturally plural societies and any media, cultural and communication studies claiming similar contemporaneity. This place is not necessarily counter-hegemonic, but it is certainly culturally plural and dynamically contending with Western forms for recognition.

There are now several claims for such public sphericules. One can speak of a feminist public sphere and international public sphericules constituted around environmental or human rights issues. They may take the form of 'subaltern counterpublics', as Nancy Fraser calls them,[11] or they may be termed 'taste' cultures, such as those formed around gay style (which does not, of course, exclude them from acting as 'counterpublics'). As John Hartley and Alan McKee put it in *The Indigenous Public Sphere*,[12] these are possibly peculiar examples of public spheres, since they are not predicated on any nation that a public sphere normally expresses. Rather, they are the 'civil societies' of nations without borders, without state institutions and without citizens.

These authors go on to suggest that such public spheres might stand as a model for developments in late modern culture generally, with do-it-yourself citizenship based on culture, identity and voluntary belonging rather than on rights derived from, and obligations to, a state. The argument here is in part a contribution to the elaboration of such a project. However, there are still undeniably relations of dominance, and 'mainstreams' and 'peripheries'. The metaphor is not simply a series of sphericules, overlapping to a greater or lesser extent. While this latter explanatory model goes some distance towards explaining the complexity of overlapping taste cultures, identity formations, social commitments and specialist understandings which constitute the horizon of many – if not most – citizen-consumers in post-industrial societies, there are broad consensus and agenda-setting capabilities that cannot be gainsaid in enthusiasm for embracing *tout court* a 'capillary' model of power. The key, as Hartley and McKee themselves identify,[13] is the degree of control over the meanings created about and within the sphericule, and by whom this control is exercised.

In contrast to Gitlin, then, this chapter argues that ethno-specific global mediatised communities display in microcosm elements we would expect to find in 'the' public sphere. Such activities may constitute valid and indeed dynamic counter examples to a discourse of decline and fragmentation, while taking full account of contemporary vectors of communication in a globalising, commercialising and pluralising world.

Ongoing public sphere debates in the field, then, continue to be structured around dualisms that are arguably less aids than inhibitors of analysis: dualisms like public–private, information–entertainment, cognition–affect or emotion, public versus commercial culture and – the 'master' dualism – public sphere in the singular or plural. What follows makes no pretence at catching up these dualisms in a grand synthesis, but rather offers a contribution to a more positive account of the operations of media-based public communication – in this case, ethno-specific diasporic sphericules – which place a different slant on highly generalised debates about globalisation, commercialisation and the fate of public communication in these contexts.

The ethno-specific mediatised sphericule

First, these 'sphericules' are social fragments that do not have critical mass. Nevertheless, they share many of the characteristics of the classically conceived public sphere. They provide a central site for public communication within globally dispersed communities, they stage communal difference and discord productively, and they work to articulate insider ethno-specific identities (which are, by definition, 'multinational', even global) to the wider 'host' environments.

Our audience research for *Floating Lives: The Media and Asian Diasporas* was conducted in communities in Australia. While Australia is, in proportional terms, the world's second largest immigrant nation next to Israel, the relatively low numbers of any individual group (at present, over 150 ethnic groups speaking over 100 different languages) has meant that a critical mass of a few dominant non-English-speaking background (NESB) groupings has not made the impact that Hispanic peoples, for example, have made in the United States. No one non-Anglo-Celtic ethnic group has reached 'critical mass' in terms of being able to operate significantly as a self-contained community within the nation. For this reason, Australia offers a useful laboratory for testing notions of diasporic communities which need to be 'de-essentialised': adapted to conditions where ethnicities and sub-ethnicities jostle in ways that would have been unlikely or impossible in their respective homeland settings or where long and sustained patterns of immigration have produced a critical mass of singular ethnicities.

Sinclair *et al.*'s study of the Chinese in *Floating Lives* posits that the sources, socioeconomic backgrounds and circumstances of Chinese immigrant arrivals in Australia have been much more diverse than those of Chinese communities in the other great contemporary immigrant-receiving countries such as the United States, Canada, Britain and New Zealand, or earlier immigrant-receiving countries in Southeast Asia, South America, Europe and Africa.[14] To make sense of 'the' Chinese community is to break it down into a series of complex and often interrelated sub-groupings based on geographical origin – mainland (PRC), Southeast Asia (Indonesia, Malaysia and Singapore), Taiwan, Indochina (Vietnam, Laos, Cambodia), Hong Kong – together with overlapping language and dialect use.

Similarly, Cunningham and Nguyen's Vietnamese study demonstrates that there are significant differences among a quite small population along axes of generation, ethnicity, region of the home country, education and class, recency of arrival and *conditions* under which arrival took place.[15] And, for the Fijian Indians in Manas Ray's work, if it was legislated racial discrimination that compelled them to leave Fiji, in Australia they find themselves 'othered' by, and othering, the mainland Indian groupings who contest the authenticity of Fijian Indian claims to rootedness in Indian popular culture.[16]

The formats for diasporic popular media owe much to their inscription within such 'narrowcast' cultural spaces and share many significant attributes: karaoke, with its performative, communal and de-aestheticised performative and communal space;[17] the Vietnamese variety music video and 'Paris/Sydney/Toronto by Night' live show formats; and the typical 'modular' Bollywood film and accompanying live and playback music culture.

Against the locus of examination of the 'diasporic imagination' as one of aesthetically transgressive hybridity produced out of a presumed 'ontological condition' occupied by the migrant subject, these are not necessarily aesthetically transgressive or politically progressive texts. Their politics cannot be read off their textual forms, but must be grasped in the use to which they are put within the communities. In *Floating Lives*, we see these uses as centring on popular culture debates, where communities contend around the politics, identity formations and tensions of hybrid popular forms emerging to serve the diasporas.

Much diasporic cultural expression is a struggle for survival, identity and assertion, and it can be a struggle which is as much enforced by the necessities of coming to terms with the dominant culture as it is freely assumed. The results may not be pretty. The instability of cultural maintenance and negotiation can lead, at one extreme, to being locked into a time warp with the fetishised homeland – as it once might have been but no longer is or can be – and, at the other, to assimilation to the dominant host culture and a loss of place within one's original culture. It can involve insistent reactionary politics. Due to the necessity to fund expensive forms of media for a narrowcast audience, it can lead to extreme over-commercialisation. Hamid Naficy cites a situation in 1987 when Iranian television in Los Angeles was scheduling over forty minutes of advertising per hour.[18] And it can also lead to textual material of excoriating tragedy, such as the (fictional) self-immolation and (actual) atrocity scenarios played out in some, respectively, Iranian and Croatian videos, as recounted by Naficy and by Kolar-Panov.[19]

Second, there is explanatory payoff in pursuing the specificity of the ethno-specific public sphericule in comparison with other emergent public spheres. Like the classic Habermasian bourgeois public sphere of the cafe society of eighteenth- and nineteenth-century France and Britain, they are constituted as elements of civil society. However, our understanding of civil society is formulated out of its dualistic relationship to formal apparatuses of political and juridical power. Ethno-specific sphericules constitute themselves as potentially global civil societies which intersect with state apparatuses at various points (immigration law, multicultural public policy and, for the irredentist and the exilic, against the regimes that control homeland societies). It follows that ethno-specific public sphericules are not congruent with international taste cultures borne by a homogenising global media culture. For diasporic groupings *were* parts of states, nations and polities, and much of the diasporic polity is about the process of remembering, positioning and, by no means least, constructing business opportunities around these pre-diasporic states and/or nations.

It is out of these realities that the assumption grows that ethnic minoritarian publics contribute to the further fragmentation of the majoritarian public sphere, breaking the 'social compact' subsuming nation and ethnicity into the state. This has been foundational for the modern nation-state. Irredentist politics and 'long-distance' nationalism, where the prime allegiance continues to be to an often defunct state or regime, are deemed non-progressive by most commentators. However, a focus on the popular culture of diasporas and its place in the construction of public sphericules complicates these assumptions, as it shows that a variety of voices contend for recognition and influence within the micro-polity, and great generational renewal can arise from the vibrancy of such popular culture.

Sophisticated cosmopolitanism and successful international business dealing sit alongside long-distance nationalism; the diasporic subject is typically a citizen of a Western country, is not stateless and is not seeking the recognition of a separate national status within his or her 'new' country, like the prototypal instances in the European context such as the Basques, the Scots or the Welsh. These sphericules are definitively transnational – even global – in their constitution, but they are not the same as emerging transnational polities and cultures of global corporate culture, world-spanning NGOs and international bodies of governments.

Perhaps the most consistent relation, or non-relation, that diasporic media have with the various states into which they are introduced is around issues of piracy. This gives another layer to the notion of civil cultures standing against the state. Indeed, given that significant amounts of the cultural production exist in a para-legal penumbra of copyright breach and piracy, there is a strong desire on the part of the entrepreneurs who disseminate such product to keep their distance from organs of the state. It is apparent that routinised piracy makes a 'shadow system' of much diasporic media, as Kolar-Panov dubs ethnic minority video circuits as they are perceived from outside, operating in parallel to the majoritarian system, with few industry linkages.[20]

Third, these sphericules reconfigure essentialist notions of community and reflex anti-commercialism. They are communities in a sense that goes beyond the bland homogeneous arcadia that the term 'community' usually connotes. On the one hand, the ethno-specific community assumes an importance greater by far than the term usually means in mainstream parlance, as the community *constitutes* the markets and audiences for the media services; there is almost no cross-over or recognition outside the specific community in most cases of diasporic cultural production. The 'community' therefore becomes an economic calculus, not just a multicultural demographic instance. The community is to an important extent constituted *through* media,[21] insofar as media performance is one of the main reasons to meet together, and there is very little else available as a mediator of information and entertainment. These media and their entrepreneurs and audiences work within a de-essentialised community and its differences as a condition of their practice and engagement.

Diasporic media are largely commercially driven media, but are not fully fledged markets. They are largely constituted in and through a commercial culture, but this is not the globalising, homogenising commercialism that has been posed by neo-Marxist political economists as threatening cultural pluralism, authenticity and agency at the local level. With notable exceptions like global Chinese popular cultural forms such as cantopop and Hong Kong cinema, which have experienced significant crossover into both dominant and other emerging contemporary cultural formations, and the Indian popular Bhangra music and Bollywood cinema, which are still more singularly based in Indian homeland and diasporic audiences, this is small-business commercialism which deals with the practical specificities of cultural difference at the local level as an absolute precondition of business viability.

Fourth, the spaces for ethno-specific public communication are media-centric, and this affords new configurations of the information–entertainment dualism. Given the at times extreme marginalisation of many diasporic groupings in public space and their lack of representation within leaderships of influence and persuasion in the dominant forums of the host country, ethno-specific media become, by default, the main organs of communication outside certain circumscribed and defined social spaces, such as the Chinatowns, the Koreatowns, the little Saigons, the churches and temples, or the local video, spice and herb parlours.

It is a media-centric space but, unlike the way that media-centricity can give rise to functionalist thinking (media are the cement that forms and gives identity to the community), it should be thought of as 'staging' difference and dissension in ways that the community itself can manage. There are severe constraints on public political discourse among, for example, refugee-based communities like the Vietnamese. The 'compulsive memoralisation'[22] of the pre-communist past of Vietnam and the compulsory anticommunism of the leadership of the Vietnamese community is internalised as unsavoury to mainstream society. As part of the pressure to be the perfect citizen in the host society,[23] there is considerable self-censorship in the public critical opinion expression. This filtering of political partisanship for external consumption is also turned back on itself in the community, with attempts by members of the community to have the rigorous anticommunist refugee stance softened (by the mid-1990s, only 30 per cent of the Vietnamese community in Australia were originally refugees) met with harsh rebuke. In this situation, Vietnamese entertainment formats operate to create a space where political and cultural identities can be processed in a self determining way, where voices other than the official, but constitutive of community sentiment, can speak.

Media-centricity also means, in this context, a constant blurring of the information–entertainment distinction, giving rise to a positive sense of a 'tabloidised' sphericule wherein McGuigan's *affective* as well as *effective* communication takes on another meaning. The information–entertainment distinction – usually maintained in the abundance of available media in dominant cultures – is blurred in the diasporic setting. As there is typically such a small diet of ethno-specific media available to these communities, they are mined deeply for social cues (including fashion, language use, and so on), personal gossip and public information as well as the entertainment of singing along to the song or following the fictional narrative. Within this concentrated and contracted informational and libidinal economy, 'contemporary popular media as guides to choice, or guides to the attitudes that inform choices'[24] take on a thoroughly continuous and central role in information and entertainment for creating a negotiated *habitus*.

Chapter 9

(2003) Actually existing hybridity: Vietnamese diasporic music video

(with Tina Nguyen)

Being originally refugees and only lately immigrants makes the Vietnamese peoples in the Western world very aware of the pull between maintaining their original cultures and adapting to their new host cultures. For most, 'home' is an officially denied category while the Communist regime continues in power, and so media networks, especially music video, operate to connect the dispersed Vietnamese communities. Small-business entrepreneurs produce low-budget music videos, mostly out of southern California, which are taken up within the fan circuits of America, Australia, Canada, France and elsewhere.

The internal cultural conflicts within the communities centre on the felt need to maintain pre-revolutionary Vietnamese heritage and traditions, to find a negotiated place within a more mainstreamed culture, or to engage in the formation of distinct hybrid identities around the appropriation of dominant Western popular cultural forms. These three cultural positions are dynamic and mutable, but, because the main cultural and social debates are constructed around them, they are a useful heuristic which can be used to organise analysis.

The Vietnamese have had a long history of migration within their immediate region but a very limited history of migration outside of Vietnam. By 1975 only about 100,000 Vietnamese were living outside Vietnam. However, from 1965 to 1975, during the height of the Vietnam (or 'American') War, over half of Vietnam's population were displaced internally, and now the Vietnamese diaspora numbers something over two million Vietnam-born throughout the world. (The current population in Vietnam is 76 million.) To this, of course, should be added a substantial second (and emergent third) generation, those born to Vietnamese parents in the host countries. Estimates of the size of these second and third generations are notoriously unreliable because census data collection in several countries follows widely variant protocols, but it is estimated at more than half a million.

About a half of the total diaspora is domiciled in the United States, with significant population centres in Orange County, San Jose, Texas, Minneapolis, Washington and Houston. Other major host countries include France, Canada, Australia, Germany and The Netherlands. Given the fraught history of the treatment of refugees in the immediate East Asian and Southeast Asian region, it is not surprising that there are very few Vietnamese resettled in the country's immediate region. Overall, there are about seventy population centres across the world with some Vietnamese presence outside the homeland.

Vietnamese diasporic music video

The live variety shows, and music video productions based on and arising from them, produced by Vietnamese-owned and -operated companies based in Southern California and exported to all overseas communities, are the only media form unique to the diaspora as audiovisual media made by and for the diaspora. This media form bears many similarities to the commercial and variety-based cultural production of Iranian television in Los Angeles studied by Hamid Naficy,[1] not least because Vietnamese variety show and music video production is also centred in the Los Angeles conurbation. The Vietnamese grouped there are not as numerous or as rich as Naficy's Iranians and so have not developed the extent of the business infrastructure to support the range and depth of media activity recounted in Naficy's study. The business infrastructure of Vietnamese audiovisual production is structured around a few small businesses operating on low margins. It is, as Kolar Panov dubs ethnic minority video circuits as they are perceived from outside, a 'shadow system'[2] operating in parallel to the majoritarian system, with few industry linkages and very little crossover of performer or audience.

To be exilic means not being able to draw on the contemporary cultural production of the home country, or at least not 'officially'. Indeed it means 'officially' denying its existence in a dialectical process of mutual disauthentification.[3] The Vietnam government asserts that the *Viet Kieu* (the appellation for Vietnamese overseas, which carries a pejorative connotation) may be fatally Westernised, whereas the diasporic populations propose that the homeland population has been de-ethnicised through, ironically, the wholesale adoption of an alien (Western) ideology of Marxism–Leninism.

The widely dispersed geography and the demography of a small series of communities frame the conditions for 'global narrowcasting', that is, ethnically specific cultural production for widely dispersed population fragments centripetally organised around an officially excluded homeland. This makes the media, and the media use, of the Vietnamese diaspora significantly different from the media consumption of large diasporas, such as the Chinese or Indian diasporas, which focus on large production centres in the 'home' countries.

These conditions also determine the nature of the production companies (Thuy Nga, ASIA/Dem Saigon, Mey/Hollywood Nights, Khanh Ha, Diem Xua and others). These are small businesses running at low margins and constantly undercut by copying of their video product outside the United States (particularly in Vietnam itself) where their ability to police copyright is restricted by not having the time or the resources to follow up breaches. They have clustered around the only Vietnamese population base that offers critical mass and is geographically adjacent to the world-leading entertainment–communications–information (ECI) complex in Southern California. There is evidence of internal migration within the diaspora from the rest of the United States, Canada and France to Southern California to take advantage of the largest overseas Vietnamese population concentration and the world's major ECI complex.

Thuy Nga Productions is by far the largest and most successful company. It organises major live shows in the United States and franchises an appearance schedule for the high-profile performers at shows around the global diaspora. Since the early 1980s it has produced over sixty two-hour videotapes as well as a constant flow of CDs, audio-cassettes and karaoke discs. President and owner of Thuy Nga, To Van Lai, was a university psychology professor before establishing Thuy Nga in 1969. Named after his wife, Thuy Nga was set up as a recording and production label that actuated To's stance as a cultural intellectual bringing traditional folk and contemporary Vietnamese music traditions into contact with popular American and French music.

Thuy Nga Productions' 'Paris by Night' series, at start-up in the early 1980s, evoked pre-1975 Saigon through its revival of cabaret music and entertainment from previously well-established Vietnamese performers, such as Elvis Phuong, Jo Marcel and Khanh Ly. Due to the rising costs of production, more public demand for live concert performances in the United States and Canada, the demand for regularisation of music video production protocols, and the fact that the majority of Vietnamese performers were living in the United States, To moved Thuy Nga production to Orange County in the late 1980s. The first Paris by Night video, produced in 1983, had been recorded in Paris and had cost about $US19,000. It consisted of eleven performances with local Vietnamese in Paris. In comparison, by the late 1990s Thuy Nga was releasing at least four videos a year, consisting usually of twenty-four performances from a range of international Vietnamese performers, a stage and technical crew of approximately 300 people, often recording in front of packed audiences. Production costs per video increased to $US500,000.

Paris by Night had the challenging task of breaking into the well-established demand for Chinese language video in the United States, which 'monopolised' the overseas Vietnamese market through the 1980s. According to To, the Vietnamese audience's 'addiction' to Hong Kong multi-tape television series had a deleterious effect on their working lives and their lifestyles.[4] Within the wider issues of dealing with the new country, the contribution of 'addiction' to Chinese videos worsened the community's social dilemmas. To Van Lai's attempt to provide an alternative to the Chinese language material began to work after 1986 with the release of its first special documentary edition, 'Gia Biet Saigon' (Farewell Saigon), which is discussed below.

The revenue and profit generated from the live performances and shows helps to fund the production of music videos, CDs and karaoke discs. To Van Lai claims sales figures per video of approximately 40,000 and up to 80,000 for 'specials' in the United States, but also says that overseas sales are not a significant or stable revenue source due to illegal dubbing of tapes.

The other most popular company committed to high production values is ASIA Productions (Dem Saigon/Saigon Nights), which was established in the United States in the early 1980s. In contrast to Thuy Nga, ASIA is not a family business but is owned by shareholders and run by a manager. ASIA reaches out beyond the established community performers, focusing more than Thuy Nga on promoting new talent in the United States and Canada. Through an annual 'star search' competition, Truc

Ho, ASIA's music director, scouts for talent, offering contracts for live shows, video taping and CD recordings for the company. The company also encourages its audience to take part in the 'quest for stardom' by testing talent using its karaoke recordings, and then sending in tapes of the performances. Short-listed singers are given the opportunity to perform in front of a live audience to get feedback on their performance. Like all other production companies, the main revenue and profit derives from the ticket sales of live shows and the domestic sale of CDs, videos and karaoke discs.

The videoscape: Texts and consumption

From data supplied by the production companies and distributors, the rates of sales and rentals derived from samples of video store retailers, and the scale of attendances at regular live variety performances, it can be surmised – in the absence of large-scale tracking surveys for which the industry does not have the resources – that most overseas Vietnamese households may own or rent some of this music video material, and a significant proportion have developed comprehensive home libraries. The popularity of the music video material is exemplary, cutting across differences of ethnicity, age, gender, recency of arrival, refugee or immigrant status, and home region. It is also widely available in pirated form in Vietnam itself, as the economic and cultural 'thaw' that has proceeded since *Doi Moi* policies of greater openness has resulted in extensive penetration of the homeland by this most international of Vietnamese expression. (Carruthers points to data from 1996 which estimated that 85–90 per cent of stock in Saigon's unlicensed video stores was foreign.)[5]

As the only popular culture produced by and specifically for the Vietnamese diaspora, there is a deep investment in these texts by and within the overseas communities, an investment by no means homogeneous but uniformly strong. The social text that surrounds, indeed engulfs, these productions is intense, multi-layered and makes its address across differences of generation, gender, ethnicity, class and education levels, and recency of arrival. 'Audiovisual images become so important for young Vietnamese as a point of reference, as a tool for validation and as a vehicle towards self identity.'[6]

The central point linking business operations, the textual dynamics of the music videos, and media use within the communities, is that the three cultural positions or stances in the communities, and the musical styles which give expression to them, have to be accommodated within the same productions because of the marginal size of the audience base. From the point of view of business logic, each style cannot exist without the others. Thus, the organisational structure of the shows and the videos, at the level of both the individual show/video and the whole company outputs, particularly those of Thuy Nga and ASIA, reflect the heterogeneity required to maximise audiences within a strictly narrowcast range. This is a programming philosophy congruent with broadcasting to a globally spread, narrowcast demographic.

This also underscores why 'the variety show form has been a mainstay of overseas Vietnamese anti-communist culture from the mid-seventies onwards'.[7] In any given live show or video production, the musical styles might range from pre-colonial traditionalism, to French colonial era high-modernist classicism, crooners adapting Vietnamese folksongs to the Sinatra era, and bilingual cover versions of *Grease* or Madonna. Stringing this concatenation of taste cultures together are the comperes, typically well-known political and cultural figures in their own right, who perform a rhetorical unifying function:

> Audience members are constantly recouped via the show's diegesis, and the anchoring role of the comperes and their commentaries, into an overarching conception of shared overseas Vietnamese identity.

> This is centred on the appeal to ... core cultural values, common tradition, linguistic unity and an anti-communist homeland politics.[8]

Within this overall political trajectory, however, there are major differences to be managed. The stances evidenced in the video and live material range on a continuum from 'pure' heritage maintenance and ideological monitoring, to mainstream cultural negotiation, through to assertive hybridity. Most performers and productions seek to situate themselves within the mainstream of cultural negotiation between Vietnamese and Western traditions. However, at one end of the continuum there are strong attempts to keep both the original folkloric music traditions alive and also the integrity of the anti-communist stance foundational to the diaspora through very public criticism of any lapse from that stance. At the other end, Vietnamese-American youth culture is exploring the limits of hybrid identities through 'New Wave', radical intermixing of musical styles. The next sections consider some textual examples of each style and audience/readership responses to them.

Heritage maintenance

Heritage maintenance embraces a range of cultural and informational productions and is closely connected to the ideological monitoring role of maintaining the salience of the anti-communist stance. Diasporic video is one of the prime sites monitored. This is borne out spectacularly in the 'Mother' issue of Paris by Night. Paris by Night Issue 40 was released in 1997 to coincide with Vu Lan, the Season of Filial Piety, a time for special veneration of parents. The video was particularly popular, but popularity turned to condemnation in the diaspora when it was discovered that a small segment of documentary war footage showing planes strafing and killing South Vietnamese civilians was actually of the Republic of

South Vietnam (RSA) air forces. Thuy Nga asserted that it was the innocent mistake of a young and inexperienced editor. Both To Van Lai and compere Nguyen Ngoc Ngan were forced to publish apologies in the main newspapers and calm very angry responses on websites, in letters to the editor, on radio and in demonstrations outside Thuy Nga's offices. Some even alleged that it was a cynical ploy by the company to establish its good name in Vietnam in advance of a greater entrepreneurial effort in the homeland.

The 'Mother' imbroglio has been extensively analysed by Carruthers. Carruthers stresses the porosity of communications flows between the diaspora and the homeland, noting that the degree of ideological border-drawing on which the identity and integrity of both the homeland regime and the diasporic community depend is increasingly difficult to sustain under the pressures of globalisation.[9] However, the 'Mother' episode illustrates the degree of psychic and ideological investment in the music video corpus and the degree to which it, like all public cultural manifestations, is monitored for deviations from the ideological foundations of the diaspora. The social text of the corpus is subtended by strong community expectations of a proper education for the young in the reasons for cultural maintenance. While much of the dissolution of boundaries between homeland and diaspora proceeds around cultural product, entrepreneurship and travel (it was estimated that about 20,000 Australian Vietnamese visited Vietnam annually in the mid-1990s), there continues to be organised resistance to such dissolution among the overseas populations. Examples include boycotts of restaurants run by government-aligned owners; a new shopping complex, known as the 'cultural court', in the heart of Westminster on Balsa Avenue, that was part-financed by the homeland sources has been conspicuously under-patronised and for a good time virtually boycotted in the months following its opening in 1996. And international attention was drawn in 1999 to the community attacks on a shop owner in the precinct who insisted on flying the official country flag and displaying pictures of Ho Chi Minh.

The main musical expression of heritage maintenance lies in the restoration and preservation of traditional Vietnamese music style (and the instruments on which they are played). Major cultural figures such as Pham Duy, often titled in American media coverage as the 'Woody Guthrie' of Vietnam, have devoted long careers to the maintenance of the received Vietnamese heritage in folk culture. (He wrote a historical treatise *Musics of Vietnam* (1973), has had several special issue videos dedicated to his corpus, and has recreated as a folk opera dubbed the 'Illiad of Vietnam' *Truyen Kieu*/The Tale of Kieu.) The purity is maintained through a scholarly attention to the traditions and their transmission to a younger, dispersed generation; the artisanal attention to the playing of traditional Vietnamese musical instruments; but also a preparedness to transmit this heritage by contemporary technologies such as CDs and the Internet. Into this category should also be placed a considerable amount of traditional folk balladry and a residual element of traditional Vietnamese opera. This form of 'pure' heritage maintenance is clearly mainly consumed by the older generation of the educated elite.

A small fraction of the music video corpus (about six to eight tapes in total) is given over to heritage maintenance. These tapes are constructed quite differently from the rest and are at the other end of the stylistic continuum from the live show formats. They are compilation documentary-style videos, and have been produced typically to commemorate historical anniversaries in the overseas communities' lives.

An early example of the historical compilation video is Thuy Nga 10, *Gia Biet Saigon*/Farewell Saigon. Made in 1986, this Thuy Nga production has none of the sophisticated production values and choreography of later productions; in fact, it is organised on quite different principles from the variety show format of most of the corpus. The organisational principle is one of popular memory, bearing all the hallmarks of a very specific address to the military, educational, business and government elites of the South Vietnam regime in the period leading to the fall of Saigon.

This principle of organisation makes it a virtually unwatchable tape for all but this specific audience. The great majority of second generation and recent arrivals who participated in focus groups and interviews asserted that historical compilation material was 'for [their] parents' or for those who 'had been through the events' being recounted. 'Farewell Saigon' is a tape of approximately ninety minutes duration, comprising historical footage of pre-1975 Saigon (together with some post-1975 footage) with studio-based musical interludes sung by performers of the same or similar generation to the target audience – performers who successfully transitioned from pre- to post-1975 as part of the diaspora.

The great majority of the time on the tape is a video essay extolling the strength, social balance, harmony and dynamism of a well-governed and stable Republic of Vietnam during the Diem and Thieu years. So much can be readily deduced from the contents and organisation of the tape. What can be *adduced* from its reception and use within the specific target audience – the original diasporic elites – is both the depth of loss and longing that the tape engenders and a still-strong politics of disavowal of the regime's complicity in its own downfall and the continued placing of blame on America as a 'great and powerful friend' which withdrew its support unilaterally, rendering the defence of the republic impossible. The vertiginous shifts from truimphalism to abjection, from very long static camera angles on impeccably suited parades of military to the hand-held chaos of the end-time of 1975 has strong parallels with the abrupt changes of tempo and testamental nature of the Croatian video analysed by Kolar-Panov.[10]

The footage combines travelogue-style panoramas of market scenes, major downtown buildings, the Presidential Palace, the main girls' and boys' schools, a compendium of religious buildings. The second set of visual materials includes a highly structured, syncopated visual hymn to the women of the republic, cut to complement the ballad 'Co gai Viet'/'The Vietnamese Lady' in a studio setting by three women performers wearing signifiers of North, Centre and South regions of a pre-Communist unified country. The third type is very extensive footage of a military parade on the National Day that was held on 26 October each year. Voice-over commentary details the different regiments in careful detail and occupies almost half an hour of the tape.

What is readable as flat 'propaganda' and inexcusably tedious editing by its non-intended audience is received very differently by its primary audience, the original diasporic elites. For them, 'Farewell Saigon' is like a home movie. There are no specific time references to anchor the footage at a particular date apart from its ambience of the late 1960s/early 1970s: it inhabits a modality of popular memory, with very specific anchors of place but not of time. In one family with whom researchers were invited to watch the video, the father had been an RSA fighter pilot and had been interned in a re-education camp for eleven years before being allowed to come to Australia under the family reunion program. 'Farewell Saigon' has footage of his military unit which he finds impossible to watch. The mother can point out the school she went to as a girl; the images of a sea of white *ao dai* (traditional dress worn by Vietnamese women) spreading gaily from the gates of the school are images of Confucian educational rectitude and the innocence of youth that are almost equally impossible to watch.

There are also those for whom the politics of this tape are to be foregrounded: 'The video brings back emotional memories of how proud and honoured Vietnamese should be with their country and not believe false propaganda and damaging accusations by foreign political analysts and the Vietcong'; and 'It was produced to remind the Vietnamese and the rest of the world that Vietnam was once an independent nation until it was betrayed in the war by its American allies'. These statements are representative of the public construction that can be placed on this material by its intended audience. It is important to note that there is nothing in the tape commentary or the visuals that directly attacks the United States, but there is a studied absence of any signifier of what was by the time of the footage an overwhelming American presence in Saigon.

There is also a very direct political sense in which 'Farewell Saigon' is like a home movie. Most of the documentary footage used in the video was smuggled out of the country just before the fall of Saigon by the Vietnamese Student Association in Paris. It was then handed over to a senior military figure who gave To Van Lai copyright clearance to use the footage in his assembly for *Gai Biet Saigon*. The footage is a virtual palimpsest of the violence of exile; such media, left behind after the fall of Saigon, would have had prime value in targeting elite members of the fallen regime.

Cultural negotiation

The auspices of the inevitable and widespread negotiation between Vietnamese and Western cultural forms are prominently the owners of the small business music video production houses and the principal well-established performers. Many of these figures were prominent in South Vietnamese cultural production before 1975 and have maintained that position in the ensuing decades. They are educated in the heritage and have maintained the popular memory as they simultaneously auspice inevitable hybridisation of this heritage under the commercial imperative. But this is to continue a well-established historical hybridisation. For the most established, there are direct links back to pre-1975 Saigon, and the continuities of such converged music forms being developed and practised well before 1975 need to be accounted for. The hybridity of Vietnamese music culture has its roots both fundamentally in millennial Chinese–Vietnamese interchange and more latterly with French interchange during the colonial period. In the 1960s it was the massive influence of American rock and roll during the war, especially in Saigon, which provided the most recent pre-exile infusion of hybrid elements. Pham Duy's historical treatise *Musics of Vietnam* (1973), even as it is committed to the identification and preservation of the country's folk traditions, shows that the south's major styles of theatrical romanticism in performance, while influenced by French and latterly American traditions, were originally a Chinese influence.[11] Vietnamese area studies could benefit significantly from a greater sense of the mutability and adaptability of their object of study, and this is nowhere clearer than in the area of popular culture. Terry Rambo, arguing this case, shows that even such an exemplary symbol of Vietnamese authenticity, the *ao dai*, is a borrowing from Chinese culture.[12]

Of the cultural positions available to the communities, that which accepts the inevitability of cultural negotiation and adaptation and fashions musical styles around that position seeks to minimise the more liminal postures of heritage maintenance or assertive hybridity. The musical styles are mainstreamed and stable in style, based on established patterns of intermixing Chinese, French and US inputs from before 1975. A major figure, Elvis Phoung – an Elvis cover singer before it became a global industry! – was an established performer in Saigon before 1975 and his career has continued unabated throughout the exile. Other major performers include Luu Bich, Tuan Ngoc and Khanh Ha. Befitting its mainstream status, probably two-thirds of the corpus is of this type, as it is predominantly easy listening or middle-of-the-road 'crooner' presentational styles that are the least confronting and of potentially broadest address across audience interests. The style of music renews audience connections to the soft melodic music and sentimental ballads often performed in bars and cabarets of the pre-1975 period. Visually, this style of presentation rarely employs documentary footage characteristic of the first style, nor does it involve the elaborate postmodern-pastiche stage settings and 'excessive' costuming of the third style. All the companies aim for this type of predominant content, as it will maximise their target audience. The other two categories occupy together roughly the other third of output.

'Hat Cho Ngay Hom Qua' ('Song of Yesterday') (in Paris by Night Issue 20, 1993), a 'Lien Khuc' (medley) with performers Elvis Phuong, Duy Quang, Anh Khoa and Tuan Ngoc, is a good example. Performed bilingually, the medley comprises popular Western songs of Elvis Presley and John Lennon, and music from the era of the Vietnam War ('Yesterday', 'Stand by Me', etc.). The performance draws upon the memories of the mature audience who lived in Saigon throughout the 1950s to the 1970s, hence the title. That audience's memories of an era of continual war, struggle and devastation are mapped gently onto the 'hardships' that are the thematic substance of the original Western songs (lost and unrequited love, etc.) and the massive disjunction is managed in the ambience of nostalgia and tasteful dinner jackets on the set.

Innovation within this style is centred on harmonious bothways adaptation: Vietnamese interpretation of foreign music or traditional Vietnamese lyrics with the influence of contemporary Western music. New songwriters like Nhat Ngan and Khuc Lan specialise in translating and interpreting Chinese and French songs into Vietnamese new wave music. Luu Bich is often linked with the latter, performing a wide range of Chinese ballads translated into Vietnamese, with one of the most popular songs being 'Chiec La Mua Dong' ('The Leaf of Winter'). Composers like Van Phung and Ngo Thuy Mien, for example, are strongly influenced by jazz and rhythm and blues. In 'Noi Long' ('Feelings') (Paris by Night Issue 39, 1997), Bich Chieu's performance of lyrics that are purely Vietnamese is revamped with a Western influence of jazz and blues. The initial reaction from one focus group of young recently arrived school students watching this was that it was 'weird' and 'un-Vietnamese'. However, after discussion and reflection they were able to appreciate the new version of the song.

The most productive means of grasping the cultural work that audiences are performing with this music is to see it as positively modelling identity transition. The simple lyrics, well known to the point of cliché ('easy listening') in Vietnamese, English or French, provide a reassuring point of recognition for those (mostly the older, more recently arrived) who find themselves displaced in an overseas community where language is the main cultural barrier; while others (mostly the young) are provided an easy way of understanding their own family's cultural environment. ASIA Productions specialises in this approach. Thanh and Jasmine, a well-educated brother and sister who are dedicated fans of the music, reflected that they were initially attracted to their own heritage by their interest in the re-mixing of traditional folklore music through the music videos of ASIA Productions.

The cultural negotiation position can also be distinguished politically from heritage maintenance insofar as it is prepared to negotiate certain emergent relationships with the homeland, a stance unthinkable within the first category. As Carruthers points out, the revered composer Trinh Cong Son, who actually lives in Vietnam but enjoys equal popularity at home and abroad, has had a long collaboration with popular diaspora singer Khanh Ly. Also, diaspora artists are now beginning to test the home market with some live performances, such as at the major Tet celebrations since 1996. Indeed, there is greater reciprocity to this emergent and problematic rapprochement than might at first appear:

> The homeland pirate culture industry has been able to take advantage of lax copyright and censorship laws to enjoy the fruits of overseas Vietnamese media companies' labours without contributing to their revenues, while overseas companies have been able to exploit the first world/third world divide by going to Vietnam to record the voices of local singers, mastering them in studios back in France and the US, and releasing the CDs at a significantly lower price than those produced entirely overseas.[13]

'New Wave' assertive hybridity

While the hybrid retains its links to and identification with its origins, it is also shaped and transformed by (and in turn, shapes and transforms) its location in the present. Belonging at the same time to several 'homes', it cannot simply dissolve into a culturally unified form. The complex achievement of the hybrid is a product of [the] obligation to 'come to terms with and to make something new of the cultures they inhabit, without simply assimilating to them'. The result . . . is a celebration of cultural impurity, a 'love-song to our mongrel selves'.[14]

The reception for performers who assertively seek to fully appropriate Western rock and pop (in a style that is dubbed 'New Wave') can be as intense as the political controversies around incidents such as the 'Mother' episode. This 'assertive hybridity' is exclusively a phenomenon of youth culture, and centres on its very specific formation at 'ground zero' in Southern California. The 'excesses' of controversial performers such as Lynda Trang Dai, Nhu Mai, The Magic or Don Ho have some precedent within the context of Californian Vietnamese-American youth culture (as evidenced by the specialist lifestyle magazines for Vietnamese-American young people such as *Viet Now*). However, the economics of live performance and music video production necessitates a much broader audience and thus a context beyond its niche age and style demographic.

New Wave, at its most basic, refers to bilingual – English and Vietnamese – song lyrics. But it is also about playful, political and increasingly ambitious appropriations or pastiches of mostly American rock and pop rendered into Vietnamese, some examples being 'Black Magic Woman', 'Hotel California' and 'Fernando'. But innovative performers like Don Ho have ranged much wider; for example, in *Paris By Night: Las Vegas* (Issue 29, 1995), Don Ho's 'Caravan of Life' performance was based on a well-known

Chinese song, translated into Vietnamese and performed in a setting that highlighted the oppression of the Nepalese.

Lynda Trang Dai is prototypical of this stance, and is a well-established but very controversial figure in Vietnamese music performance. She has established a profile since the mid-1980s modelling herself on Madonna, reprising most of Madonna's personae, from the fishnet stockings–crucifix–white trash–material girl to the toned gym junkie and the feminine-Vogue look. It is entirely possible to see Lynda's confrontational personae as doubly mapped onto the provocations Madonna posed to sexual/musical/religious representations over this period, given that her career has been entirely played out within the Vietnamese community. Her influence can be measured by her pioneering 'assertive hybridity' and by the strength of audience response, which in its extremes is *sui generis* in the Vietnamese music industry. It is not only in sexual Westernisms that this occurs: there is much more stress in this style of music on the dramatic/excessive *surfaces* of performance, costume and reprising contemporary Western rock, pop and rap than on traditional Vietnamese music's emphasis on subtly coded variations of voice and face.

Thanh, a young proprietor of a karaoke coffee shop who is extremely knowledgeable about all aspects of the Vietnamese music scene, offered this analysis:

> Lynda is the first Vietnamese to do that [fashion a form of extreme hybridity] when she came out. It was a clash of cultures especially with the older generation. They were giving her a bad name. But guys like her performances. Now everyone [that is, Vietnamese performers] just copies Lynda while she continues to copy Madonna. Lynda was daring to do that because Vietnamese performers at that time were more traditional and very influenced by the Vietnamese culture.

Over time, Lynda has – and very importantly in the Vietnamese community – officially 'earned respect' in terms of her longevity and solid track record of performance, and a typical introduction to a Lynda performance by a compere might now be the respectful coding 'a Vietnamese woman with a Western style of performance', or this saying quoted by one of the MCs linking the performances on Paris by Night Issue 36, 'khau za ma tam phat'/'although the mouth speaks badly, the heart speaks of goodness'. Nevertheless, at the level of gossip and rumour in the unofficial culture, a figure like Lynda is the occasion for much boundary-marking.

On the one hand, it is very difficult for young people to appreciate the heritage maintenance and cultural negotiation positions, particularly those young people without Vietnamese language skills and/or sufficient background in the formal poetic rhetoric of much of the music embodying the positions. The Westernised/Americanised posture of a Lynda offers some purchase into Vietnamese culture. For Thanh and Jasmine (Thanh's sister, who runs the grocery store adjacent to Thanh's coffee shop), the single most crucial factor in excluding potential fans of this music video is high-enough levels of language competence. On the other hand, Lynda will often bring out an 'ultra-Vietnamese' reaction, with gossip about face lifts, corruption of the language through sloppy lyrics and 'inability to sing rather than just perform', and dismissal of her claims to feminist credentials on the basis that 'women's rights are a Western issue' – which is precisely why, for the New Wave youth following, the latter should be foregrounded.

'Cyber Queen' (Paris by Night Issue 32, 1995) is Lynda's reprise of Madonna in her Gaultier cyborg phase. Lynda and her backing singers and dancers are costumed as steely cyborgs, the women sporting conical bras. The English lyrics are consistent with the choreography of the piece, but there is a complete disjunction with the Vietnamese lyrics, which speak in traditional coding of 'winds and waterfalls'. There is also a disjunctive gesture midway through the song when Lynda unveils the Republic of Vietnam flag under one arm and the United States flag under the other. This nationalistic gesture would be characteristic of a heritage maintenance performance but is received with some bewilderment as part of this style.

Don Ho is one of the most popular performers for younger Vietnamese. His performances are noted for their elaborate choreography, set design, costuming and innovation, along with sophisticated cover versions of a wide range of exclusively Western songs. 'I Just Died in Your Arms' (Paris by Night Issue 36, 1996) was a Western hit song in the late 1980s and, in this instance and compared with 'Cyber Queen', there is a close conjunction between the English and the Vietnamese 'translation' from the English. The Vietnamese lyrics, being a translation and not a lyrical sequence or song in its own right in the language, are, for some, a stronger provocation to Vietnamese lyrical traditions and to traditional models of romance and sexual relations. The song embraces without reservation the iconic degeneracy, the female sexual predation, sex and death equivalences and the eviscerated manhood that are at the centre of the European vampire mythologies. And, by and large, the Vietnamese lyrical component is drawn directly into this field of meaning.

There is nothing that compels identification as Vietnamese in either the staging or the referencing in the lyrics. One focus group of young school-aged, recently arrived migrants were generally consensual about Don Ho being 'American' rather than 'Vietnamese' because the mannerisms in which he performs are 'foreign', such as his dress, the Western songs he sings, the way he dances, the fact that there are back-up dancers performing with him and particularly in this performance, and the stage design being European Gothic (coffins, chandeliers, the crepuscular smoke, female vampires with extended incisors, black capes and ghostly make-up). Others in the group commented that he is a 'lai', a 'half-breed' as a performer.

In 'going too far', the assertive hybridity position provokes criticism and risks losing at least part of its intended audience. A music store owner catering primarily to Vietnamese youth argues that the young listen primarily to Western techno and house music and may regard the more radical performers and styles as in fact assimilationist, as they are 'cheap imitations' of dominant Western styles. If they want to 'be' Vietnamese in their music tastes, they will turn to the more middle-of-the-road material of cultural negotiation which engages identifiably distinct Vietnamese traditions.

Conclusion

> Each time I view these videos, the feeling I am left with afterwards is one of complete exhilaration or of absolute sadness. There is no in between. It is either one extreme or the other.
>
> Having left Vietnam as a child of 7 years of age in 1976, I do not have a strong recollection of the physical landscape of Vietnam, of the traditions, the tastes, the smell, the sights, the sounds of this 'homeland'. Every image that comes on screen builds for me the 'reality' of what Vietnam is and was. And it is these images that I collect and refer to when I speak of Vietnam. It is not the Vietnam that once existed or the country as it is now that swims in my head. Vietnam becomes for me a collection of images I have been immersed in through media.[15]

The rate of immigration from Vietnam slowed appreciably over the late 1990s. The proportion of those who were originally refugees also diminished appreciably, while the numbers of those visiting Vietnam for business or family purposes rose. Although the official culture of the diaspora continues to remain strongly anti-communist and anti-homeland government, growing numbers of particularly the young are forging 'hypenated' ('Asian-American', 'Asian-Australian') identities which owe less to the past and more to a globalising present. For such small communities, there is a remarkable diversity in both the population and their economic, social and cultural circumstances. It is arguable that diasporic communities provide examples of cultural formations at their most mutable, with political change in both the homelands and the host countries, inter-generational tension a key given the recency of departures from the homeland, and very sharp socio-economic differences between the successful and the struggling. The media consumed by overseas Vietnamese people, rather than resolving the conflicts thrown up by such mutability, as a functionalist model of media–social relations would have it, tend rather to 'stage' them, give them voice and manage them in a productive tension. Western claims to cultural pluralism would be more plausible if the 'shadow system' of diasporic video, music and popular culture was to come into a fuller light.

Part 4 The cultural policy debate

Perhaps the position I am most well known for is the argument laid out in *Framing Culture*: that cultural studies may be actually detrimental to the formation of progressive cultural policy rather than being benignly irrelevant to it or merely a 'handmaiden' of it. The controversies this and related positions (such as those of Tony Bennett and Ian Hunter) stirred up were dubbed the 'cultural policy debate' and have reverberated to the present. The two essays in this part capture the argument in its first and most concise formulation ('Cultural studies from the viewpoint of cultural policy') and then reflect on the immediate set of critical responses to it, and my reply to them ('Re-framing culture').

Essentially, my arguments in the cultural policy debate were designed to assess academic work in the field against its claims to be a politically informed critical practice. In 'Re-framing culture' the problem is named as cultural studies' tendency to underestimate 'the positive role the state may play in shaping and supporting cultural activity that would otherwise not be viable in unregulated or minimally funded markets, a tendency to downplay the achievements of Australian cultural expression from within commercial and corporate environments, and minimal participation in the ongoing policy debates that are framing our cultural futures'. I enjoin on the field a politics of reformist social democracy. To articulate this kind of politics to the politics of representation, discourse and systemic suspicion of the state and the corporation was, as I readily admitted at the time, a big ask. For many critics, the attempt to place academic practice and mainstream political principle in lock-step was a step too far.

But, interestingly, over time since the eruption of the cultural policy debate, critical cultural studies has become somewhat more comfortable with the notion of culture as what Tony Bennett calls 'a reformer's science'.[1] While there remains a volatile debate about the varying politics of particular stances – as independent critical intellectual assessing cultural policies, as pedagogue dispassionately introducing students to the field, as advocate for policies and for the importance of policy as an object of study, or as consultant to or researcher for cultural policy apparatuses – substantial international contributions such as those of Jim McGuigan, Justin Lewis, Toby Miller and George Yúdice[2] make the field a robust one. Yúdice, for example, in a nuanced account of the politics of culture in Latin and South America, argues that culture should be regarded as a resource, as something to be maintained and invested in. This is not for its artefactual nature – the preservation of cultural heritage – or excellence in aesthetic attainment, but for its expedient value in the management of populations. This allows Yúdice to be as at home advocating governmental expansion into any area of culture as providing powerful accounts of sophisticated resistance strategies by marginalised groups.

Meanwhile, cultural policy studies remains one of the key elements in the fields of media, communications and cultural studies in Australia today.

Chapter 10

(1993) Cultural studies from the viewpoint of cultural policy

As the discipline of cultural studies moves into a phase of consolidation and some respectability, it is being questioned from three broad directions. In placing these on a left-to-right continuum, it is worth noting that one of the things at stake in the current climate is the viability of just such a political set. We might well remember the wonderful caveat issued by Jean-Luc Godard and Anne-Marie Mieville in *Numero Deux*: 'This is not a film of the left or right, but a film of before and behind.'

To the left is a position that seeks to question the orthodoxies of academic cultural studies in the name of a more authentic critical and political practice, or in the name of a more thoroughgoing deconstruction of postmodernism. This position can invoke the powerful trope of recalling cultural studies to its origins as a brave intervention in established literary and social science orthodoxies.

Meaghan Morris's 'Banality in Cultural Studies', for example, attacks the wilful calling into being of progressiveness in texts, and resistance in audiences – a cheerful populism that often collapses criticism into little more than fandom.[1] She also suggests that the critical stances of the traditional humanities disciplines have not been so clearly dispelled as might once have been imagined.

On the right, emerging from the social sciences, is a position that views the early 1990s' sea-changes in Eastern Europe and the USSR, the longer-term global shifts towards internationalisation and the collapse of movement politics of various kinds as calling into question the continuing relevance of the neo-Marxist 'motor' of cultural studies. From this perspective, the anti-capitalism, anti-consumerism and romanticisation of subcultural resistance embodied in the classical texts of cultural studies are no longer adequate responses to the big questions confronting the articulation of politics and culture in modern Western societies.

With these political reassessments has come a revaluation of empirical detail, aligned with a piecemeal approach to the articulation of ideology and culture. There is a 'beyond ideology' flavour about much of this work. John Kelly's discussion of Stuart Hall's key text on left renewal in Britain, *The Hard Road to Renewal: Thatcherism and the Crisis of the Left*, is a frontal attack on a politics of grand theory that lacks credible empirics.[2] With rhetorical naivety, Kelly poses the ultimate empirical question: 'How does Hall *know* any of these things?' (emphasis added).

The ranks of apostates from neo-Marxist orthodoxies have swelled, especially in Britain (though in the United States the field of cultural studies is still on a growth surge, and substantial questioning of the assumptions of the field from within will not come very soon or very readily). It seems that something more than a faddish search for The Next Thing is afoot.[3]

There is also a 'centrist' policy orientation. This approach seeks to position the perspectives of cultural studies within fields of public policy where academic critical protocols do not have priority. Like the 'left humanities' position, it is aware of the limits of academic discourse. While seeking to respond to the same global concerns as the 'right-social-science' position, it is not as concerned to discredit the foundational posture of cultural studies, if that posture is distilled down to the central Enlightenment values of liberty, equality and solidarity.[4] Indeed, it seeks to revivify these core values as the central motor of reformism that can be appealed to in the public sphere of contemporary Western societies. This is the position that this chapter advances as a way forward for cultural studies.

What relations should exist between cultural studies and cultural policy? The term 'cultural studies' (or 'cultural criticism') is employed as a convenient shorthand for work that treats film, the arts, media and communications, as well as lived, everyday cultures, and is driven by the major strands of neo-Marxist, structuralist, poststructuralist and postmodernist thought. Cultural policy embraces the broad field of public processes involved in formulating, implementing and contesting governmental intervention in, and support of, cultural activity.

The commonsense reaction to the question, one likely to be offered by most of those outside the academy who might be inclined to consider it, would be that the former serves as a kind of 'handmaiden', developing rationales for those engaged in public policy. Theory, analysis and commentary should undergird practice; practice implements theory. On closer inspection, however, the relations are far less harmonious than this model suggests. Indeed, in many ways, contemporary practices flatly contradict received wisdom.

Cultural studies, from the viewpoint of cultural policy, are rather like the curate's egg – good in parts – but even the good parts mightn't be very good. Liz Jacka has written of the 'widening gap between cultural critique and cultural policy'.[5] Taking a cue from this, the chapter canvasses some recent issues in Australian cultural and communications policy where practical opportunities for cultural analysis have been forgone, or worse.

Australian content on television

The Australian Broadcasting Tribunal's exhaustive inquiry into Australian Content on Commercial Television concluded its main considerations in December 1989 with the introduction of a new Television Program Standard. The inquiry ran for about five years, with a break of three years in the mid-1980s.[6]

One of the members of the tribunal, Julie James-Bailey, commented that during the inquiry there was virtually no input from academic cultural critics and analysts.[7] There *was* one such contribution, however, from John Docker, who employed an array of contemporary theory to attack the legitimacy of regulation of Australian content on television.[8] Docker argued that regulation actually means the imposition of (British) high cultural values onto popular cultural forms whose appeal is indifferent to national variations and registrations. What viewers actively embrace in television culture, according to Docker, is the carnivalesque overturning of statist official culture and the celebration of working-class values and interests. These values and interests are transnational, and subvert state interventions to preserve national registrations of popular cultural forms.

It is probably just as well that Docker's arguments had no effect on the outcomes of the inquiry. But it is alarming that Docker's was the only significant contribution that presented any of the theoretical issues that have concerned theorists, critics and historians for decades. Docker's view of popular television and its audiences may be idiosyncratic, but it is, in Graeme Turner's words, 'directly licensed' by current strands of cultural theory.[9] To applaud Docker's irrelevance could be tantamount to applauding the irrelevance of critical and theoretical input to the policy-making process in general.

Advertising and national culture

The tribunal's inquiry addressed Australian content provisions covering all television programming, including advertising. The regulations for television advertising are different from those for other program material. They are directed at prohibiting more than 20 per cent of any advertising being produced overseas, unless Australian crews travel overseas to obtain the footage. They constitute a very high level of protection for local content, and, because they have been in place for thirty years, they have been extremely influential in underwriting the television advertising industry in Australia.

The inquiry into foreign content in advertising has operated virtually as a sidelight to the main act. It is not hard to see why. Advertising is the unworthy discourse, as far as both criticism and policy are concerned. If there has been an outstanding consensus among critics of various persuasions it is that advertising panders to patriarchy and consumerism. This consensus sits comfortably with moves to deregulate a 'blatantly' protected industry. Regulation against foreign advertising content has been the subject of concerted attack from industry – primarily from transnational advertisers – as well as high-level economic rationalist sources of advice to government. A report by the Industries Assistance Commission (now the Industry Commission) attacks the 'virtual embargo' on foreign-produced ads: 'the sector enjoys an extremely privileged position relative to nearly all other economic activity in Australia'.[10]

The main rationale for continued regulation has been the argument that advertising has a role in the formation of national cultural identity. The argument for making a positive connection between advertising and national culture can be mounted in two basic areas. From the viewpoint of policy, the weaker argument is the appeal to the effects of deregulation in the area of advertising on the drama production industry. It is clear that drama production could not have developed its present scope and depth without the industrial infrastructure of the Australian advertising industry. Evidence for this link is widely accepted, and pieces of it are often cited in film and television histories.[11] For this reason, if for no other, deregulating television advertising would have major cultural consequences.

The central argument, however, has to grasp the nettle – the positive contribution advertising itself may make to national culture. In its present forms, cultural studies is spectacularly unsuited to this task.

Two main patterns of criticism have remained foundational to the cultural critique of advertising. The first is diachronic, focusing on the history of advertising as an agent of American cultural imperialism. Jeremy Tunstall's *The Media Are American* and Mattelart and Dorfman's *How to Read Donald Duck* established the parameters of this pattern, and the general critical perspective on advertising has never seriously deviated from it. The other pattern is synchronic; informed by the early semiotic guerrilla tactics of Roland Barthes's *Mythologies*, it focuses on the cultural reproduction of dominant ideological values embedded in bourgeois culture. In spite of an increasingly strong emphasis on feminism, the cultural studies approach to advertising, both in critical writing and in curricula, has not advanced significantly beyond the works of Barthes, Tunstall and Mattelart and Dorfman in the 1950s to 1970s.

Under the umbrella of the tribunal's content regulation, Australian television advertising has developed a strong grammar of national imaging that parallels film and television fiction but has a considerably greater permeation of the mass market. Advertising occupies an average of about three and a half hours a day on each commercial metropolitan television station, compared with typical Australian drama content of about two hours a week. By dint of repetition, saturation coverage across the most popular networks, and sophisticated textual strategies that increasingly link programs with their commercial 'environment', advertising must be seen as having considerable cultural valence.

Such indicators of cultural permeation, though crude and problematic from a critical perspective, are important in policy formulation. The real issue is: to what extent can a positive character be imputed to them? This is not simply a question of putting the Mister Sheen gloss on what critics have regarded as a tawdry business. It is a matter of evaluating the contribution of television advertising in terms that are not just a matter of marking ideological ticks and crosses. It is to describe the impress and influence of advertising in terms that accept that its ideologically regressive elements – its sexism, its chauvinism, its rowdy populism – are bracketed within a more neutral, descriptive cultural and audio-visual history.

Such a history would focus on the central role that advertising has played in the development of a popular audiovisual 'grammar' of national identity during the 1970s and 1980s. The so-called 'new' nationalism of this period was most visibly expressed in advertising campaigns, despite the large claims made for the contribution of film and television drama. These campaigns were at key moments explicit attempts at social engineering – for instance, the 'Life. Be In It' campaign and the 'Advance Australia' campaign of the late 1970s and early 1980s. This is clear in the published aims of 'Advance Australia': 'To heighten community and public awareness and pride in Australian skills, achievements and potential. To highlight the role of individual enterprise in the economy. To encourage improvements in quality design, marketing and other characteristics of Australian identity.'[12] This advertising campaign, and others that came in its wake, sought to redress what attitudinal research had identified as a widespread lack of 'pride in country' and support for Australian manufacturing.[13]

This kind of public-service advertising has had its counterparts in purely commercial campaigns, which over the last fifteen years have invented a popular audiovisual grammar of nationalism. Prestige national advertising campaigns now routinely incorporate this established repertoire of Australianist tropes. The fact that this repertoire is used for evidently contradictory purposes, from promoting health to flogging beer and tobacco, and uses images that range from the unacceptably sexist to the innovative, even progressive, simply registers the modularity of advertising's nationalism.

There is very little substantial critical appraisal of this enormous portfolio of material, and what there is does little to articulate a position sensitive to the policy issues. There are critical exercises of the traditional kind, such as Stephen Alomes's less than trenchant putdown of the course of Australian nationalism ('from jingoism to jingle-ism') in *A Nation at Last?* or Noel King and Tim Rowse's critique of television populism in the 'humanity' ads.[14] But the 'sophisticated theory of consumption' called for by Kathy Myers in Britain,[15] or the magisterial descriptivist account of 'advertising as social communication' given by William Leiss, Stephen Kline and Sut Jhally in North America,[16] have no Australian counterparts. Such approaches must be applied to the question of Australian national identity in advertising if we are to advance beyond reflex ideological critique and begin to address urgent and practical policy issues.

Feminist cultural theory and bureaucratic reform

Australia lags behind Canada and some Scandinavian nations in implementing strategies to modify sexist representations in the mass media, but in the last few years there have been significant initiatives here. The Office of the Status of Women has acted as the coordinating secretariat for a body called the National Working Party on the Portrayal of Women in the Media, a body consisting of representatives of the advertising industry, community groups and government departments.

To my knowledge, little or nothing arising from feminist scholars' sophisticated repertoire of theories of representation has been brought to bear on questions of bureaucratic reformism. Indeed, the most willing and effective advocates of institutional change use 'outdated', reflectionist and empiricist research to drive evidence for change, and a liberal humanist feminism to ground their campaigns.

It is not hard to see why advanced feminist theories of representation have weighed so lightly, despite the considerable body of literature that has been developed around exactly the sorts of questions that animate reformist policy initiatives. As Leiss, Kline and Jhally argue, 'representation' critiques of advertising have been subjective and non-quantitative, and have reduced the specificity of advertising to a generalised social critique.

From the viewpoint of policy, such critiques depend to an unacceptable degree on methods that are difficult to replicate without a high level of interpretative training. Semiotic method is powerful and convincing in the hands of a Barthes or a Williamson, but there has been a lot of obfuscated and redundant 'normal science' in the area. Representation critiques also depend too heavily on extrapolated pertinence – the findings are not underwritten by content analysis based on accepted sampling techniques. And they are guilty of simply using advertising, because it is arguably the most visible and most insistent form of commercialism, as a springboard into a generalised critique that is of little use within the protocols of piecemeal reformism. For all these reasons, representation accounts have been of little value in policy calculation, even for those predisposed to accept the assumptions from which they stem.

Media ownership and cultural power

Cultural studies has increasingly moved away from the orthodox political economy model's concern with questions of ownership and control of the mass media. The cultural power that is interesting now resides with audiences and, to a lesser extent, producers of media content itself. Set over against these interests are what appear to cultural theorists as rather hackneyed and predictable arguments for greater diversity and less concentration of media ownership. The calls of a David Bowman, a Paul Chadwick or an

Eric Beecher appear hackneyed and predictable because they are voiced within very narrow terms of cultural debate, and partake of what Walter Benjamin memorably called 'left-wing melancholy'. This miserabilism, this prophetic nay-saying, is something that cultural studies is now resolutely rejecting.

The exercise of political and cultural power through media control, however, remains one of the key blind spots of public policy in Australia. There is considerable evidence that the issue cuts through established party and factional allegiances and is beginning to create intolerable anomalies for public policy.

This issue will certainly not go away in a postmodernist flush of audience sovereignty. Indeed it will increase in centrality as media converge and narrow their focus ever more powerfully towards precise demographic and psychographic fine-tuning. Not only that, but the current theoretical fashion for championing the active audience finds an ironic echo in the rhetoric of consumer sovereignty that is offered by media owners and deregulators.

Unambiguous economic and political power will increasingly be translatable into unambiguous cultural power. Those who are best positioned to benefit from enhanced technologies of audience targeting, from the convergence of media of carriage and from pro-competitive public policy parameters are precisely those who now exercise enormous power through control of the traditional media. Unless it allies itself with social-democratic advocates of media reform, cultural studies could well become irrelevant in the near future.

Now, just wait a minute!

The 'handmaiden' model is easy picking for those inside the academy. Most people trained in the politics of cultural studies would view their primary role as critics of the dominant political, economic and social order. When such cultural theorists do turn their hands to questions of policy, their command metaphors of resistance, refusal and opposition predispose them to view the policy-making process as inevitably compromised, *ad hoc*, incomplete and inadequate, controlled by people who are inexpert and ungrounded in theory and history, or who wield gross forms of political power for short-term ends. These people and processes are then called to the bar of an abstrusely formulated cultural idealism. Critical idealism would retort that it is the critical theorists who are the mealy-mouthed voice of liberal bourgeois compromise.

A more reflective critique of the position being advanced would raise the issue of the long-term leavening effect of critical idealism. Tomorrow's public debate and potential consensus may well issue from today's utopian, abstruse, left-of-field thinking. The clearest example of this is the 'sourcing' of femocrat reformism by feminist movement politics. Similar sourcing relationships hold between the environmental movements and green politics, or between ethnic advocacy and official discourses of multiculturalism. A more pragmatic variant of the same objection is that, if cultural studies doesn't hold to the humanities' traditional critical vocation, who will – particularly in the wake of the breakdown of more broadly based social movements?

These objections seem reasonable, so they require a careful response. First, the model of prophetic critic is not to be discounted; the role of prophetic critic is the essential prerequisite of critical practice. It is, however, rather disingenuous for the academy to don this mantle, as a great deal of the critical work performed within the academy cannot plausibly claim such prophetic status. The most effective public intellectuals on issues of culture in the Australian polity are not vanguard theorists, but those who work within the terms of a given (and, one might readily concede, narrow) set of public-interest, liberal-democratic and social-democratic norms. Vanguard theory, on the evidence we have to date, is less than likely to translate into prophetic criticism.

The second response proceeds from the first. To get to the nub of the problem: what is cultural studies' understanding of its political vocation? What is its vision of a better, more just, equitable, participatory, cultural order? What measures are cultural theorists and analysts taking to have this vision articulated widely? What alliances are they forming with cultural activists and policy agents and players? To what extent are they informing themselves about the historical, existing and emergent policy agenda, and identifying where they might fit?

In an interesting interchange between John Fiske and an unnamed interlocutor, published in Fiske's *Reading the Popular*, Fiske asserts that 'internal or semiotic resistance . . . is an essential prerequisite of social change'.[17] This statement brings to the fore the politics of Fiske's influential model of resistive populism. The resistive strategies imputed to consumers of popular culture, by definition, are never mobilised into organisations that might seek to influence change in any institutional arrangement or professional practice by which cultural meaning is produced and delivered. The resistance Fiske champions actually undermines the strategies of organised reform movements because it sets itself against ideal standards of professional media practice and against empirical audience measurement. Both are essential if reformism is to gain some purchase in public policy processes.

The missing link is a social-democratic view of citizenship and the training necessary to activate and motivate it. A renewed concept of citizenship should be increasingly central to cultural studies as it moves into the 1990s. Political science, government, sociology, journalism, organisation studies, to say nothing of traditional professional training such as law, all have particular mobilisations of citizenship embodied in their curriculum. Despite this, the emerging evidence for an attention to citizenship in cultural studies signifies an important advance. It demonstrates that cultural studies is coming to terms with its neo-Marxist heritage as it realises that other political postures can be as radically reformist as neo-Marxism without employing a totalising and confrontational rhetoric. For this reason, the perspectives of Australian social-democratic thinkers like Hugh Stretton in social theory, Donald Horne, Peter Wilenski and H. C. Coombs in cultural and communications areas, or Francis Castles in economics, should assume as great an importance for rethinking the vocation of cultural studies as the international fathers (and mothers) of the discipline.

Replacing shop-worn revolutionary rhetoric with the new command metaphor of citizenship commits cultural studies to a reformist strategy within the terms of a social-democratic politics, and thus can connect it to the wellsprings of engagement with policy. Even though, as Ham and Hill show,[18] the policy process in modern capitalist states has arisen within a liberal pluralist problematic, it need not be limited by liberalism's underdeveloped ideas of power and of the necessity of struggle for access to decision-making processes.

This concept of citizenship does not by any means imply a politics of the status quo – a sort of primary-school civics. Donald Horne uses it to advance his Lockean notion of the 'cultural rights' of the citizen in modern social democracies.[19] Graham Murdock and Peter Golding use it to invite thinking about information poverty in our age of increasingly privatised communications.[20] It is also being employed to pose questions about new forms of citizenship that may embrace larger units than the individual nation-state, such as the emergent European community. Similarly, in a 1984 report to the French Ministry of Culture, Mattelart, Delcourt and Mattelart proposed a linguistic–cultural transnational community – a 'latin audio-visual space'.[21] Such concerns have been abroad for decades in the continuing debate in UNESCO concerning the New World Information and Communications Order (NWICO).

Third, the greater proportion of cultural studies work is performed within academic arrangements that either prioritise vocational training or seek to marry a liberal arts education with gestures towards such training. These institutional orientations will become more established, if not necessarily accepted, under current government policies. Pragmatically, then, there are powerful reasons to review the current state of cultural studies.

The calls to introduce a policy orientation into cultural studies became louder in the early 1990s.[22] We hear that cultural studies remains fixated on theoretical and textual orientations that provide little to equip students with knowledge and skills for citizenship and employment in the 1990s. The gap between textually based studies and policy cannot be bridged merely by further refinements in theories of representation, in new understandings of the audience or the 'progressive text', or in notions of subcultural resistance.

Indeed, two British cultural studies 'apostates', Geoff Hurd and Ian Connell, have argued that cultural critique, as a governing educational model, has actively deskilled students:

> While we accept there is a need for cultural appraisal and reconstruction, we would also suggest that the predominant view of the cultural organisations within cultural studies has been misleading and that criticism has been placed before understanding. In short, cultural studies has been critical of enterprises whose modes of operation and social significance it does not properly comprehend.[23]

Questions of policy do circulate at the margins of the traditional core curricula of cultural studies. In Trevor Barr's words, moving those marginal interests towards the centre of the curriculum ultimately has to do with 'political empowerment'.[24]

A focus on policy, if extended to both types of communications curricula – semiotics-based cultural studies on the one hand and business communication, journalism, public relations, marketing and advertising on the other – has the potential to bridge the yawning gaps between these traditions. Its integration into liberal arts and media production programs would encourage a firmer grasp of the social and vocational implications of cultural struggle as embodied in governmental and industrial processes. On the other hand, its integration into industry-driven courses would draw students into a broader appreciation of the politics and ethics of their vocations and the reasonable legitimacy of state intervention.

Finally, many of our protocols are disabling because they take scant account of the local conditions in which theory must be developed. It might seem a truism to state that different emphases should emerge in cultural studies in different parts of the world. Because Australia is a net importer of ideas as much as goods and services, it is crucial for an Australian cultural studies program to be self-critical about its agenda, lest the agenda be set, by default, elsewhere. It cannot be put better than the report of the Committee to Review Australian Studies in Tertiary Education, which said that Australianising tertiary education would prevent the intellectual cringe that slides 'between a vacuous cosmopolitanism and an apologetic provincialism'.[25]

To Australianise is not to call for a form of intellectual tariff blockade. On the contrary, it implies a much stronger and more perspicacious engagement with imported traditions. And it in no way implies an *a priori* defence of the status quo, or a rejection of the possible benefits flowing from greater internationalisation of inquiry. It does suggest that an Australian cultural studies engaging with policy issues that affect the future of Australian culture would involve reconceptualising certain general theories, upgrading the focus on regulation as a positive underpinning of cultural production, and rethinking the politics of culture in a non-British, non-North-American setting.

Importing British cultural studies has meant privileging subcultural resistance to a repressive and class-defined state. This has much to do with Thatcherism's far-reaching influence on the agenda of the British left, the anti-statist tone of much cultural studies and the subsequent search for positive markers of the intrinsic subversiveness of everyday life. The libertarianism implicit in this approach might find a greater echo in the United States (where the state has willingly abetted rather than mollified economic and cultural imperialism) than it ever should in Australia, or for that matter many other countries where state regulatory activity has struggled to achieve an equitable flow of economic and cultural goods and services.

Consider the perennial issue of the nation as an illustration of the importance of localism in intellectual work. The ascendant current of macro-level thought in cultural studies today lays to rest the nation-state and invites practitioners to link opportunities for internationalism with a renewed communalism. This may be appropriate for cultural thought in the present European context, but it is inappropriate in virtually any context outside the First World, including Australia.

There are high stakes involved in the arguments for internationalism and community against the nation. All the major cultural industries in Australia (film, television, the major arts and the many community-based arts programs sponsored by the Australia Council) derive their policy justification from their being national in scope. It is too early, if indeed it will ever be politically strategic, to pit the internationalist–communalist position against the nation in Australia.

Ultimately, despite a Byzantine tripartite system of government that makes Australia one of the most 'governed' countries in the world per capita, it is at the national level that debate on cultural futures has to be staged. The future of cultural production is unavoidably bound into the future of national cultural policies. In terms of the intellectual resourcing of policy development, and in the myriad ways that local, state and subcultural sites of activity depend on national provision and support, the national arena will remain the engine room for cultural policy initiatives. For its part, cultural theory must take greater stock of its potential negative influence on progressive public policy outcomes and, if it is to orient itself in a more valuable way towards policy imperatives, must attend to the tasks of consolidating the legitimacy of policy rhetorics that sustain a national cultural infrastructure.

Implications and conclusions

Is it possible to regard a policy orientation within cultural studies as simply an add-on element, one more offering in the interdisciplinary smorgasbord? Not really. It has been suggested that the political rhetoric undergirding cultural studies would have to be re-examined. This alone would indicate a more thoroughgoing review of the cultural studies enterprise than the smorgasbord model would permit.

Nothing in what has been said here should be taken to indicate a less critical vocation for cultural studies. What would count as the critical vocation, however, would change. A cultural studies that grasps and sustains links with policy will inquire across a greatly expanded field, but with methods far less totalising and abstract, far more modest and specific, than those to which we are accustomed.

To treat cultural policy adequately from a critical perspective, it is necessary to appreciate the combined impact of economics, administrative law, cultural history, entertainment financing, government and parliamentary procedures on the development of public policy. This means a more subtle and context-sensitive re-education in the roles of the state in mixed capitalist economies, away from monolithic and wooden grand theories inspired more by critical purism than by the requirements for piecemeal reformism. Critical policy research thus implies more, rather than less, critical understanding than is found in the traditions of cultural criticism developed exclusively within humanities-based disciplines, and a significantly greater sensitivity to the extra-academic contexts within which such research must circulate for it to exercise its potential leavening function.

In summary, then, a policy orientation in cultural studies would shift its 'command metaphors' away from rhetorics of resistance, oppositionalism and anti-commercialism on the one hand and populism on the other, towards those of access, equity, empowerment and the divination of opportunities to exercise appropriate cultural leadership. It would not necessarily discount critical strategies and priorities, but may indeed enhance and broaden them. It is not a call simply to add another 'perspective' to the academic sideboard, but it would necessitate rethinking the component parts of the field from the ground up. It offers one major means of rapprochement across the critical/vocational divide that structures the academic field of cultural and communication studies. Finally, it would commit us to a genuine localism, against the abstract theoreticism that usually passes as the currency of international academic exchange.

Chapter 11

(1993) Re-framing culture

To coin a well-turned phrase, writing *Framing Culture: Criticism and Policy in Australia* seemed like 'a good idea at the time'. I was working outside the academy, as a researcher and policy analyst at the Communications Law Centre, a public interest advocacy unit working at the interface between community groups, unions and researchers on the one hand and government and the bureaucracy on the other, to advance public interest inputs and outcomes in communications policy. While I had been appointed in part because of my background in academic cultural analysis of film and television, to my increasing dismay I found that the protocols of such analysis were often not simply different but at odds with the work of public interest advocacy in culture and communications. As one of my co-workers at the Centre, when I asked for her thoughts on the relations between cultural critique and cultural policy and my prospects for writing a book about them, said famously, 'not many and not much'.

Framing Culture looked at the rapid growth of tertiary courses in media studies, communications studies, cultural studies and film studies in the context of Australia's move towards an information society, with its media of communication playing an increasingly central role in delivering information, entertainment and education and in offering opportunities to develop a shared public culture. In large measure, the new orientations to communications and cultural studies in the humanities and social sciences have been informed by a politics based on a radical questioning of the state and corporate power and strategy and a suspicion of cultural forms that issue from, partake in or seek to legitimise that power or those strategies. This has resulted in an engaging portfolio of concerns for marginalised voices and cultures and for redressing the asymmetries of power between advantaged and disadvantaged groups in society.

However, it has also resulted in an underestimation of the positive role the state may play in shaping and supporting cultural activity that would otherwise not be viable in unregulated or minimally funded markets, a tendency to downplay the achievements of Australian cultural expression from within commercial and corporate environments, and minimal participation in the ongoing policy debates that are framing our cultural futures. Indeed, in some instances, cultural theorists and critics seek actively to undermine state regulation or commercial cultural activity on principle. So, *Framing Culture* looked at this new interdisciplinary field and its relationship, or rather lack of relationship, to the institutional structures and ethos that contribute to the making and analysis of cultural policy in Australia.

It examined the impact of increasing globalisation in communications on small nations with 'import cultures' like Australia. A generation of neo-Marxist and postmodernist cultural criticism has engendered a suspicion of constructed unities, the largest of which is the 'imagined community' of the nation. Such critical suspicion is now beginning to dovetail in unlikely ways with international political, economic and technological developments that are bringing national unity and sovereignty into question with great effect. There is a strange convergence between the posture of criticism and ascendent doctrines of 'rational' economic and social restructuring. Cultural studies should develop more appropriate accounts of national identity that can support policy development in the context of increasing internationalisation, the book argued.

Similarly, there has long been regulation in Australia to ensure that television advertising is predominantly undertaken by nationals, and this has contributed significantly to the growth not only of that industry but of the film and television drama production industry as well. However, such regulatory support was diminished in the early 1990s, with potential effects on Australian audiovisual production across the board. Traditionally, cultural theory on advertising has been uniformly hostile, treating it as perhaps the most 'unworthy discourse' of all. Cultural theories of advertising need to be developed in order to build a policy-oriented account of the positive contribution that television advertising may have made to Australia's national identity.

Equally, the discipline of cultural studies has tended to neglect analysis and advocacy about communications futures, such as the introduction of pay television in Australia. The book therefore attempted to extend the relation between criticism and policy to embrace procedures usually foreign to the critical enterprise – – experimental modelling, options analysis, and normative argument rather than *post facto* critique – and sought to map the way arguments about the relation of cultural to economic and technological precepts can work in the formulation of policy for future, rather than existing, industries.

The book also looks at the way social issues like violence in the media are treated in contemporary policy development, suggesting that these could be used to renovate and enliven academic debates which, despite several decades of research, have failed to deliver outcomes that can be implemented in pluralistic democratic societies. It concludes with several suggestions about the shape of curricula and of research that might take up the challenge of policy issues.

The main reason that *Framing Culture* attempted to articulate policy to the new fields of inquiry in the humanities and social sciences is that a 'cultural mandate' is the key rationale for the continued legitimacy of government intervention and support in areas of the arts, television, film and heritage. It retains more legitimacy than arguments for economic multipliers arising from the cultural industries and has been a more persuasive argument than employment protection. It seems that communications and cultural studies are the fields where these questions can be taken up most productively in universities today. *Framing Culture* advocated that a cultural politics of reform and participation should be developed in a dialogue with the politics of opposition – a cultural politics that connects the academic to wider communities of interest and action.

Befitting my co-worker's famous last words, the career of the book's reception has been turbulent to say the least. (In what follows, reference is made to several reviews and commentaries on *Framing Culture*.) The most enthusiastic endorsements of the thrust of *Framing Culture* were from outside the academy or from those already professionally committed to its broad remit,[1] perhaps worryingly so in the light of Meaghan Morris's comment that '[t]he image of cultural studies in the book is largely fantasmal; it is as though the text were addressed to someone who already thought that it was a wank but wanted some reassurance'.[2]

The more sober but mainly positive accounts were from those already predisposed to regard the argument as a useful one in the light of either the pressing nature of the policy questions the book addressed or the viewpoint of its calling cultural studies to account.[3] Those who were pretty much even-handed in their criticisms and endorsements were so because they at least provisionally began from a similar point to me, while the conclusions they drew differed constructively from mine.[4] The strongest ripostes issued from those most closely identifying with my target, fantasmal or not, of critique.[5] And some were just tired of all the self-centred peacock-puffing displays: 'humanities intellectuals arguing about ... humanities intellectuals, like a bad day on the Oprah Winfrey show'.[6]

So, there was a range of responses that threw up substantial, possibly central, issues in the future agenda for cultural, media and communications studies. In what follows, I concentrate on some themes of the politics of culture that were not treated in my earlier review of responses to the book.[7]

Perhaps quite rightly, the most significant challenge that the critics served up to *Framing Culture* was the view of a political vocation which it enjoined on cultural studies. I say 'quite rightly' because *Framing Culture*, to be more declarative than the book itself was, is ultimately about the political grounding of cultural studies, and the policy orientation can be seen as the platform for raising those questions. I would readily concede that I did not make nearly as much as I could have of the oppositional position which public interest advocacy perforce must take in the context of policy debates, and that the degree of swerve in my interests from policy *advocacy* – the attempt to put marginalised positions in the context of overt power relations – to policy *studies*, or, better, the attempt to run the two in parallel in the book, was taking on too much. The articulation of my perspective to social and advocacy movements, both established and nascent or potential, was underdeveloped. It is time to try to redress this.

The formation of the Communications Law Centre was indebted to US models of organised public interest group activity developed in one of the great 'stateless states', in Michael Pusey's words,[8] where the citizen's voice was muted in public forums. The development of parastatal organisations to fill the gap between the state and civil society had been dominated by extremely well-organised and well-funded para-political think-tanks of a right-wing persuasion.

In Australia, there was also the recognition that the role of the state was ramifying, with elements directing it towards the American model. As the state began to interface more and more widely with domains of what was formerly thought of as civil society, both the opportunities and the threats that this posed were brought to the fore. On the one hand, the ramifying activities of the public bureaucracies meant that they were becoming both progressively more powerful and more permeable to community response on a routine basis. Although this is to read him somewhat against the grain, Pusey's landmark analysis of the Canberra bureaucracy shows both elements at play: its power, in that the bureaucracy can no longer be regarded, if it ever was, as 'neutral in the policy process and transparent to a political will expressed elsewhere',[9] and its greater permeability, in Pusey's focus on the increasingly conflictual structure of the client-oriented departments versus the central agency departments. Activism through organised pressure groups responding to and exploiting the diversifying interfaces between state and civil society was becoming an adjunct to activism through political parties.

The most proximate developments that undergirded this kind of reformism included the rise of investigative journalism and organs of informed critique for the professional middle classes such as *Nation* or the *National Times*, and the embracing of so-called middle-class concerns like the anti-Vietnam movement or conservation by activist unions (leading to the green bans, the inner-city resistance to development projects and the anti-freeway movements of the 1970s, which have grown to the fully fledged green politics of the present), and the professionalisation and widening of what counted as legitimate union activity. The administrative law changes of the mid-1970s which opened up formerly closed governmental and bureaucratic processes of decision making to some degree of public participation and response were also a moment with long-term implications for bureaucratic reformism.

These were part of the complex of developments that constituted the enduring political energy emanating from the New Left of the 1960s, those elements which had not succumbed to what was usually called 'cooptation'. They should be contrasted with the newer politics of gender, sexual orientation, ethnicity and race which grew from a critique of the New Left. One political disposition took the posture of the New Left on the long march through the institutions, the other regarded that posture as deeply flawed, however much it would stand on the shoulders of the New Left to pursue its own visions.

This is an important element of the broad historical–political hinterland within which the social reformism subtending *Framing Culture* was conceived. To caricature it, it was the politics and ethos of Labor lawyers, the peak consumer and social service bodies like ACOSS and the Australian Consumers Association, the lobby groups, the green alliances perhaps more than movement radicals, a politics of bureaucratic reform borrowing, if it ever turned (and it rarely did) to theoretical support, from American elite theory rather than the European discourse and neo-Marxist theory of Althusser or Foucault. It seeks to exploit the tensions between the actual *exercise* and the public *legitimation* of power in liberal democracies. Hester Eisenstein captures the spirit of this politics well in her account of femocracy, the most significant political phenomenon that has suggested possible rapprochments between the two traditions that I have outlined. She argues that any bureaucratic reformism perforce works within the framework of liberalism or social democracy. 'One is taking the rhetoric of the liberal democratic state at its word.' Those 'academic analysts of state power that tend to turn up their noses at this kind of a framework', she suggests, 'will wind up dictating the outcome rather than actually taking account of the lived reality of the struggle that is taking place at a number of significant levels'.[10]

In setting out, as *Framing Culture* did, to articulate this kind of politics to the politics of representation and discourse was, as they say, a big ask. The former was an outgrowth of a modernist Enlightenment project which is capable of embracing the politics of gender, ethnicity and race and class, but which does not depend on any one of them for its central ethos, depending as it does on pragmatic admixtures of Fabianism, social democratic redistributive statism as practised in the Scandinavian countries and, at times, in mixed economies like Canada and Australia under reforming governments, and, at the limit, the democratic socialism of Western Marxism. The latter, on the other hand, is a project that is indebted to the major twentieth-century critiques of the Enlightenment, such as psychoanalysis, deconstruction, subaltern cultural studies and queer theory, together with strong if ambivalently positioned elements of postmodernism.

Issues of political groundings run across most commentary on *Framing Culture*; Boris Frankel's wide-ranging critique of postmodern and post-Fordist prophets in *From the Prophets Deserts Come* is one substantial contribution, although it is not a full-ranging rebuttal of the book. It includes a concerted attack on what he calls the 'Left technocrats' advancing cultural policy as a way forward in the face of the dispiritment of the Left.[11] Frankel's critique shares many elements of Morris's, summed up in her withering epithet 'desperately gung-ho corporatism' as a description of my posture in *Framing Culture*.

In Chapter 7, Frankel defends the great traditions of modernist cultural forms, particularly the left *avant garde* which produced high culture with enduring transcendental value. This he pits against the cultural relativism of the left technocrats, on which basis they are able comfortably to assimilate all questions of cultural value to industry and economic valuation. This is surely wrongheaded. The work of cultural policy advocacy and formulation tries to ensure that a basically anthropological grounding of cultural activity is maintained in the context of a mixed economy – it doesn't enter into questions of aesthetic valuation. Which is not to say that debates about the relative cultural, ideological and aesthetic value of popular cultural forms should not be and cannot be debated, just that the work of policy participation does not consciously enter into them, even though they might strongly need to rely indirectly on them.

Frankel expects cultural policy and planning rhetorics to remain a close cousin to and dependent on cultural criticism. This it cannot do in its operational forms *as* cultural policy and planning. But this is not to say that value is not embedded strongly in such operational forms. Frankel accords too little transformative weight to rhetorics like diversity and quality, access and equity. These can represent real platforms for democratising and empowering cultural activity finally unencumbered with the debilitating aesthetic dead weight of the past represented in political left modernism that he subscribes to at this point of his book. His argument is almost entirely waylaid by the retreat to notions of aesthetic value which are pitted against the cultural 'relativism' of the policy push. This misunderstands the quite limited nature of policy planning which does not attempt to preordain the ways in which for instance youth arts might develop their ethos, their normative contents. By and large, the 'Left technocrats' are on the side of marginalised cultural forms, like youth arts, or strategically focus on vulnerable issues of cultural maintenance, like Australian content regulations.

Whatever the failings of the Accord in industry and wages policy, calling policy protagonists 'Accordists' and meaning by this that they are in the throes of unrestrained market forces by buying into arguments about 'productive culture' is far wide of the mark. The arguments for culture as industry are much needed arguments to win in a mixed economy like Australia, precisely because they represent 'industry' sectors outside, or only partially articulated to private sector market forces, and will always be so. Far from being assimilated willy-nilly to entrepreneurial 'productive culture', they are industries fashioned out of state support, and arguments for them as industries come from the strategic arguments for continued state support.

Frankel's overly generalised critique blinds him to the particularities of how, why and to what audiences 'culture as industry' arguments are made. These should not be reducible to the grand sweep of theoretical decay surveyed in *From the Prophets Deserts Come.* In bewailing the loss of the ironic and critical edge that Adorno and Horkheimer's original formulation of the term 'culture industries' carried, Frankel wishes to collapse cultural and political scenarios separated by decades of difference.

What can we learn from this debate and what is worth continuing with? It would be little more than a sterile exercise in raking over merely warm coals if my purpose here was not to lay out what I think are the enduring questions that this debate points us towards.

The work to 'fill in', to give substance to central policy rhetorics such as diversity, quality, access and equity as they apply to media, culture and communications, is a major challenge. *Framing Culture* did little more than point in this direction. 'Thick' descriptions of what is and is not brought into social representation by the media and cultural production can contribute to a fuller sense of diversity and access.

If, in John Hartley's elegant words, cultural studies 'has yet to convince activists and adversaries alike that discourses organise practices, that the real is constructed',[12] activists (and adversaries) must return the compliment to cultural studies in saying that the practices organised by discourses are complex institutional realities that are not comprehensively amenable to change, or even perhaps to understanding and participation, through discursive analysis alone. If the real is constructed, what is it constructed *as* and *for*, and how do we go about constructing alternative and oppositional realities? These questions and propositions, as Toby Miller ultimately concludes in his wide-ranging review of the 'present moment' of cultural policy studies,[13] should lead us to a sense of shared tasks across many disciplinary divides. It is a sense I share, beyond the (however necessary) polemic of *Framing Culture*.

If there is another persistent strain running through most of the critiques of *Framing Culture*, it is the insistence on the relative autonomy of the critical from other domains. In these accounts, the policy push has become a putsch, the debate a 'head-kicking exercise'.[14] Tim Rowse offers a constructive way forward and a far better formulation than mine when he says that 'the differences between social democracy and its radical Other can be recast as differences among cultural studies intellectuals' audience orientations'.[15] While in teaching we may deem it important to problematise all social representation, in other domains, of policy participation and analysis for instance, closure around notions of the national popular, for example, are equally important. 'Both moments, that of problematising and of closure, are essential to the project of an engaged cultural criticism.' It is impossible not to agree with this formulation, while at the same time wishing to recall the instances highlighted in *Framing Culture* of the patent lack of awareness of both sides of this political coin on the part of cultural studies.

And, needless to say, the more specific issues that inspired the case studies in *Framing Culture* have not gone away, and in some ways they have intensified and will intensify further. There is continuing pressure to relax the Australian content regulations, now administered not by the Australian Broadcasting Tribunal, a body created out of the mid-1970s Whitlamite moment of greater public participation in policy formation, but by the Australian Broadcasting Authority, one newly fashioned out of the deregulatory enthusiasms of the late 1980s.

The lineaments of pay TV policy continue to confound the rational-comprehensive model of the policy process, fuelling critical habits of decrying policy participation as inevitably compromised, the arena of dirty deal making. The longer term and bigger picture, however, tell us that embracing or opposing the effects of pay TV on viewing habits and activities, and on the established media landscape of free-to-air broadcasting and the production industry, will continue to be a battleground between those who embrace a postmodernist social aesthetic of fragmentation and volitional microcultural taste cultivation and those who wish to defend the vital contribution the oligopolistic mainstream broadcasters make to whatever can be said to be the public sphere in contemporary society. This is a difference between traditional social responsibility models of mass media and the embrace of the potential of 'information-rich microcultures': a modernist Habermasian defence of a national public sphere and a postmodernist Baudrillardian embrace of global and the local. (The most likely major programming inputs into an Australian pay TV system, when considered along with the additional inputs of the community-based sixth channel services, will be of this nature.)

The challenge to articulate the concerns of 1980s audience analysis in cultural studies to an awareness of the wider questions of information richness and poverty remains an utterly open one, with few takers. The central issue for audience studies in the 1990s, I would argue, is the citizenship question of how well media audiences and cultural consumers will be served by deregulated and increasingly convergent communications forms. To contribute to the understanding of these wider social and technological developments, cultural studies would need to take a textually based and partially ethnographic set of protocols and findings established in the 1980s and widen them to connect with the broad issues of information richness and poverty, which are being addressed mainly in telecommunications research.

Ultimately, the task, if anything of the spirit of *Framing Culture* is to be forwarded, will be contributing to a sharper, more widely shared, more evidentially based sense of what cultural citizenship means in a country like Australia. In short, to turn the phrase again, the whole exercise still seems like a good idea.

Part 5 Creative industries and beyond

Most of my work in recent years has been devoted to tracing a movement from cultural policy to creative industries and then to innovation policy. The rationale for this is laid out in summary form at the start of Chapter 12, 'The creative industries after cultural policy'. The rationale has been motivated by cultural, social and technological change: the decline of cultural nationalism, the parallel changes in the nature of the Australian screen industries and the composition of their content, the explosion of the Internet and of web 2.0 and the growth of new, mobile and Internet media around it. This has led to a recognition of the limits of regulation as a stimulant of and protector for content creation, and to a greater focus on where that stimulus might come from – the wellsprings of creativity, the prime economic conditions and technological affordances under which they might flourish, and the most forward-looking policy frameworks that focus on and facilitate such conditions.

Consider the changing conditions for what was a central plank of the argument of *Framing Culture*: cultural regulation for Australian television content. There is a cloud over its future in part due to the fact that much cultural rationale for television content regulation is based as much on an industry development or protection basis as on a sophisticated cultural rationale. General transmission quota regulation (stipulating how much total air-time is devoted to Australian content) is based on a broad, generic cultural remit (national culture is represented by whatever content is found on television – the anthropological account of culture). But regulation for specific forms of national television, such as high-end fictional drama and social documentary, is based on cultural exceptionalism. The official argument goes that high-end fictional drama is a key genre of the national culture because it heightens, dramatises and narrativises national stories while also providing crucial alternatives to the US hegemony in audiovisual fictional drama. The official argument has to be of this more intense (culture as art) nature, because such content may not be produced without state intervention. The rationale then becomes one of market failure to provide such high-end genres, because of their cost relative to imported hegemonic content.

However, if there is evidence that there is a decline in audience demand for high-budget series and one-off TV dramas, the market failure argument is weakened, and specifically cultural policy for television is no longer based on a popular cultural mandate but is pushed back to more of an 'arts and audience development' strategy. The trend away from nation-defining drama to reality TV, from authored texts to branded experiences, is both a cultural, generational shift and a corporate response to the long-term ratings crisis of the television industry driving unit costs of content creation inexorably down in the face of the challenge of the Internet, the exploding multi-channel marketplace, and the consequent fragmentation of the audience base.

Regulation is a necessary but less sufficient condition for the health of content creation in all its ramifying forms in the time of web 2.0, electronic games, the blogosphere, and social networking software, and all this on top of the established forms of content production and distribution. How can we most usefully appropriate the rhetorics of the new economy to advance a contemporary understanding of the production and consumption of creative and informational content? Can the concept of creativity be broadened, but not so much that it becomes everything and nothing – the newest business literature fad and just as ephemeral as the rest – such that claims for its role as a driver of economic growth can be sustained? Can the analytical and research context for 'experiential' or 'cultural' consumption, in Rifkin's[1] terms – core business for cultural, media and communications studies academics – be helpfully developed through new economy models?

These are the questions addressed in the last two essays in the book. The first tracks the way culture and content are, and could be, treated within cultural policy, a 'services' or industry approach, and a 'knowledge-based' or innovation framework. These grids of understanding have served, or could serve, as rationales for state intervention in support of the content and creative industries as well as the sector's own understandings of its nature and role. The argument therefore mixes descriptive analysis of trends and normative claims about 'preferred futures' through linking content and creative industries to the innovation agenda.

The second, Chapter 13, 'What price a creative economy?', traces the history of the idea of creative industries from its inception and its take-up in numerous countries to its being folded into a broader notion of the 'creative economy'. This is where the research agenda in this field is now, and it requires an engagement with contending varieties of economics, which this book has already identified as a 'third way' between political economy and cultural economics.

Chapter 12

(2004) The creative industries after cultural policy

This chapter takes an explicitly policy-oriented line and tendentiously tracks a genealogy and some possible preferred futures for the creative industries, beyond their framing within a cultural policy problematic. The fate of creative and informational content is tracked as it passes across three grids of understanding: 'culture', 'services' and 'knowledge'. These grids also serve as historical and/or possible rationales for state intervention in the creative industries, as well as industry's own understandings of their nature and role.

Currently, cultural policy fundamentals are being squeezed by the combined effects of the 'big three' – convergence, globalisation and digitisation – which are underpinning a services industries model of industry development and regulation. This model, despite the dangers, carries advantages in that it can mainstream the creative industries as economic actors and lead to possible rejuvenation of hitherto marginalised types of content production.

But new developments around the knowledge-based economy point to the limitations for wealth creation of only microeconomic efficiency gains and liberalisation strategies, the classic services industries strategies. Recognising that such strategies won't push up the value chain to innovation and knowledge-based industries, governments are now accepting a renewed interventionary role for the state in setting twenty-first century industry policies.

But the content and creative industries have not to this date been thought of as sectors requiring attention in R&D and innovation strategies. The task is, first, to establish that the content industries indeed engage in what would be recognisable as R&D and exhibit value chains that integrate R&D into them. The second task is to evaluate whether the state has an appropriate role to support such R&D in the same way and for the same reasons as it supports science and technology R&D.

Culture

Culture is very much the home patch of the content proselytisers – where many of us grew up intellectually and feel most comfortable. Also, it has been around as a fundamental rationale for government's interest in regulation and subsidy for decades. The 'cultural industries' was a term invented to embrace the commercial industry sectors – principally film, television, book publishing and music – which also delivered fundamental, popular culture to a national population. This led to a cultural industries policy 'heyday' around the 1980s and 1990s, as the domain of culture expanded. (In some places it is still expanding, but it is not carrying much heft in the way of public dollars with it, and this expansion has elements trending towards the (perfectly reasonable) social policy end of the policy space, with its emphasis on culture for community development ends.)

Meanwhile, cultural policy fundamentals are being 'squeezed'. They are nation-state specific in a time of the World Trade Organisation and globalisation. Cultural nationalism is no longer in the ascendency socially and culturally. Policy rationales for the defence of national culture are less effective in the convergence space of new media. Marion Jacka[1] shows that broadband content needs industry development strategies more than cultural strategies, as broadband content is not the sort of higher-end content that has typically attracted regulatory or subsidy support.[2] The sheer size of the content industries and the relatively minute size, economically speaking, of the arts, crafts and performing arts sub-sectors within them[3] (John Howkins estimates the total at $US2.2 trillion in 1999, with the arts at 2 per cent of this) underline the need for clarity about the strategic direction of cultural policy. Perhaps most interestingly, and ironically, cultural industries policy was a 'victim of its own success': cultural industry arguments have indeed been taken seriously, often leading to the agenda being taken over by other, more powerful, industry and innovation departments.[4]

Services

This doesn't get talked about much in the cultural/audiovisual industries 'family', but it's *sine qua non* in telecommunications and in much of the rest of the economy. All OECD countries display service sectors that are by far the biggest sectors of their respective economies (the services sector in Australia is 65 per cent of total businesses, 63 per cent of total gross value added, and 73 per cent of employment), and the relative size has generally been growing steadily for decades. This is the broad sectoral basis for thinking through a new approach to industry development in the creative industries sector.

Much convergence talk has it that a potent but as yet unknown combination of digital television and broadband will become a, if not *the*, prime vehicle for the delivery or carriage of services. Education, banking, home management, e-commerce and medical services are some of the everyday services that interactive television and broadband might deliver.

But for media content to be considered as part of the service industries takes the convergence tendency to a new level. For most of its history, media content and the conditions under which it is produced and disseminated have typically been treated as issues for cultural and social policy in a predominantly nation-building policy framework. They have been treated as 'not just another business' in terms of their carriage of content critical to citizenship, the information base necessary for a functioning democracy and as the primary vehicles for cultural expression within the nation.

In the emerging services industries policy and regulatory model (which some – for example, Damien Tambini[5] in talking about the United Kingdom's recent communications bill – might dub 'new' public interest), media content could be treated less as an exception ('not just another business') and more as a fundamental, yet everyday, part of the social fabric. Rather than television's traditional sectoral bedfellows (cinema, the performing arts, literature and multimedia), media content is seen as more related to telecommunications, e-commerce, banking and financial services and education.

The model carries dangers. It subjects all television systems to a normative, globalising perspective and thus weakens the specifics of a cultural case for national regulation and financial support. Its widespread adoption would see the triumph of what might be called the US regulatory model, where competition is the main policy lever and consumer protection rather than cultural development is the social dividend. The application of this model across the board is not a universal panacea for all industry regulatory problems, as most mid-level and smaller countries need to, or do, acknowledge.

However, there are also possible advantages. Hitherto marginal programming could be significantly upgraded in a services industries model. Programming produced for and by regional interests might be as fundamental as the guarantee of a basic telephone connection to all regardless of location. The need for programming inclusive of demographics such as youth and children might be as fundamental as free and compulsory schooling. Moves in various jurisdictions, including the European Union and Canada, to give greater weighting to regional, infotainment, youth and children's programming signal a shift in priority of content regulation to include these alongside a continuing emphasis on drama and social documentary.[6] While the latter advance core cultural objectives such as quality, innovation and cultural expression, the former warrant greater consideration in a services industries model of media content regulation in terms of their contribution to diversity, representation, access and equity.

The knowledge economy

We are not nearly as comfortable with this association. This is higher up the value chain than the service industry sector. Our sector needs to learn to see itself as part of the knowledge-based economy and as an integral and arguably central part of any decent innovation or R&D agenda, and to begin to win some degree of recognition for this association.

From where has this new macro-focus emerged? In part, it has been around for a long time, with notional subdivisions of the service or tertiary industry sector into quaternary and quinary sectors based on information management (4th sector) and knowledge generation (5th sector). But the shorter-term influence is traceable to new growth theory in economics which has pointed to the limitations for wealth creation of only microeconomic efficiency gains and liberalisation strategies.[7] These have been the classic services industries strategies.

Governments are now attempting to advance knowledge-based economy models, which imply a renewed interventionary role for the state in setting twenty-first century industry policies, prioritisation of innovation and R&D-driven industries, intensive reskilling and education of the population, and a focus on universalising the benefits of connectivity through mass ICT literacy upgrades.

Every OECD economy, large or small, or even emerging economies (such as Malaysia) can try to play this game, because a knowledge-based economy is not based on old-style comparative factor advantages but on competitive advantage – that is, what can be constructed out of integrated labour force, education, technology and investment strategies (e.g. Japan, Singapore, Finland).

But the content (and, as a sub-sector of them, the creative) industries *don't as a rule figure* in R&D and innovation strategies. When they do, it is as last-minute concessions to dogged lobbying, and they are usually damned with faint praise or condescended to with benign indifference. There are several recent examples in this country: *Backing Australia's Ability* (2001), *Knowledge Nation* (2001), Queensland's Department of Information and the Information Economy (DIIE) R&D Strategy Paper (2002), and 'Developing National Research Priorities: An Issues Paper' (May 2002).[8] I will discuss just two of these.

Knowledge Nation

'Knowledge Nation' was the Labor Party's compendium of policy options for stimulating a knowledge-based economy and society leading into the federal election in November 2001. For 'Knowledge Nation', the creative industries are coterminous with the arts. The result of this conflation is that recommendations for advancing the creative industries are residual at best, being lumped in with some afterthought as recompense for the university's humanities and social sciences rather than upfront in the document as the sector that will deliver the content essential for next generation information and communication sector growth. (ICT is seen as one of five key knowledge-based growth hotspots of the Australian economy into the future, along with biotechnology, environmental management, medical services and education export.)

While 'Knowledge Nation' can claim against its political rivals that 'There was not one mention of the creative industries – the arts – in the Howard government's innovation statement', the patent limitations of complete equivalence of the arts and the creative industries has at this time escaped Australian Labor.

DIIE's Queensland R&D Strategy Paper

The DIIE paper is clearer and more explicit than *Knowledge Nation* about the relevance of creative industries to the broad R&D field. In the paper, ICT infrastructure or the 'enabling technologies' for R&D includes multimedia, broadcasting, 3D and games. And 'creative retail' like the arts and entertainment are also acknowledged as 'applications fields' for R&D. However, none of these areas acknowledged as R&D or R&D-influenced sectors has been targeted under an R&D label for state-level investment to this date. Indeed, the term 'creative industries' is used only once in the entire document.

And yet the principles on which Queensland wishes to build its R&D profile, such as opportunities to leverage private sector investment through strategic state involvements, and the value of leveraging existing infrastructure and traditional industries (such as the broadcasting infrastructure that exists today in Queensland), could be centrally addressed by R&D in the creative industries in Queensland. The need to develop virtual clusters and bandwidth capacity would also be addressed in significant ways if the creative retail or consumer consumption end of demand for broadband in the broader business and consumer sectors was engaged with by an R&D strategy as much as in the research community.

Why should the content industries be considered as a knowledge-based sector with R&D integral to its value chains?

Worldwide, the creative industries sector has been among the fastest growing sectors of the global economy. Several analysts, including the OECD,[9] the UK government through its Creative Industries Task Force,[10] Jeremy Rifkin in *The Age of Access*[11] and John Howkins in *The Creative Economy*,[12] point to the crucial role the sector plays in the new economy, with growth rates better than twice those of advanced economies as a whole. Entertainment has displaced defence in the United States as the driver of new technology take-up, and it has overtaken defence and aerospace as the biggest sector of the Californian economy.

Rather than being relegated to marginal status in the new economy, sociologists Lash and Urry[13] and business analyst John Howkins claim that creative production has become a model for new economy business practice (outsourcing, the temporary company, the 'producer' model of project management, just-in-time teams, etc.). Rifkin claims that cultural production will ascend to the first tier of economic life, with information and services moving to the second tier, manufacturing to the third tier and agriculture to the fourth tier.[14]

Most R&D priorities reflect a science- and technology-led agenda at the expense of new economy imperatives for R&D in the content industries, broadly defined. The broad content industries sector derives from the applied social and creative disciplines (business, education, leisure and entertainment, media and communications) and represents 25 per cent of the US economy, while the new science sector (agricultural biotech, fibre, construction materials, energy and pharmaceuticals), for example, accounts for only 15 per cent of the economy.[15] In fact, all modern economies are consumption-driven (60 per cent of GDP in Australia and 62 per cent of US GDP)[16] and the social technologies that manage consumption all derive from the social and creative disciplines.

We can no longer afford to understand the social and creative disciplines as commercially irrelevant, merely 'civilising' activities. R&D strategies must work to catch the emerging wave of innovation needed to meet demand for content creation in entertainment, education and health information, and to build and exploit universal networked broadband architectures in strategic partnerships with industry.

Not only is R&D in the applied social and creative disciplines required for its own commercial potential, but such R&D must also be hybridised with science and technology research to realise the commercial potential of the latter. Commercialisation depends on 'whole product value propositions' not just basic research.

Why don't the content industries figure as knowledge industries with R&D needs?

Now, we can 'curse the darkness' or we can 'light a candle'. We can rehearse the reasons, deeply embedded in our Western cultures, for the chasm that separates the arts and sciences that C. P. Snow rehearsed decades ago.[17] But instead let us 'light a candle' by trying to understand the problem from the other side, as it were.

Services versus R&D
It should be acknowledged that the great majority of the 'good news' economic data adduced to point to the economic dynamism and centrality of the creative industries to the new economy are services sector data. They relate to creative retail rather than to any R&D process that may be argued to be essential to the generation of creative content. That part of the large and growing creative industries sector that is also a part of an emerging

industries sector (that is, one requiring R&D-style investment in experimental technologies or applications – the arena inscribed by the 'digital applications for creative industries') is not big enough to justify any but marginal policy focus supported by mainstream economic data.

Not recognised and justified before as R&D
Both the digital applications sub-sector and the larger sector from which it is growing have been supported by public subsidy and, in those sectors where there is a fully industrialised and commercial focus, such as film, television, games and music, Australia is a significant net importer of the sectors' product. So their dynamism has real social and cultural benefit for a country but problematically established direct economic benefits. This can be sharply contrasted with the communications and IT sector, which is perceived to drive significant productivity growth throughout the economy and to be a substantial sector in its own right, with greater export potential.

But a small, peripheral country cannot afford to bow to a perceived iron law of comparative advantage enjoyed by the United States and the United Kingdom in creative industries pre-eminence. (Note that all of Howkins's creative industries sectors are dominated by the United States and the United Kingdom, with very few exceptions.) This fact is well accepted in the science, engineering and technology fields, where relative competitive advantage is *constructed*, in part through state interventions.

The government's role is to seed risky innovation in those sectors with the most potential for growth and wealth creation – just as in science, engineering and technology R&D. To be schematic, we progress from the cultural to the services frame by the application of contemporary *industry* policies. We progress from the cultural and the services to the knowledge frame by the application of *R&D* policies.

The commercial nature of the big creative industries

Another reason has to do with the *thoroughly* commercial nature of R&D investment in the big creative industries. There might simply not be robust enough arguments for state interventions in what are, after all, massive multinational commercial enterprises and sectors. The argument against this is essentially the same as the one above. While this may be to a significant (but by no means complete) extent true of the US economy, it is true of probably no other economy. While the private sector is the major driver of creative industries such as film, broadcasting, music, games, leisure software, architecture and so on, smaller economies always need public sector involvements. This is reinforced by the risk-averse nature of private sector investment in smaller economies like Australia's. R&D, properly defined, for the creative industries will always be in need of public sector understanding and involvement.

The creative industries are intrinsically hybrid

The creative industries can be thought of as intrinsically hybrid in their nature. They are at once cultural, service-based – both wholesale and retail – R&D-based, and part of the volunteer, community sector. In this sense, one can make a general case for the creative industries being central in a knowledge-based *society*. But their specific, focused connection to the knowledge-based *economy*, and to public policy interventions specific to it, might, to some, remain diffuse.

Practical problems with R&D investment in the creative industries

Access to capital through seed and venture funding is often particularly difficult within this sector. Where venture capital players are looking for intellectual property that can be exploited and thereby result in substantial growth, the intellectual resources in the creative industries sectors are often the people themselves rather than a new product or service. This represents a more difficult assessment process for investors, with higher risk factors and often lower growth potential. But it could also mean that industry departments need to structure their programs of assistance better in order to engage this sector.

Concluding comments

The services model for understanding the emerging role of content is valuable, as it tells the story of the ever-deeper embedding of content in the mainstream economy. But it won't get the creative industries up the value chain to R&D investment and innovation.

The task is, first, to establish that the content industries indeed engage in what would be recognisable as R&D and exhibit value chains that integrate R&D into them. The second task is to evaluate whether the state has an appropriate role to support such R&D in the same way and for the same reasons as it supports science, engineering and technology R&D.

Major international content growth areas, such as online education, interactive television, multi-platform entertainment, computer games, web design for business-to-consumer applications, or virtual tourism and heritage, need *research* that seeks to understand how complex systems involving entertainment, information, education, technological literacy, integrated marketing, lifestyle and aspirational psychographics and cultural capital interrelate.

They also need *development* through trialling and prototyping supported by test beds and infrastructure provision in R&D-style laboratories. They need these in the context of ever-shortening innovation cycles and greater competition in rapidly expanding global markets.

Perhaps it can be said better, and finally, if it is said that the creative industries are simultaneously *cultural* industries delivering crucial representation, self-recognition and critique in a globalising world. They are *service* industries delivering basic information and entertainment services in a converging services environment and *knowledge* industries requiring very significant levels of R&D to continue to innovate and to provide content and applications that 'make the wires sing'.

Chapter 13

(2006) What price a creative economy?

What is this thing called a creative economy?

Of course, the creative economy is the brilliant movies for which our directors, set and fashion designers, cinematographers and actors have received such high international acclaim, marking out Australia as a talent pool of the highest order. It is also the interface designers who have worked in the finance industry to make huge changes in how we do our banking and make investments. This has been one of the most dramatic and rapid changes in mainstream business models seen in a major service sector.

Naturally, it includes our great writers, novelists, playwrights, poets and lyricists, who continue to find ways to reflect back to us our life and times through their exacting and engaging prisms. It is also the 'technical' writer, whose job it is to produce online education and training materials that contribute to Australia's education export successes – Australia's fourth biggest export earner, now worth $6.9 billion to the economy. The film industry earned $2 million from international sales in the same period.

It obviously includes our artists who have made it to the top of tremendously demanding professions and who represent the top echelon of creative talent winnowed through innumerable filters. As Harvard economist Richard E. Caves has written, many hear the call but few survive the round-up.[1] The creative economy is also about the growing legions of amateur and 'pro-am' creatives – bloggers, flash animation mavens, webmeisters – creative and technologically literate *wunderkinder*, who are not inclined to wait till the gatekeepers tell them how they can reach an audience.

The creative economy is a hard fish to catch, a difficult category to nail down. But it is bigger and broader than we think, and is much more than culture and the arts. This chapter is about why those who support culture and the arts might be interested in the 'creative economy'.

This chapter is not an argument for or against a better deal for the arts in today's Australia. But I have great sympathy for the idea that far too much negative emphasis is placed on public funding for the arts. In quantum terms, the tax dollar spent on the arts is very small indeed and judicious increases are certainly called for. The Productivity Commission, the government's principal review and advisory body on microeconomic policy and regulation, estimates that Culture and Recreation, the sector where the arts are placed, received less than 1 per cent of its income from the public purse. Compare this with the enormous 14.3 per cent allocated to some manufacturing sectors, and the 9.5 per cent to textiles, clothing and footwear. Clearly, the idea that the arts are more heavily subsidised by our hard-earned tax dollar than other sectors is laughable. Thanks to the efforts of excessively influential lobbyists, the amount of corporate welfare routinely thrown at failing industries and mendicant companies is massively greater than that given to the arts. According to the Productivity Commission, tax breaks and handouts that the federal government gave to business last year amounted to $4.6 billion.

As John Holden cheekily points out, no one speaks of the 'subsidised' defence industry, the 'mendicant' education sector or a health system 'propped up' by government funding.[2] Yet all these sectors are funded substantially or wholly by our tax dollars and are subject to the same supposed regime of market failure as are the arts and culture. For better and for worse, it is always open season on the arts and culture because they are intimately bound up with controversial inquiries into meaning, purpose and human understanding.

The usual arguments in favour of support for the arts have served us well for a long time. For fifty years or more, cultural economists have given governments good reason to subsidise the arts, with usually bipartisan goodwill. The idea of the cultural industries – the large, mostly commercial, businesses in broadcasting, music and film that deliver popular culture – has given governments reasons to regulate and develop modern cultural policies to support them, and they have done so since the 1960s with a similar commitment. However, the arts now struggle to grow their consumption and support base, while the business models of the cultural industries are facing confronting challenges. The three Ts – technology (the Internet, games and mobile devices), taste (Generations X and Y and the 'millennials' are not into the mass media in the same way as their elders were), and talent (creatively and technologically literate young people are finding other creative channels) – are presenting a formidable challenge to the traditional arguments.

What is urgently needed is a forward-looking view of what a 'creative economy' might look like, and what it might take to strengthen it. It is my contention that fresh arguments and evidence can be found for renewing the case for public investment. Not that this is the only way forward, but it does take up the case on economic grounds, which is where it typically needs to be built in the contemporary policy process.

The chapter begins by examining the idea of the 'creative industries' as a broad alliance of activities with creativity at their heart – one that is becoming more central to economic policy and planning, and being entertained seriously in many parts of the world. It then looks at the impact this idea has made in Australia. The subsequent parts of the chapter explore the challenges of capturing the full value of the creative industries, particularly when there are so many questions being asked of traditional approaches to culture. It turns then to a discussion of new economic approaches that might inform the debate, before finally looking at the shape of the policy agendas that are emerging around the culture, creativity and digital content landscape. The 'price' to be paid for a creative economy is that the case for arts and culture will become less about their special or exceptional difference, and will become diffused into the need for creativity across the economy and society. To reach our destination, we must take the long way round.

The creative industries idea around the world

The idea of creative industries is quite recent.[3] It was developed in the United Kingdom in 1998 by a Creative Industries Taskforce of interdepartmental and industry representatives set up by the incoming Blair government.[4] The British definition – 'activities which have their origin in individual creativity, skill and talent and which have the potential for wealth and job creation through the generation and exploitation of intellectual property' – has remained broadly acceptable world-wide.[5]

It is a definition that encompasses no fewer than thirteen industry sectors: advertising, architecture, arts and antique markets, crafts, design, designer fashion, film, interactive leisure software, music, television and radio, performing arts, publishing and software. Its scope is impressive in its ambitiousness. Indeed, it may be thought too broad to be coherent. At the same time, however, it insists that there is a connection between all thirteen sectors: each has its origin in individual skill, creativity and talent, and each has the potential for wealth and job creation through the exploitation of intellectual property.

When Tony Blair became prime minister in 1997, he restructured Britain's Department of Heritage into a Department of Culture, Media and Sport, with the intention of repositioning the United Kingdom as 'cool Britannia' for trade and the intention of reasserting the country's pre-eminence as a creative-industries powerhouse in the world. But there was a further aim, to highlight the value for advanced economies of the fact that the creative industries were already a significant component of GDP, exports and jobs. Indeed, they had been growing at twice the rate of the rest of the economy.

In addition to internal British action in Scotland and the English regions, several other countries have rapidly developed creative-industries strategies.[6] East Asia, Australia and New Zealand are 'hotspots' of these developments.

Korea's approach has seen investment in major infrastructure.[7] The Digital Media City development in Seoul is an attempt to bring together government and corporate infrastructure development and to construct a large cluster of related creative industries in a new precinct. Korean film, television, games and animation productions are currently riding the crest of the so-called Korean Wave.[8] While Japan built its success predominantly on analog media, Korea has excelled in new media, and is seeing a whole range of renewed creativity flow through the economy. At 75–85 per cent penetration, Korea is significantly ahead of any other country in broadband connectivity. The Korean animation industry, which was organised originally as a low-cost sweatshop for Hollywood animation, is now growing its own indigenous content and films. In general, Korea exhibits all the characteristics at both a policy and a practice level of moving well beyond being a Cold War client state of the United States.

In the context of a National Development Plan, Taiwan is linking a more 'humanistic and sustainable' approach to development to 'culturally creative industries'.[9] Its goals are to nurture creative skills and promote the combination of culture with entrepreneurship characteristic of the creative industries approach. This necessitates the establishment of a promotional organisation, cultivating a creative workforce for art and design and nurturing design and culture-based industries. There is major new R&D investment in such key areas as design and digital content and incentives to cooperate among industry, academe and research institutions. In the light of a contracting and narrow export industry base, the creative industries are being considered as a way forward. The semi-conductor industry in Taiwan – which is the major export sector and is based largely in one area of the country – is considered to be too narrow an export base, particularly with the recent worldwide downturn of the information and communications technology (ICT) sector.

Particular strategies have been implemented in Hong Kong to address the fading eminence of its film and television industries and to reinforce advertising, design and publishing, aided by a particularly rigorous policy research base.[10] Having invested heavily in ICTs, Singapore now wants to use content and creativity to push the next wave of development beyond its undoubted technocratic excellence.[11] New Zealand has positioned creative industries as one of three key sectors (along with biotechnology and ICT) in its 'growth and innovation framework' that captures the new economy growth strategies.[12] It is a strategy that crisply focuses on the innovative nature of creative design and screen production, boosting the New Zealand brand overseas.

Renewal
There is a view that the creative industries idea might be the flavour of the month and that it will fade along with fashionable rhetoric overhyping other 'sunrise industries'.[13] But there is no evidence yet of that. In fact, two current developments suggest the opposite. One is that it is starting to be taken up in China, the other that it is being strongly refocused in its original home, the United Kingdom.

WHAT PRICE A CREATIVE ECONOMY?

Creativity is widely understood as embodying distinctive attributes in the arts, in business, in technology and the sciences – and also in the broader economy. In China the word for creativity, *chuangyi*, is mostly used in the world of the arts but also in the advertising, multimedia and design industries. More recently, it has found its way onto educational curricula.

On the other hand, the Chinese term for innovation, *chuangxin*, carries great national freight. Correlations are evident between China's ongoing economic reforms and the national innovation-systems policy, which was officially instituted in 1998 as the 'knowledge innovation program' (*zhishi chuangxin gongcheng*). Accession to the World Trade Organisation in December 2001 signalled a need for broad institutional reform, and, in the eyes of radical reformers, a tide of 'creative destruction' was necessary. Entrepreneurs were admitted into the Chinese Communist Party in 2003.

In January 2006 President Hu Jintao articulated the concept of autonomous innovation (*zizhu chuangxin*).[14] This has led to a broader-based innovation philosophy (*chuangxinxing guojia*). Broadening innovation from its science, engineering and technology base has started to bring to the fore creativity and imagination in other economic and social spheres. We are beginning to see China ready to embrace, or at least accept, creative entrepreneurialism 'from below', while it continues to obey a national imperative imposed 'from above' that it be more industrially and educationally innovative. The economy that is already reshaping geopolitics and economic strategy – and one Australia is formidably dependent on – is already changing from 'made in China' to 'created in China'.[15]

In the United Kingdom, after almost ten years, two major reviews and a political makeover have refocused the creative industries idea and a dedicated junior minister's portfolio has been created within the Department of Culture, Media and Sport. This is the responsibility of James Purnell who, as Minister for the Creative Industries and Tourism, has instituted a Creative Economy

Programme,[16] which is refocusing creative industries towards higher growth business development and clearer differentiations of economic and cultural goals. Major national reviews this year have recommended creativity/innovation 'centres of excellence' in all regions and a close look at the whole canvas of intellectual property law as a precondition for a healthy knowledge-based society and economy. An ancillary development is the further embedding of the idea in higher education and training. Indeed, several universities are currently expanding their 'creative industries' portfolios and advertising professorships in the field.

London has built one of the most rigorous evidence bases for the importance of the creative industries. It shows that creative industries are second only to business services in driving the London economy. The industry represents the second largest sector employer, with 600,000 people working either directly in creative industries or in creative occupations in other industries. They contribute more than 4 per cent of Britain's export income and provide jobs for over two million people.[17] Estimates put the world market at over $3.04 trillion in 2005, a figure that may have doubled by 2020.[18]

These are data to die for. But what is the situation in Australia?

The situation in Australia

The creative industries idea has been in play in Australia since the late 1990s. It was preceded by an intense period of policy thought represented by *Commerce in Content, Excellence in Content*, the Broadband Services Expert Group (BSEG) reports and, of course, *Creative Nation* in the mid-1990s.[19] While current policy formulation has yet to translate into significant federal government action, the level of activity shows that this sector is more visible on Canberra's radar now than at any time since the mid-1990s.[20]

Since 2001, there has been a comprehensive Creative Industries Cluster Study, a Digital Content Industry Action Agenda, a Prime Minister's Science, Engineering and Innovation Council inquiry into 'Creativity in the Information Economy' and a Creative Innovation Strategy from the Australia Council.[21] What we are seeing is the development of an innovation framework appropriate for creative content. The focus has shifted towards the 'digital content and applications' aspect of the creative industries and raised a greater understanding that creative industries *outputs* and creative occupations are becoming a more important *input* into manufacturing and the wider service industries, such as health, education, government and business services.

In 2001, Senator Richard Alston, at the time Federal Minister for Communications, IT and the Arts, inaugurated the Creative Industries Cluster Study (CICS). And it is CICS that, at a national level, has seen a shift from a cultural policy framework to an industry policy framework. This change in approach views the creative and digital content industries more in terms of industry policy than purely arts or cultural policy. The various reports in the CICS examined the agglomeration characteristics of creative industries. The study considered company structure and performance, particularly issues of fragmentation in the industry. It also examined export issues, broadband infrastructure and the role of cultural institutions in facilitating industry development. One of the reports – entitled 'Research and Innovation Systems in the Production of Digital Content and Applications' and written by Cutler & Company and a Queensland University of Technology (QUT) team – applied, for the first time, an innovation systems approach to building the digital content and creative industries. This is looked at in greater detail later in the chapter.

Queensland took some innovative action: the state government teamed with QUT to build a $60 million Creative Industries Precinct. Seeking to make the creative industries idea a physical reality, this project brought together on a single site higher education,

R&D, creative businesses, arts and new media display and exhibition. In operation since 2004, the precinct houses most of the Creative Industries faculty's staff and students, plus their facilities; eleven small and medium-sized creative enterprises; a company promoting business links with creative talent and research capacity; a professional theatre company (La Boite) and the Roundhouse Theatre; Australia's only Co-operative Research Centre in interaction design and an ARC Centre of Excellence in Creative Industries and Innovation, the only such centre outside the sciences. The Queensland government has built on this, producing a splashy creative industries strategy, *Creativity Is Big Business*.[22]

The most recent national initiatives have been a Prime Minister's Science, Engineering and Innovation Council (PMSEIC) inquiry into 'Creativity in the Information Economy', which was held in 2005, and a Digital Content Industry Action Agenda, released in March 2006. The recommendations of the PMSEIC inquiry included the establishment of a local version of the United Kingdom's National Endowment for Science, Technology and the Arts (NESTA), in order to develop better cross-disciplinary educational opportunities, and to extend the country's heavy investment in science and innovation so as to include creativity and the creative industries. The Digital Content Industry Action Agenda has been devised to double the value of the digital content industry to the Australian economy, to a total of $42 billion by 2015. Its recommendations are aimed at improving private investment in the sector by such strategies as the development of stronger export performance, the strengthening of links between industry and skills and training providers and with R&D institutions, and by ensuring that intellectual property regimes keep pace with technological and social change. The Agenda also wants much better sources of timely data that can inform planning by both industry and government.

The Australia Council's Creative Innovation Strategy seeks to capture these policy trends for the creative community it serves.[23]

The term 'creative innovation' itself makes the point that what the sciences call innovation the arts and humanities call creativity; so, to align the two is to urge stronger links between what are otherwise thought to be disparate sectors. The new strategy shows the Australia Council to be reaching out to forge formal and informal partnerships with R&D centres, industry players and artists' peak bodies, and demonstrates its determination to be a contributor to contemporary innovation policy.

Why is this important? From creative *industries* to creative *economy*

As we have seen, the creative industries idea has gained wide purchase in contemporary policy and industry debate, its proponents seeking to reshape relations between old and new media and the cultural sector, and to reposition media, communications and culture as a driver, rather than a passenger, in the knowledge economy. Their further aim is to connect the sector to national innovation agendas and thereby move it into the sphere of research-based, knowledge-intensive industry policy. What defines creative industries in the economy is the proposition that 'creativity' is their *primary* source of value, something that is becoming increasingly important for growth in post-industrial, knowledge-based societies. In other words, the aim is to foreground the sector's economic potential and make the creative industries the 'sparkplugs' of next generation, post-industrial growth.[24]

A creative industries approach brings together a range of sectors that have not hitherto been linked and thus it has expanded greatly the domain of what is typically counted, throwing settled categories like arts, media, culture and cultural industries into a more dynamic process. To give one, admittedly extreme, example, John Howkins defines the creative economy as simply 'financial transactions in creative products', whose economic value is secured through copyright, design, trademark and patents, and therefore includes the sciences, engineering and technology (SET) sectors along with the arts, media, new media, design and architecture.[25] On this basis, the creative economy in 1999 accounted for US$2.2 trillion, or about 7.3 per cent of the global economy. The contribution of the creative and performing arts, however, a mere 1.7 per cent of this total, has shrunk to virtual insignificance. Apart from science R&D, which massively – and, in my view, undeservedly – expands the economic quantum of the sector, the real powerhouses are publishing, software and broadcasting.

Furthermore, the sectors within creative industries – the established arts (theatre, dance, music, visual arts), the established media (radio, film, TV), the large design and architecture sectors, and new media (software, games, e-commerce and mobile content) – range from the resolutely non-commercial to the hightech and commercial. It is also a spectrum that encompasses not only the culturally specific and often location-specific but also the globalised and generically creative, inviting such questions as how creative inputs drive wider industry sectors, and how sectors with very different business models, revenue sources, demand drivers and scale and purpose can coexist productively elsewhere than in a policy-maker's dream.

This continuum is less coherent than our traditional, neat definitions of the arts, media and cultural industries, but more dynamic and relevant to contemporary policy-making. One reason why the idea of creative industries has been taken up widely is that it connects two key contemporary policy clusters: on the one hand, elements of the high-growth ICT and R&D-based *production in the new economy* and, on the other, those types of *consumption in the new economy* redolent of cultural identity and social empowerment. Critics of the creative industries idea are fearful that, by introducing into the rationale for supporting culture too great an emphasis on economics, it might marginalise the traditional arts sectors. However, the benefits of mainstreaming culture and media into policy powerhouses of industry development and innovation arguably outweigh the drawbacks.

We need to understand better the full dimensions of the creative industries, as there is a tendency to systematically underestimate their size and economic impact in official counts. But we need also to move from an emphasis on understanding creative *outputs* (culture) to creative *inputs* into the wider economy. Much of the real growth dynamics will be found in this move. The creative *industries* constitute one sector of the economy; the creative *economy* is formed when we move from sector-specific arguments to creative occupations as inputs into the whole economy, and creative outputs as intermediate inputs into other sectors. Indeed, the central aim of the present essay is to urge that, mindful of the example of ICTs in recent decades, people acknowledge that creativity too has the potential to be a powerful enabler of economic growth.

This takes us into territory recently investigated by Richard Florida, who, instead of analysing industry sectors, concentrates on occupational statistics in order to measure a city's or a region's potential for, or success as, a creative 'hotspot'.[26] While Florida's work may be open to criticism, it is undeniable that his focus on *occupation* and *qualification* counterbalances the usual dependence simply on *industry* statistics in industry development debates. To stress occupation statistics and the place of the creative industries in the wider economy is tantamount to saying that creative skills have become economically significant and are growing in value to the broader economy.

Florida's work on the 'creative class' has highlighted the wider economic significance of creative human capital, especially in underpinning high technology industry development. The following 'creativity index', prepared in 2002 by National Economics, compares Australia and the United States in terms of population diversity, high-tech output, innovation and human capital.[27]

Creativity index: Top ten regions (Australia and the US)

Australia	Score	United States	Score
Global Sydney	992	San Francisco	1057
Melbourne Inner	985	Austin	1028
ACT	831	San Diego	1015
Perth Central	744	Boston	1015
Adelaide Central	735	Seattle	1008
Sydney Inner West	733	Raleigh–Durham	996
Brisbane City	720	Houston	980
Melbourne South	606	Washington–Baltimore	964
Sydney Outer North	535	New York	962
Melbourne East	519	Dallas	960

The table shows that if Sydney and Melbourne were ranked among US cities they would be in seventh and eighth positions respectively.

Further comparison indicates that, as a percentage of the population, the United States' 'super creatives' (Florida's term for the core of the class) outrank Australia's by approximately two percentage points. However, the reverse holds for the second-tier creative professionals in business services, health and education, in which sector Australia is superior. Australia also out-performs the United States on both Florida's Bohemian Index of arts workers as a proportion of population and on his Diversity Index (which measures cultural and lifestyle diversity). The areas in which Australia lags significantly are innovation (patents per capita), human capital talent (the percentage of the population with a higher degree) and high technology production.

While National Economics' Australian survey confirms and replicates the US findings of Richard Florida regarding the correlation between concentrations of creative populations and the location of high-tech industries, it is also apparent that Australia is not levering its creative capital with economic outcomes as successfully as the United States. This suggests that there are significant points of failure in Australia's national innovation system.

Recent work with new field research and substantial data-gathering and data-mining, conducted by the ARC Centre of Excellence for Creative Industries and Innovation, tries to take this analysis forward.[28] Evidence from its research projects, *Mapping Queensland's Creative Industries* and *Creative Digital Industries in Australia*, demonstrates that these sectors are significantly underestimated in official statistics, whose categories lag badly behind the growth of, particularly, the digital end of this industry sector. The projects have refined official categories into which the data fits in a way that reflects the changing realities of these industry sectors. They have also counted much more comprehensively the economic contributions of creative people and organisations by correlating industry sector with occupation.

Most mapping studies have naturally been focused on industries and therefore gathered data about the specialist firms operating within each specific segment. But measuring the creative 'impact' on the economy needs to encompass both specialist creative *industries* activity and the breadth of specialist creative *occupations*. There is frequent movement between these types of activity. For example, an individual might operate solo as an independent film producer and then move to work for a government film agency, or an independent designer might sign a three-year contract to work for a bank or an advertising agency.

The direct economic impact of creative industries has been significantly underestimated. For example, the Centre of Excellence's analysis has shown that, because so many designers are embedded in other industries and because design is defined and counted in such an unhelpful way, the design sector is undercounted by some 36 per cent.

Design consulting activities are often subsumed into much broader business services, or technical services, or even clothing manufacturing classifications. And when specialist occupations *are* tallied, the failure to take into account the support and management staff that work within specialist creative firms still results in total employment being underestimated by as much as 33 per cent.

The measurement of all three axes has been dubbed the 'creative trident', which is the total of creative occupations within the creative industries ('specialist'), plus the creative occupations employed in *other* industries ('embedded'), plus the *support* occupations employed in creative industries.

Total Australian employment within the creative trident (Census, 2001)

		Industry		
		Employment within creative industries	Employment within other industries	Total employed
Occupation	Employed in core creative occupations	Specialist: 138,623	Embedded: 159,476	298,099
	Employed in other occupations	Support: 147,891		147,891
	Total employed	286,514	159,476	445,990

This means that 138,623 people were employed in creative occupations within the *core* creative industries, another 159,476 in creative occupations within *other* industries, and a further 147,891 in *support, managerial* or *sales* occupations within specialist creative industries. People who are 'embedded', that is, employed in creative occupations outside of specific creative industries, and are spread across all industry divisions, constitute almost 2 per cent of the total Australian workforce.

Total trident employment amounted to almost 446,000 people in Australia in 2001, which is substantially higher than the estimated employment figure of 211,638 used in the 2003 *Creative Industries Cluster Study: Cottages to Corporations Report* and 100,000 higher than the estimate of 345,000 used in the 2002 *Creative Industries Cluster Study: Stage One Report*.[29] The *Stage One Report* included employment in related industries such as distribution. Based on their earnings as recorded in the census, the people employed made an annual contribution in wages and salaries of over $21 billion directly to the Australian economy.

Apart from this revaluation of the quantum of creative people and activity in our economy, there are other important pointers to a different profile for the sector that have been produced from this research. The 'creative trident' represents approximately 5.5 per cent of Australian employment, 5 per cent of GST-paying enterprises and 8 per cent of non-GST-paying enterprises. These percentages are all markedly higher than those given in standard statistical analyses. The detailed work on *The Ecology of Queensland Design* is one of many international studies that focus on the input value of the design occupation. Design is one of the leading examples of creative inputs into the broader economy, including, and especially, manufacturing.[30] The study found that the 'creative trident' for design activity in Queensland resulted in a count of twice that of standard statistical analyses.

The whole sector has a mean income 34 per cent higher than the economy as a whole, which suggests a different profile for creatives than the widespread understanding of a low-wage, high-volunteer sector. In the Queensland study, it was found that exports and gross value added are higher than average sectorally, and that creative industries tend to be more knowledge-intensive in that they spend more on knowledge-based workers as a percentage of their total wages than do other sectors.

These findings are suggestive rather than definitive, but they do provide pointers in the direction of the movement from a sector-specific focus to an economy-wide focus. Just as the ICT sector benefited from the input-value it was shown to afford the economy as a whole, so the data suggest that a similar value can begin to be seen with creative inputs.

Shifting policy rationales, shifting economics

The established economic approaches to culture and the arts may have been thrown a curveball by the notions of creative industries and economy. However, creative-industries theory, analysis and policy have a way to go before they establish a robust economic framework that compellingly captures the value of the creative sector and thereby provide fresh rationale for public support for the sector. They must first engage with cultural economics, that established sub-branch of neo-classical economics, and then with the economic thinking that underlies the concept of the 'cultural industries'.

Cultural economics analyses largely settled industry sectors and focuses on microeconomic analysis of choice in established markets. It concentrates on the exceptional character of these markets or quasi-markets which is held to be due to the unusual nature of choice and decision making by both suppliers and purchasers in these markets. The traditional approach to the arts and culture employs an argument for public support based on 'exceptional' economic activity in which there will always be market failure.

Cultural economics has typically focused on the arts end of the creative industries spectrum, often because these arguments and assumptions work best at that end. David Throsby is Australia's foremost exponent of cultural economics. In *Economics and Culture*, his most comprehensive exposition of his position, he builds in a working assumption that 'the creative arts as traditionally defined' are the core sectors in a cultural industry model because they are the 'locus of origin of creative ideas'.[31] Throsby reiterates this argument in his recent Platform Paper,[32] where he argues that a flourishing arts sector is 'one of the most enduring foundations' on which to build the cultural industries.

This notion, while often seen and adopted in various forms, conflates static and dynamic models of economic analysis in that it assumes that, because some sectors have more creatives as a proportion of the whole workforce in that sector, they must be the 'locus of origin of creative ideas'. Also built into the model is the dubious assumption that the more sectors produce both cultural and non-cultural goods and services (such as the large industrialised creative industries), the less 'core' they are. Given the capacity for 'creative ideas' to diffuse further when they are embedded into other products and services, and given the data that show that more creatives are found in other industry sectors than in specialist sectors, the opposite could have been a more interesting hypothesis. The sources of innovation propelled by creatives will be found across the creative industries and increasingly across the wider economy. The 'enduring foundation' lies more where creative qualifications and occupations are deployed than in particular output/industry sectors. (Of the total population with 'creative' qualifications at the last census, it was estimated that about 70 per cent of those employed were working outside the specialist creative industries.) This suggests a human capital model, rather than an 'exceptional sector' model, for the importance of creativity in the economy.

The foundations of public support for the cultural industries – the large, mostly commercial, businesses in broadcasting, music and film, which deliver popular culture – are somewhat more complex. They lie in a combination of cultural sovereignty, market failure and natural monopoly/oligopoly. The cultural sovereignty part asserts that it is important to project Australian content into those media where most Australians are consuming their culture. But imported content is much cheaper to buy and comes with inbuilt publicity and momentum. Thus, the local product needs support to level the playing field, as it were. This is the market failure part which justifies public investment. The need for content regulations that require commercial radio and television to broadcast certain amounts of Australian product is a variation on the natural monopoly argument. Broadcasters enjoy very significant protection from competition because they use a scarce public resource, the electromagnetic spectrum. The quid pro quo for this 'natural oligopoly' is the cultural dividend extracted through content regulation.

In fact, the cultural rationale for content regulation has a generally unacknowledged weakness. Most television transmission quota regulations are based on a broad, generic cultural remit: that national culture is represented by whatever content is found on television. This is an *anthropological* account of culture. But regulation for specific forms of television, such as expensive fictional drama and social documentary, is based on cultural exceptionalism. According to the official argument, fictional drama is a crucial genre in our national culture, because it narrates, heightens and dramatises national stories, while also providing crucial alternatives to US dominance. The official argument has to be of this more intense nature – *culture as art* – because such content may not be produced without state intervention. The rationale then becomes one of market failure to provide such expensive programming, because of its cost relative to imported content.

However, with emerging evidence that there is a decline in audience demand for high-budget series and one-off TV dramas, the market failure argument is weakened, and specifically cultural policy for television is no longer based on a popular cultural mandate but is pushed back to more of an 'arts and audience development' strategy. Is the trend away from nation-defining drama to reality TV, from authored texts to branded experiences, a cultural, generational shift? Or has it to do with the corporate strategies of the television industry driving unit costs of content creation inexorably down in the face of the exploding multi-channel marketplace and the fragmentation of the audience base? While the latter is undoubtedly the case, it is too early to say whether the former, the cultural shift, is irreversible.

Such endogenous challenges to the regulatory settlement are now more than matched by exogenous change. These include shifts in what might count as popular culture (as we will see in the next section) as well as a *deus ex machina* such as the Australia–United States Free Trade Agreement (FTA). The FTA has effectively capped such initiatives as government might take to extend content regulation and even public investment into emerging new media environments.

Before looking at versions of economics that might be used to understand the emerging creative economy, we need to consider the rationale for investment in public-service broadcasting – the ABC and SBS – which is by far the largest single outlay for cultural industries in this country.

Government appropriation to the ABC (about $800 million per annum) is more than six times larger than that to the Australia Council. The ABC's position in the bustling marketplace of popular culture is under significantly greater threat than that of bodies which enjoy basically bipartisan political support and are usually at the margins of governments' financial radar. It is not for nothing that the ABC is often claimed to be Australia's most important cultural institution: it potentially links modernist culture (nation-building, linking regional and rural with the cities; its education and arts remit; the centrality of news and current affairs) with the postmodern, with innovative technology and creative R&D, and not least with artists' career development – and all this under a charter that retains the essence of public service in the best, traditional sense. It has distributional muscle and has shown it can lead in innovation (ABC Online); it can bring broad-based content to the people; it can break out of the inner-city latte belt. That it is under continuing attack is a sign of the ABC's enduring importance in the Australian polity and culture.

We need economists here, because the tried-and-tested argument for government action around culture – market failure – doesn't apply at all neatly to public-service broadcasting (PSB). The ABC and SBS operate in an abundant marketplace that does not lack for any of the program formats produced by these broadcasters. PSB's core *raison d'être* is not market failure, but is more complex and important. It is to be found in its complex of nation-building (or nation-maintaining) roles: delivering key information and news and current affairs unburdened by commercial interests and thus performing a key informal educative function (thus maintaining a 'trust' relationship in a 'risk' society); and providing essential R&D into the Australian cultural landscape by being able to innovate, take risks, and connect creative people to a broad-based audience. That it is not doing much of this well at the moment – due to relentless attacks, financial starvation and being placed at the nerve-centre of the culture wars – is cause for the highest priority concern. The economics that might help to secure the future for public-service broadcasting would be focused not only on efficiency or market failure but on its role in innovation.[33]

The culture, it is a-changin'

Looking ahead, what are some of the key emergent cultural practices in the twenty-first century? What is likely to gain ground and drive innovation? Consumption drives post-industrial economies more and more, and its nature is changing. More and more consumer activity around media and culture is do-it-yourself, user-generated content. There is huge growth in peer-to-peer activity and a more 'participatory' culture. Some of the neologisms that capture this phenomenon blur the lines between production and consumption: there is now 'prosumption', engaged in by 'produsers'.

There is more user-generated content on the Internet than professionally produced and corporate content. User-led innovations, such as SMS, have changed the business model for mobile devices, one of the most dynamic growth-sectors of the economy, leading to successful MMS (picture cameras) uptake and heavy R&D and investment in mobile content, which in turn has led to expanding opportunities for creatives.

There is the Wikipedia for knowledge production, Meetup and MyPlace for civic formation, OhMyNews for citizen journalism, Orion's Arm – an online science-fiction, world-building project – for identity formation, and Amazon and eBay Web Services for independent market advice. Twenty-five per cent of all Internet users in the United States are also blog readers. There is Digital Storytelling, where all those with life stories but no prior access to media technologies can engage in a process of releasing those stories, in the case of the world-leading practice in the Capture Wales program, onto BBC TV and websites, a form of vernacular literacy in which virtually anyone can participate.

There is Flash, the animation software which is virtually ubiquitous on networked computers as an enabling platform for global vernacular creativity. And there is Current TV (www.current.tv). Launched in the United States in mid-2005, already about a quarter of its air-time is user-generated and it publishes some of the best DIY production guides for viewers to become 'produsers'.

Of course, we might get carried away with user-led innovation. Might it not go the way of the dotcom bubble? Is it not just another of those new media 'moments' which always seem to promise revolution – the Internet as the end of social dislocation and hierarchical media relations, TV as the world's demotic educator, and so on? But when Rupert Murdoch starts talking about digital 'natives' and 'immigrants' (in his 2005 address to the American Society of Newspaper Editors) and acknowledges that News Corp has underestimated the impact of Internet-based news sourcing and the social logic or 'collective intelligence' (not to mention the impact on the bottom line) of peer-to-peer communication, then, as Eric Beecher surmised recently, 'Something seismic is going on. Seismic, but unpredictable'[34] Reputedly, Murdoch was scared into this position by data such as those presented by the Carnegie Foundation, demonstrating that 'new forms of newsgathering and distribution, grassroots or citizen journalism and blogging sites are changing the very nature of who produces news' and that the 18–34 demographic is creating this inexorable momentum.[35]

What are the deep implications of this new take on culture? First, it disrupts the linear value chain of professional modes of production. Second, the innovations are as much about distribution as production.

One way to understand this emergent paradigm shift is to consider Richard Caves' brilliant summary of the 'Basic Economic Properties of Creative Activities' that constitute the mainstream arts and media today – and then consider how these properties need to change in order to deal with 'future culture':

1. *'Nobody knows'/demand is uncertain* (There is radical uncertainty about the likely demand for creative product, due to the fact that such products are 'experience goods', about which buyers lack information prior to consumption, and the satisfaction derived is largely subjective and intangible.)
2. *'Art for art's sake'/creative workers care about their product* (Creative producers derive substantial non-economic forms of satisfaction from their work. This makes them

vulnerable to exploitation and to supply almost always outstripping demand, thus fundamentally distorting market equilibrium.)
3. *'Motley crew'/some products require diverse skills* (Creative production is mostly collective in nature. Hence the need to develop and maintain creative teams that have diverse skills, and often also diverse interests and expectations about the final product.)
4. *'Infinite variety'/differentiated products* (There is a huge variety of creative products available, both within particular formats (rental-store videos, for example) and between formats. Each creative output is to a greater or lesser extent a prototype of itself, and thus as much or more effort has to go into marketing as production, if it is to stand a chance for success.)
5. *'A-list/B-list'/vertically differentiated skills* (All creative sectors display great difference between the bright stars and the 'long tail' and this plays out in both remuneration and recognition and also in the ways in which producers or other content aggregators rank and assess creative personnel.)
6. *'Time flies'/time is of the essence* (Most industrial forms of creative production need to coordinate diverse creative activities within short time-frames.)
7. *'Ars longa'/durable products and durable rents* (Many cultural products have great durability, their producers having the capacity to continue extracting economic rents (for example, copyright payments) long after the period of production.)[36]

Of these principles, at least four must be rethought in the light of 'produsers', 'prosumption' and user-generated content. The vast gap between the famous few and the long tail ('A-list/B-list/ vertically differentiated skills') is radically challenged. There is competition for recognition and often a desire for commercial success, but participatory culture is a much more level playing field. 'Nobody knows/demand is uncertain' is turned on its head as supply is starting to come from the demand side. 'Art for art's sake/creative workers care about their product' will continue, but with a possible vengeance as their care about their product may be translated into a lesser willingness to accept the asymmetrical contracts which place most risk and most profit in the hands of the mainstream aggregator. 'Infinite variety/differentiated products' becomes less a major obstacle to effective and cost-efficient marketing and to risk management than a challenge to find enough 'market' bits to make low-cost, low entry production and distribution viable. The growing confidence of models for independent distribution of creative content see the Internet as having unique potential for constituting newly viable markets.

Emerging varieties of economics

In contrast to the static reallocation model of cultural economics, an economics that captures the dimensions and trends in the creative economy needs to be dynamic, focusing on sources of novelty and change and on both the way industries grow (rather than their size at any one particular moment in time) and what drives them to grow. Much of this novelty and change may increasingly be found in the demand rather than the supply side of the equation, if the previous section's argument tells us anything. Analysis may also be redirected away from resource allocation arguments and towards the ways in which the creative industries function as a bellwether for structural change in modern economies. Several bodies of economic thought need to be tapped to engage this challenge, among them transaction-cost economics, growth theory, and evolutionary and information economics. This process has only begun.

Examples of this kind of work applied to the economics of creative industries have sought to steer economic analysis in some interesting and *prima facie* surprising new directions. The first of these analysed information imperfections and asymmetries in agents and markets under the heading of the new information economics and the modern transactions cost theory of organisations. The best example of this – indeed, a definitive work on the organisation of the arts industries – is Richard Caves's *Creative Industries*, which uses transactions-cost theory developed in the 1970s to explain the logic of the complex, time-dependent contracts and organisational forms in an industry characterised by extreme uncertainty and highly mobile factors of production. The transaction-cost approach highlighted the fact that the creative industries were exceptional, less in their cultural goods aspects than in the evolution of highly complex contractual forms and their ability to live in a rapidly changing market environment through the constant production of novelty.

This line of work has been further developed by Arthur De Vany in his *Hollywood Economics: How Extreme Uncertainty Shapes the Film Industry*, which uses complexity theory from the late 1980s to show how the pattern of economic outcomes of firms and cultural products like movies conforms to the characteristic power–law signatures that are ubiquitous in evolutionary processes.[37] (Power–law signatures include the long tail, the 'A-list/B-list' phenomenon, and very high rates of company entry and exit from the industry.) Again, this reinforces the message that the economics of creative industries might be understood in terms of their complex industrial and enterprise dynamics and their similarity to the high-tech end of the economy. Both Caves and De Vany provide fresh insight into the dynamic structure of the arts industries and the ways in which markets and organisations cope with the volatility inherent in this industry.

Over the last ten years a new, 'evolutionary' approach to economic analysis has taken shape, which places particular focus on the dynamics of the economic system under conditions of variety generation, enterprise competition and selection and self-organisation. Stan Metcalfe, Brian Loasby and Jason Potts have all published readable accounts of these developments.[38] Most of the empirical and theoretical work so far undertaken in modern evolutionary economics has focused on manufacturing and high technology sectors, as have most analyses of the sources of innovation in contemporary economies. Unfortunately, there is little yet that seeks to apply this new framework to the economic analysis of creative industries, although some of the most interesting is focused on the broader question of innovation in services.[39] The core advance that this approach might facilitate is to understand creative industries as an emergent, innovative part of the services sector of the economy, rather than presenting them as an exception to mainstream industries, as 'not just another business'. The professional interest group Focus on Creative Industries (FOCI) in the UK captured this well:

> Whilst FOCI welcomes the recognition of the strong economic contribution made by the creative industries in terms of wealth creation and employment, we would also keenly stress that this sector is very different from traditional industries. They deal in value and values, signs and symbols; they are multi-skilled and fluid; they move between niches and create hybrids; they are multi-national and they thrive on the margins of economic activity; they mix up making money and making meaning. The challenge of the creative industries is the challenge of a new form of economic understanding – they are not 'catching up' with serious, mainstream industries, they are setting the templates which these industries will follow.[40]

The evolutionary approach places a focus on the ways economies *grow* as complex open systems rather than by optimising allocative efficiencies. It also offers a clearer understanding of the way in which new technologies are integrated into an economy and the restructuring of organisations, industries, markets and consumer lifestyles that the evolutionary growth process requires. The creative industries' complex contractual and organisational structures, inherent uncertainty, power–law revenue streams, and high rates of experimentation – not unlike some of Caves's 'basic economic properties of creative activities' – suggest that they may be 'pure' cases of service-based competitive enterprise in a fundamentally uncertain environment.

Evolutionary economics may therefore hope to provide a new basis for assessing the significance of the creative industries by focusing analytic attention on how the industry is dynamically structured and how it changes. This may furnish us with a clearer view of how it is able to adapt to change and explore niches available to it, as well as how it feeds variety into the economic system that other industries and sectors can further exploit. We are seeking to better understand the organisational, market and industrial dynamics of how the creative industries grow and change, as well as the effect this has on the dynamics of other parts of the economy. We will be particularly interested to see how the creative industries integrate and transform new technologies into new services and how variety in the economy is regenerated by the continuous flows of novelty (in content or design, for example) into all parts of the economy.

The value of such novelty or variety is negligible in a static analysis, but from the dynamic perspective it is grist to the mill of economic growth and evolution. To properly understand their role, the creative industries need to be evaluated in terms of the way in which they both induce and facilitate the ongoing process of economic transformation. For the discipline of economics, this is where their true value might lie, not in appeals 'beyond the market' to notions of un-revealed preferences or cultural value.

Compare this approach with the types of evidence presented earlier from the ARC Centre of Excellence for Creative Industries and Innovation mapping analyses. This time the focus would be not on the size of the sector but on indicators of how the creative industries inject dynamic influences into the economy. For example, why is design important? One might say that aesthetic values are important, or that in an enterprise economy – in which all firms must continually introduce new and better goods and services just to stay in the market – good design provides a competitive edge in better performance and in attracting the consumer's attention. Design, however, is irrelevant in a static economy, because nothing new is ever being introduced and firms are not competing in this manner of rivalry and enterprise. The value of design will always be highest in an innovation-driven, enterprise economy. A further example: why is user-originated content and user-led innovation important? It is not necessarily the size of the sector – games are bigger than film, there is more user-generated content on the Internet than professionally produced and corporate content, and so on – though that indicates something significant. It is that they provide a classic instance of 'creative destruction', upsetting the business models of the established communications conglomerates, introducing novelty into the system, and leading even Rupert Murdoch himself to presage the end of the days of the media mogul.

Evolutionary analysis also defines why it is so hard to capture the creative industries within standard classification systems such as the Australian and New Zealand Standard Industry Classifications (ANZSICs). The classification crisis is itself evidence of a sector that is rapidly changing and subject to greater and greater differentiation and specialisation. This is the hallmark of what evolutionary economics would call the *growth* of knowledge – the hallmark of a knowledge-based economy. Inside these classification conundrums lies the disruptive emergence of many new species of industry.

What is to be done?

If we accept that creative industries may benefit from being positioned less in the realm of cultural policy and more towards the idea of creativity as an input into the broader economy and towards the knowledge-intensive dimensions driving innovation and change, a raft of policy domains and programs comes into play. There are implications for education and R&D policy and innovation policy (including export, tax and intellectual property) as well as cultural policy. (Bringing these into better alignment is the goal of the new ARC Centre of Excellence for Creative Industries and Innovation.) It is a great challenge for governments and industry to deliver joined-up initiatives to support holistic or systemic approaches. And the amount of activity is not the only issue; it is also and equally about coordination, about getting the linkages working better.

As we have seen, there have been many policy recommendations made recently which it is not necessary to rehearse here. Rather, this section draws on the substantial analysis conducted recently by Cutler and Company and a Queensland University of Technology team, which applied, uniquely for Australia, an innovation systems approach to building the digital content and creative industries.[41]

There are many *elements* of an innovation and industry development system in place. Australia has a very large education and training sector producing skilled graduates and trainees. There are large market organisers and industry players, in both the public sector (broadcasters, funding agencies, and cultural institutions such as museums and galleries) and the private sector (commercial broadcasters, publishing houses, telecommunications firms and advertising). There is a strong and growing demand for such a system, in retail consumer demand and in the role of digital content as an enabler across a growing range of industries, particularly in the services and manufacturing sector.

However, the *quality of linkages* and the *lack of clear public policy signals and frameworks*, together with a number of other critical issues, mark the innovation system as, at best, embryonic. Public policy needs to address the shifts required to capture the innovation potential of digital content industries by moving, for example, from unrelated cultural and higher education policies to a more dynamic mix of coordinated program initiatives.

Several strategies exist to improve the situation. A Digital Content Industry Action Agenda has been developed to establish a framework for alignment of existing policy regimes with digital content industries. A primary focus of the innovation agenda must be to better align cultural policies with industry development and R&D policies. What are needed now are nationally funded centres of research to promote university and industry linkages that will establish *tripartite* interfaces between cultural institutions, universities and content industries. Such an initiative would create incentives for, and legitimise the role of, cultural institutions in research collaborations. Such an R&D initiative might invite a levy from participating industry sectors to fund innovation, which would then trigger government funding. This is the model adopted by many established R&D boards for primary industries. The industry levy might apply to broadcasters, publishers and distributors, and could be limited to firms with a turnover above a floor level, to exempt emerging small and medium-sized enterprises. Levy contributions could also offset, or replace, some or all existing broadcasting licences and other imposts. In the event of any major changes to cross-media or ownership rules, the scheme could be extended to offset any wind-back of existing local production requirements. An essential element of such a centre (or R&D corporation) would be a national information and resource brokerage centre for the sector to address the serious and endemic information asymmetries and structural weakness in the innovation system.

Equally necessary is a suite of reforms to research digital content and the creative industries, and higher education policies to accommodate them, including campaigns targeting young people with the message that knowledge entrepreneurship – a 'creative career' – is a viable and attractive option. Supporting and promoting exports is important as the only way to sustainable growth. Equally important is the fact that only hard evidence of sustainability and scalability will make the sector attractive to private investors and break the vicious cycle of under-investment.

The role of broadcasting and broadband in the innovation system is crucial, as the gateway between established and emergent *content creation* (popular media's migration to interactivity and mass customisation) and *industry structure* (from highly centralised distributional models to more networked and distributed models). Understanding the interaction between the potent legacy of broadcasting and the potential of convergent broadband media is the key, if content creation is to remain close to the mainstream of popular cultural consumption and not be siphoned off into science or art alone.

Major technology-related reforms include national investment in content and metadata standards and supporting systems, thus limiting the huge transaction costs for both producers and users created by the current 'bottom up' approach to standards. They also include tax credits for R&D investment in technology infrastructure in emerging content areas. Both are crucial missing pieces in the innovation jigsaw.

Open content repositories, or public domain digital content, are the content industries' equivalent of open source software. They *selectively* address barriers to production and unintended cultural outcomes of prevailing copyright and intellectual property regimes through an alternative *opt-in* model that can operate in parallel with existing regimes. As such, it can be a powerful structural mechanism to support a rich 'digital sandpit' for creative content producers. The measure facilitates the active re-directing and re-use of digital content assets. Misuse of this public domain material would be protected under the provisions of a general non-exclusive Public Licence scheme.

In short, an innovation systems approach to the creative industries opens up central policy territory which, until now, has been the preserve of science, engineering and technology. It seeks to move culture into mainstream policy calculations by connecting culture to the most trenchant current rationale for active government involvement in industry shaping.

What price a creative economy?

There are, and will be, plenty of critics of this line of argument about the creative industries and a creative economy. They worry that it might marginalise the traditional arts sectors and introduce an untoward economism into rationales for support for culture. It will be said that if we put our faith in economic data we are sure to fail, as we argue on 'their' turf. John Holden, for one, argues for a return to 'intrinsic' justifications for the arts as a way of solving their 'crisis of legitimacy'.[42] The proposition that policy should be fashioned from the self-understanding of creative people is attractive, but the critical spirit that constitutes the creative community makes it doubtful that there would be a robust and enduring consensus about what an 'intrinsic' justification is. Would it be strong enough to withstand the processes that contemporary public funding must go through? What is intrinsically important about culture? *Pour épater le bourgeois*? Indigenous social laws and beliefs? Aesthetic excellence before all else? National projection? A good night out?

And there is always the flipside to intrinsic arguments stating the essential benefits that flow from culture and the arts – an essentialism of the dark side, as it were. George Steiner put it most forcefully when he asked how the Nazi genocide could have been perpetrated by lovers of Beethoven and Mozart. So did John Carey when he asked recently, *What Good Are the Arts?*[43] The danger of essentialist arguments is that the gun can be turned on you.

I would prefer a pragmatic approach, involving a defence of the innovations, the fresh knowledge and the new friends for culture that come from close attention to what are usually called the 'ancillary' benefits of culture and creativity, such as economic opportunity and innovation, social inclusion and educational advantage. It is best to keep moving forward on several fronts, lest one be outflanked or forced into retreat.

This chapter, then, has stressed the opportunity to significantly broaden the support base, from culture and the arts to the creative community (or class). Richard Florida is very aware of the problems associated with galvanising a consciousness among such a diverse group;[44] and, nevertheless, while it is a group that may have little of the solidarity evidenced by artists, it is the object of much state attention. This gives us the opportunity to 'mainstream the claims', to emphasise a small-business and demand-driven ethos as a strong complement to the charismatic, supply-side ethos of the national artistic leadership. This places emphasis on career development and opportunities through occupation as much as industry sector – combining the arts with market-driven, commercial ventures and employment and emphasising sustainability and impact as functions of an economy-wide vision.

The 'price' to be paid is that the special status attributed to the arts and culture is folded into the need for creativity across the economy and society. To reach our destination, we must take the long way round.

Thanks to Terry Cutler, Greg Hearn, Mark Ryan and Michael Keane, co-authors with me of Research and Innovation Systems in the Production of Digital Content, from which some of the policy analysis in the penultimate section was taken. Thanks to Jason Potts, to whom I am indebted for insights on applying evolutionary economic analysis to the Australian creative industries; to Peter Higgs, who has done the hard data-mining yards; to Michael Keane for the update on the China situation; and to John Hartley and Kate Oakley for the same on the United Kingdom.

Notes

Introduction

1. Tom O'Regan, *Australian National Cinema*, Routledge, London, 1996.
2. John Frow and Meaghan Morris, 'Introduction', in John Frow and Meaghan Morris (eds), *Australian Cultural Studies: A Reader*, Allen & Unwin, St Leonards, NSW, 1993, p. viii.
3. Rosemary Neill, 'And then there was one – Lost for words', *Australian*, 2 December 2006, and 'Debate on Aussie literature a horror story for our greats', *Australian*, 22 March 2007. See also Peter Holbrook, 'Lost literature refound', *Australian*, Higher Education, 15 August 2007, p. 25, and Imre Salusinszky, 'Literary rescue mission', *Australian*, 8 August 2007, p. 15.
4. Meaghan Morris, *The Pirate's Fiancee: Feminism, Reading, Postmodernism*, Verso, London, 1988.
5. Robert Dixon, 'An agenda for our own literature', *Australian*, 28 March 2007, p. 37.
6. Any number of John Hartley's works maintain this campaign, but see, for example, *Popular Reality: Journalism, Modernity, Popular Culture*, Arnold, London and New York, 1996, *Uses of Television*, Routledge, London and New York, 1999, and *A Short History of Cultural Studies*, Sage, London, 2002.
7. See Stuart Cunningham, *Featuring Australia: The Cinema of Charles Chauvel*, Allen & Unwin, Sydney, 1991.
8. Colin Johnson [Mudrooroo], 'Chauvel and the Centring of the Aboriginal Male in Australian Film', *Continuum: The Australian Journal of Media & Culture*, vol. 1, no. 1, 1987.
9. But see, for example, J. Landman, *The Tread of a White man's Foot: Australian Pacific Colonialism and the Cinema, 1952–62*, Pandanus Books, Research School of Pacific and Asian Studies, ANU, Canberra, 2006, for a treatment of Australian neo-colonialism and screen in the south Pacific.
10. Two major survey volumes came out in the same year: John Frow and Meaghan Morris (eds), 'Introduction', in *Australian Cultural Studies: A Reader*, Allen & Unwin, St Leonards, NSW, 1993, pp. vii–xxxii; Graeme Turner, 'Introduction: Moving the Margins: Theory Practice and Australian Cultural Studies', in *Nation, Culture, Text: Australian Cultural and Media Studies*, Routledge, London and New York, 1993, pp. 1–13. Later, the discipline field was featured in Australian Academy of the Humanities, *Knowing Ourselves and Others: The Humanities of Australia into the 21st Century. Volume 2: Discipline Surveys*, Australian Research Council Discipline Research Strategies, April 1998: Commonwealth of Australia. Volume 2 contains both an overview of cultural studies (by Tony Bennett) and media and communication studies (by Graeme Turner).This was one of three volumes published at the same time. Volume 1 contained a 'context and commentary on the humanities in Australia' and Volume 3 contains 'reflective essays' on themes in humanities research. John Frow wrote a detailed and updated account in 'Australian Cultural Studies: Theory, Story, History', *Australian Humanities Review*, <http://www.lib.latrobe.edu.au/AHR/archive/Issue-December-2005/Frow.html>. Helen Wilson's '30 years of MIA: a commemorative editorial', *Media International Australia*, no. 119, May 2006, pp. 3–20, is a personal history of the media studies scholarly community associated with the leading journal *Media International Australia* since its inception in the 1970s.
11. Bruce Molloy and June Lennie, *Communication Studies in Australia : A Statistical Study of Teachers, Students and Courses in Australian Tertiary Institutions*, Communication Centre, School of Communication, Queensland University of Technology, 1990; Peter Putnis, *An Investigation of the Growth and Current Status of Communications and Media Studies Courses in Australian Universities*, DEST Evaluations and Investigations Programme, 2000.
12. 'Review of research in the Humanities and Creative Arts discipline grouping', Australian Research Council 2004, unpublished draft, especially Part 5, 'Research leaders surveys', pp. 67–94.

13 Graeme Turner, 'Introduction: Moving the Margins', pp. 11–12.
14 John Frow and Meaghan Morris, 'Introduction', p. xiv.
15 John Frow, 'On Literature in Cultural Studies', in Michael Berube (ed.), *The Aesthetics of Cultural Studies*, Blackwell Publishing, Malden, 2005, p. 45.
16 Alan McKee (ed.), *Beautiful Things in Popular Culture*, Blackwell, Malden, MA, 2007; Alan McKee, *Australian Television: A Genealogy of Great Moments*, Oxford University Press, South Melbourne, Vic., 2001; Graeme Turner, *Ending the Affair: The Decline of Television Current Affairs in Australia*, UNSW Press, Sydney, 2005.
17 See, for example, John Fiske, *Reading the Popular*, Unwin Hyman, Boston, 1989; John Hartley, *Communication, Cultural and Media Studies: The Key Concepts*, Routledge, London, 2002; Nicholas Garnham, *Capitalism and Communication: Global Culture and the Economics of Information*, Sage Publications, London, 1990; Peter Golding and Graham Murdock (eds), *The Political Economy of the Media*, Edward Elgar, Cheltenham, England, 1997.
18 Yochai Benkler, *The Wealth of Networks*, Yale University Press, New Haven, 2006.
19 Graeme Turner, 'Introduction: Moving the Margins', p. 124.
20 Nicholas Garnham, 'From Cultural to Creative Industries: An analysis of the implications of the creative industries approach to arts and media policy making in the United Kingdom', *International Journal of Cultural Policy*, 11, 2005, pp. 15–29.
21 Toby Miller, 'In the blue corner – creative industries. In the red corner – critical cultural-policy studies' in Jennifer Holt and Alisa Perren (eds), *The Media Industry Studies Book*, Blackwell, forthcoming 2008; and see also 'A View from a Fossil: The New Economy, Creativity and Consumption – Two or Three Things I Don't Believe In', *International Journal of Cultural Studies*, vol. 7, no. 1, 2002, pp. 55–65.
22 See Nicholas Garnham, 'Concepts of Culture: Public Policy and the Cultural Industries' [1987], in Ann Gray and Jim McGuigan (eds), *Studies in Culture: An Introductory Reader*, Arnold, London, 1997, pp. 54–61.
23 Nicholas Garnham, 'Concepts of Culture', p. 16.
24 ibid., p. 20.
25 Stuart Cunningham, 'Creative industries as policy and discourse outside the United Kingdom', *Global Media and Communication*, vol. 3, no. 3, December 2007, pp. 345–49.
26 Stuart Cunningham, review of Tony Bennett and David Carter (eds), *Culture in Australia: Policies, Publics and Programs*, in *International Journal of Cultural Studies*, vol. 5, no. 2, 2002, pp. 253–6.
27 See, for example, Stuart Cunningham, John Banks and Jason Potts, 'Cultural economy: the shape of the field', in Helmut Anheier and Raj Isar (eds), *Cultural Economy*, Sage, Thousand Oaks and London, 2008; and Stuart Cunningham and Jason Potts, 'New economics for new media', in Gerard Goggin and Larissa Hjorth (eds), *Mobile Media Reader*, Routledge, London, forthcoming 2008.
28 Quoted in Thomas K. McCraw, *Prophet of Innovation: Joseph Schumpeter and Creative Destruction*, Belknap Press of Harvard University Press, Cambridge, Mass., 2007, pp. 349, 6.
29 Chris Anderson (*The Long Tail: Why the Future of Business Is Selling Less of More*, Hyperion, New York, 2006) and Mark Pesce (http://www.mindjack.com/feature/piracy051305.html) exposit the limitations of the mass market mentality that can be addressed by Internet-based harvesting of the 'long tail' and exploitation of 'hyperdistribution'. Charles Leadbeater's *We-Think: The Power of Mass Creativity* (http://www.wethinkthebook.net/home.aspx) explores diverse domains where the power of socially networked collective creation and communication is at work. Recent studies by Henry Jenkins (*Convergence Culture: Where Old and New Media Collide*, New York University Press, New York, 2006) and Yochai Benkler (*The Wealth of Networks*) suggest that consumers' participation in new media production practice now generates significant economic and cultural value. Media production may be shifting from a closed industrial model towards a more open network in which consumers are participatory co-creators of media culture product. Henry Jenkins

is careful to remind us that this is not simply a direct outcome of technology but a significant cultural phenomenon in which we're seeing what happens when the means of cultural production and distribution are co-evolving between producer, aggregator and user. He is aware that this 'bottom-up' process plays out in the context of 'an alarming concentration of the ownership of mainstream commercial media, with a small handful of multinational media conglomerates dominating all sectors of the entertainment industry' (p. 18).

30 Cf David McKnight, *Beyond Left and Right: New Politics and the Culture Wars*, Allen & Unwin, Crows Nest, NSW, 2005.
31 John Hartley (ed.), *Creative Industries*, Blackwell, Malden MA, 2005.
32 Andrew Ross, *No-Collar: The Humane Workplace and Its Hidden Costs*, Basic Books, New York, 2002; and *Fast Boat to China: Corporate Flight and the Consequences of Free Trade-Lessons from Shanghai*, Pantheon, 2006; Vintage, 2007.
33 These points are sourced from Christopher Warren, Federal Secretary, Media, Entertainment & Arts Alliance, at a forum on the future of journalism at *Sydney Morning Herald*, 14 September 2007.
34 Peter Higgs, Stuart Cunningham, Greg Hearn, Barbara Adkins and Karen Barnett, 'The Ecology of Queensland Design', 2005, p. 41, Creative Industries Research and Applications Centre, Brisbane <http://eprints.qut.edu.au/archive/00002410/>, last accessed 21 August 2007.
35 Analysis by ARC Centre of Excellence for Creative Industries and Innovation of custom table from the Australian Bureau of Statistics 2006 Census of Population and Housing, Industry of Employment (ANZSIC06) by INCP Individual Income (weekly) and EMPP Number of Employees, for Person Records, Employed, Owner/managers.
36 Ruth Bridgstock, 'Success in the Protean Career: A Predictive Study of Professional Artists and Tertiary Arts Graduates', PhD, Centre for Learning Innovation, Faculty of Education, QUT, 2008.
37 David Gauntlett (ed.), *Web.studies: Rewiring Media Studies for the Digital Age*, Arnold, London, 2000; and David Gauntlett and Ross Horsley (eds), *Web Studies*, Arnold, London, 2004.

Part 1

Introduction

1 Meaghan Morris, *The Pirate's Fiancee: Feminism, Reading, Postmodernism*, Verso, London, 1988; Tom O'Regan, *Australian National Cinema*, Routledge, London, 1996.
2 Richard Dawkins, *The Selfish Gene*, Oxford University Press, Oxford, 1989.
3 I am indebted to Mark David Ryan for these estimates, in 'A dark new world: Producing contemporary Australian horror films', PhD-in-progress, QUT.
4 Pauline Webber, 'It's time to grow up: Our industry lacks range and adult story-lines', *Weekend Australian Review*, 8–9 September 2007, p. 21.

Chapter 1 The decades of survival

1 See John Tulloch, *Legends on the Screen: The Narrative Film in Australia 1919–1929*, Currency Press and Australian Film Institute, Sydney, 1981, and *Australian Cinema: Industry, Narrative and Meaning*, Allen & Unwin, Sydney, 1982. Stuart Cunningham's 'Australian Film History and Historiography', *Australian Journal of Cultural Studies* vol. 1, no. 1, May 1983, places these ground-breaking books within the traditions of Australian film history.
2 John Tulloch, *Australian Cinema*, p. 40.
3 ibid., p. 174 (original emphasis omitted).
4 *Everyone's*, 6 March 1935.

5   This is the title of a study of the National venture; see Joy Willis, 'National Studios: The Last Colonial Dream?', BA (Hons) thesis, Griffith University, 1984.
6   Bill Routt, 'Videocrit: The Cinema of Charles Chauvel' [videorecording], Australian Film and Television School, North Ryde, N.S.W, 1982.
7   Sylvia Lawson, 'Towards Decolonization: Film History in Australia', in Susan Dermody, John Docker and Drusilla Modjeska (eds), *Nellie Melba, Ginger Meggs and Friends*, Kibble Books, Malmesbury, 1982; Bruce Molloy, 'Before the Interval: An Analysis of Some Aspects of Australian Social Mythology in Selected Australian Feature Films, 1930–1960', PhD thesis, Griffith University, 1984; Graham Shirley and Brian Adams, *Australian Cinema: The First Eighty Years*, Angus & Robertson and Currency Press, Sydney, 1983; and Andrew Pike, 'The Past: Boom and Bust', in Scott Murray (ed.), *The New Australian Cinema*, Nelson, Melbourne, 1980.
8   For more detailed studies of outstanding feature productions of the period, see the articles by Tom O'Regan and Stuart Cunningham in 'Australian Film in the 1950s', *Continuum*, vol. 1, no. 1, 1987, and Stuart Cunningham, 'To Go Back and Beyond', *Continuum*, vol. 2, no. 1, 1988.
9   'On *The Back of Beyond*: An Interview with Ross Gibson', *Continuum*, vol. 1, no. 1, 1987, p. 83.
10 ibid., p. 82.
11 Thomas Elsaesser, 'Primary Identification and the Historical Subject', *CineTracts*, vol. 3, no. 3, 1980.
12 *Sydney Morning Herald*, 30 September 1946.
13 For the fullest treatment of these issues, see Tom O'Regan, 'The Politics of Representation: An Analysis of the Australian Film Revival', PhD thesis, Griffith University, 1985.
14 Simon Brand, 'Picture Palaces and Flea-pits', in *The Australian Screen*, Dreamweaver Books, Sydney, 1983.
15 Bob Larkins, *Chips: The Life and Films of Chips Rafferty*, Macmillan, Melbourne, 1986, p. 57.
16 *Variety*, 5 August 1959.
17 Andrew Pike and Ross Cooper, *Australian Film 1900–1977*, Oxford University Press, Melbourne, 1981, p. 309.

Chapter 2 Approaching Chauvel

1   Robert C. Allen, 'Film History: The Narrow Discourse', and Edward Buscombe, 'A New Approach to Film History', Film Historical Theoretical Speculations, *The 1977 Film Studies Annual, Part Two, Pleasantville*, Redgrave, New York, 1977.
2   For example, the collections of essays 'Metahistory of film', *Film Reader*, no. 4, 1979, and Patricia Mellencamp and Philip Rosen (eds), *Cinema Histories, Cinema Practices*, American Film Institute Monograph Series, vol. IV, University Publications of America, Frederick, MD, 1984.
3   David Bordwell, 'Our Dream Cinema: Western Historiography and the Japanese Film', *Film Reader*, no. 4, 1979, p. 58.
4   ibid.
5   Robert C. Allen and Douglas Gomery, *Film History: Theory and Practice*, Alfred A. Knopf, New York, 1985.
6   ibid., p. 76 (original emphasis).
7   ibid., p. v.
8   ibid., p. 61.
9   ibid., pp. 82–3.
10 For example, Fernando Solanas and Octavio Gettino, 'Towards a Third Cinema', in Bill Nichols (ed.), *Movies and Methods*, University of California Press, Berkeley, 1976, pp. 44–64.

NOTES

11 For example, Edward Buscombe, 'Film History and the Idea of a National Cinema', *Australian Journal of Screen Theory*, nos 9/10, 1981, pp. 141–53.
12 David Bordwell, Janet Staiger and Kristin Thompson, *The Classical Hollywood Cinema: Film Style and Mode of Production to 1960*, Routledge and Kegan Paul, London, 1985.
13 Edward Buscombe, 'Film History and the Idea of a National Cinema', p. 141.
14 See, for example, Thomas H. Guback, *The International Film Industry: Western Europe and America since 1945*, Indiana University Press, Bloomington, 1969; Douglas Gomery and Janet Staiger, 'The History of World Cinema: Models for Economic Analysis', *Film Reader*, no. 4, 1979, pp. 35–44; and Kristin Thompson, *Exporting Entertainment: America in the World Film Market 1907–1934*, British Film Institute, London, 1985.
15 See, for example, Eric Rentschler, *West German Film in the Course of Time: Reflections on the Twenty Years since Oberhausen*, Redgrave Publishing Company, Bedford Hills, NY, 1984; and Timothy Corrigan, *New German Film: The Displaced Image*, University of Texas Press, Austin, 1983. An untheorised Australian example of this approach is Diane Collins, *Hollywood Down Under. Australians at the Movies: 1896 to the Present Day*, Angus & Robertson, North Ryde, 1987.
16 David Bordwell, 'Lowering the Stakes: Prospects for a Historical Poetics of Cinema', *Iris 1*, no. 1, 1983, p. 15. See also Allen and Gomery, pp. 78–91.
17 Thomas Elsaesser develops the notion of the 'social imaginary' in his various studies of German cinema. See Thomas Elsaesser, 'Film History and Visual Pleasure: Weimar Cinema', in Patricia Mellencamp and Philip Rosen (eds), *Cinema Histories, Cinema Practices*, American Film Institute Monograph Series, vol. IV, University Publications of America, Frederick, MD, 1984, pp. 47–84; Thomas Elsaesser, 'Primary Identification and the Historical Subject', *Cine-Tracts 3*, no. 3, 1980, pp. 43–52; Thomas Elsaesser, 'Myth as the Phantasmagoria of History: H.J. Syberberg, Cinema and Representation', *New German Critique*, nos 24/25, Fall–Winter 1981–82, pp. 108–54; and Thomas Elsaesser, 'Lulu and the Meter Man', *Screen*, 24, nos 4/5, July–October 1983, pp. 4–36.
18 Allen and Gomery, p. 167 (original emphasis).
19 *Australian Silent Films: A Pictorial History of Silent Films from 1896 to 1929*, Lansdowne Press, Melbourne, 1970; *The Talkies Era: A Pictorial History of Australian Sound Film Making 1930–1960*, Lansdowne Press, Melbourne, 1972; *History and Heartburn: The Saga of Australian Film 1896–1978*, Harper and Row, Sydney, 1979; *The Australian Cinema*, Pacific Books/Angus & Robertson, Sydney, 1970; *Forgotten Cinema*, producer and director Tony Buckley, script Bill Peach, 1967; *The Pictures that Moved*, producer Commonwealth Film Unit, director Alan Anderson, script Joan Long, 1968; and *The Passionate Industry*, producer Commonwealth Film Unit, director and script Joan Long, 1972. The scripts of the latter two films are included in Joan Long and Martin Long, *The Pictures that Moved: A Picture History of the Australian Cinema 1896–1929*, Hutchinson, Melbourne, 1982.
20 It is estimated that 'of about 250 silent feature films made in Australia between 1906 and 1930, little more than 50 survive in whole or in part today'. Ray Edmondson and Andrew Pike, *Australia's Lost Films: The Loss and Rescue of Australia's Silent Cinema*, National Library of Australia (NLA), Canberra, 1982, p. 9.
21 John Baxter, 'Preface', *The Australian Cinema*, Angus and Robertson, Sydney, 1970.
22 Andrew Pike, 'The Past: Boom and Bust', in Scott Murray (ed.), *The New Australian Cinema*, Nelson, Melbourne, 1980, p. 11, and see also Andrew Pike and Ross Cooper, *Australian Film 1900–1977*, Oxford University Press, Melbourne, 1980.
23 This formulation is based on Tom O'Regan, 'Australia Film Making: Its Public Circulation', in Anne Hutton (ed.), *The First Australian History and Film Conference Papers 1982*, Australian Film and Television School (AFTS), Sydney, 1982, p. 228.
24 Sylvia Lawson, 'Towards Decolonization: Some Problems and Issues for Film History in Australia', *Film Reader 4*, 1979, and in Susan Dermody, John Docker and Drusilla Modjeska (eds), *Nellie Melba, Ginger Meggs and Friends: Essays in Australian Cultural History*, Kibble Books, Malmsbury, 1982; Susan Dermody, 'Rugged Individuals or Neo-Colonial Boys?

The Early Sound Period in Australian Film, 1931/2', *Media Papers*, no. 12, New South Wales Institute of Technology; Susan Dermody, 'Two Remakes: Ideologies of Film Production 1919–1932', in *Nellie Melba* ..., pp. 33–59; and Graham Shirley and Brian Adams, *Australian Cinema: The First Eighty Years*, Angus & Robertson and Currency Press, Sydney, 1983.

25 John Tulloch, *Legends on the Screen: The Narrative Film in Australia 1919–1929*, Currency Press/AFI, Sydney, 1981, and *Australian Cinema: History, Narrative and Meaning*, Allen & Unwin, Sydney, 1982.
26 John Tulloch, *Australian Cinema*, p. 41.
27 ibid., pp. 40, 8, 41.
28 There is an extensive literature on dependency theory. See the bibliographies in Malcolm Alexander, 'The Political Economy of Semi-Industrial Capitalism: A Comparative Study of Argentina, Australia and Canada, 1950–1970', unpublished PhD thesis, McGill University, 1979, and John Sinclair, 'From Modernisation to Cultural Dependence: Mass Communication Studies and the Third World', *Media Information Australia*. No. 23, February 1982.
29 See, among others, Malcolm Alexander, 'Political Economy of Semi-Industrial Capitalism'; Malcolm Alexander, 'Dependency Theory and the Structural Analysis of Australian Society: A World Systems Perspective', Paper No. 41, Department of Sociology, La Trobe University, August 1977; Peter Cochrane, *Industrialization and Dependence: Australia's Road to Economic Development 1870–1939*, University of Queensland Press, St Lucia, 1980; Philip Ehrensaft and Warwick Armstrong, 'Dominion Capitalism: A First Statement', *Australian and New Zealand Journal of Sociology*, 14, no. 3, Part 2, October 1978; and David Clark, 'Australia: Victim or Partner of British Imperialism?', in E. L. Wheelwright and Ken Buckley, *Essays in the Political Economy of Australian Capitalism*, Vol. 1, ANZ Book Company, Sydney, 1975.
30 John Tulloch, *Legends*, p. 269, and Programme Notes to Charles Chauvel Retrospective, Queensland Cultural Centre, February 1987.
31 Sylvia Lawson, 'Towards Decolonization', p. 65.
32 John Baxter, *Australian Cinema*, pp. 54, 65.
33 John Hill, 'Charles Chauvel', *Sydney Cinema Journal*, no. 3, Winter 1967, p. 26.
34 Eric Reade, *History and Heartburn*, p. 48.
35 John Baxter, *Australia Cinema*, p. 65.
36 Bruce Molloy, 'Salute', p. 48.
37 Andrew Pike, 'Early, Commercial and Good Film', *Hemisphere* 20, no. 1, (1976), p. 4.
38 Sylvia Lawson, 'Towards Decolonization'.
39 Bill Routt, 'The Cinema of Charles Chauvel', *Videocrit*, Australian Film and Television School, 1982; Bill Routt, 'On the Expression of Colonialism in Early Australian Films – Charles Chauvel and Naive Cinema', in Albert Moran and Tom O'Regan (eds), *Australian Film Reader*, Currency Press, Sydney, 1985, pp. 55–66; Tulloch, *Legends*, ch. 7; and Bruce Molloy, 'Before the Interval: An Analysis of Some Aspects of Australian Social Mythology in Selected Australian Feature Films, 1930–1960', PhD thesis, Griffith University, 1984, ch. 6.
40 Bill Routt, 'The Voice of the Exploited: Naive Style in Australian Films', unpublished manuscript version of 'Charles Chauvel and Naive Cinema', p. 2.
41 John Tulloch, *Legends*, p. 269 (original emphasis).
42 Bruce Molloy, 'Before the Interval', pp. 315, 316, 318.
43 David Bordwell, *The Films of Carl-Theodor Dreyer*, University of California Press, Berkeley, 1981, p. 9.
44 David Bordwell, *The Films of Carl-Theodor Dreyer*, p. 9.
45 David Bordwell, *The Films of Carl-Theodor Dreyer*, p. 23, 24.
46 See, for example, Eric Irvin, *Australian Melodrama: Eighty Years of Popular Theatre*, Hale and Iremonger, Sydney, 1981.

47 Peter Brooks, *Melodramatic Imagination: Balzac, Henry James, Melodrama, and the Mode of Excess*, Yale University Press, New Haven, 1976, p. 41.
48 ibid., p. 199.
49 This position is argued in Stuart Cunningham, 'The "Force-Field" of Melodrama', *Quarterly Review of Film Studies*, 6, no. 4, Fall 1981. See also Peter Brooks, *Melodramatic Imagination*, especially ch. 1, and Routt 'The Voice of the Exploited'.
50 The title of a personality profile on the Chauvels, in *TV News Times*, 4 October 1958.
51 Charles and Elsa Chauvel, *Walkabout*, W.H. Allen, London, 1959, p. xiii.

Chapter 3 Apollonius and Dionysus in the Antipodes

1 O. Mannoni, *Prospero and Caliban: The Psychology of Colonization*, Praeger, New York, 1964; Franz Fanon, *The Wretched of the Earth*, Penguin, London, 1969.
2 Benedict Anderson, *Imagined Communities*, Verso, London, 1983.
3 I borrow this fine phrase from David Thomson's essay on Robert Flaherty in *A Biographical Dictionary of Film*, 2nd edn, William Morrow, New York, 1981, p. 193. The parallel is in some ways reasonable.
4 Never published, but a great many held in the National Library Manuscripts section. Several extracts are to be found in *Hurley at War: The Photography and Diaries of Frank Hurley in Two World Wars*, The Fairfax Library, Sydney, 1986.
5 See David P. Millar, *From Snowdrift to Shellfire: Capt. James Francis (Frank) Hurley 1885–1962*, David Ell Press, Sydney, 1984, p. 138.
6 Herc McIntyre, 'In Retrospect', in Elsa Chauvel, *My Life with Charles Chauvel*, Shakespeare Head Press, Sydney, 1973, p. 191.
7 ibid.
8 See Andree Wright, *Brilliant Careers*, Pan Books, Sydney, 1986, p. 47. However, as I argue in *Featuring Australia: The Cinema of Charles Chauvel*, Allen & Unwin, North Sydney, 1991, this partnership doesn't amount to a full case of 'dual' authorship.
9 See, for the industrial politics and policy background, John Tulloch, *Legends on the Screen*, Currency Press/AFI, Sydney, 1981, pp. 286–91.
10 See David P. Millar, *From Snowdrift to Shellfire*, ch. 9.
11 See John Tulloch, *Australian Cinema: Industry, Narrative and Meaning*, Allen & Unwin, Sydney, 1982, pp. 157ff and 204.
12 Andrew Pike and Ross Cooper, *Australian Film 1900–1977*, Oxford University Press, Melbourne, 1981, p. 171-2.
13 See John Tulloch's discussion in *Australian Cinema*, pp. 202–5.
14 The production was prevented from shooting in Papua by a last-minute decision of the Australian government that 'it would be harmful to show whites and blacks together'. See Pike and Cooper, *Australian Film 1900–1977*, p. 171.
15 Charles Chauvel, *In the Wake of 'The Bounty' to Tahiti and Pitcairn Island*, Endeavour Press, Sydney, 1933, pp. 37–8.
16 ibid., pp. 11–12.
17 Elsa Chauvel, *My Life with Charles Chauvel*, p. 47.
18 Bill Routt, 'The Cinema of Charles Chauvel', AFTRS Videocrit series, 1982.
19 They also established contact with some of the islanders 'outside' the film; their correspondence is moving. Charles and Elsa's daughter, Susanne Carlsson, travelled to Pitcairn and wrote an 'update' on the fortunes of the community. It is also an appropriate anecdote to quote Elsa saying that Charles held to a kind of benign assimilationism through intermarriage as an ideal mode of containing the fractious master–slave dialectics of cultural contact. See Papers of C. E. Chauvel, Mitchell Library, MSS 666/1; 'Pilgrimage to Pitcairn', *Australian Women's Weekly*, February 1985, pp. 39–45; also Elsa Chauvel, interview with Graham Shirley, 12 August 1976, typescript, NFSA.

Chapter 4 Hollywood genres, Australian movies

1. See, for example, Rick Altman (ed.), *Genre: The Musical. A Reader*, Routledge and Kegan Paul, London, 1981, especially the articles by Thomas Elsaesser, Mark Roth, Robin Wood, Denis Giles, Jane Feuer and Richard Dyer.
2. Richard Dyer, 'Entertainment and Utopia', *Movie*, no. 24, Spring 1977, reprinted in Altman, *Genre: The Musical*, p. 177.
3. ibid., p. 175.
4. ibid., p. 175.
5. ibid., p. 70.
6. Raymond Williams, *Marxism and Literature*, Oxford University Press, Oxford, 1977.
7. Richard Dyer, 'Entertainment and Utopia', p. 185.

Part 2

Introduction

1. The title of my extended essay on Kennedy–Miller's *Vietnam*, 'Jewel in the Crown', *Filmnews* May 1987, pp. 8–9.
2. *Curtin*, ABC and Apollo Films, screened on 22 April 2007. Producers Andrew Wiseman and Richard Keddie, writer Alison Nisselle, director Jessica Hobbs. *Bastard Boys*, ABC TV and Flying Cabbage Productions, screened on 13–14 May 2007. Writer Sue Smith, director Ray Quint.
3. Chris Scanlon, 'The History Trap: Chris Scanlon on ABC TV's *Bastard Boys*', *real time + on screen*, no. 79, June–July 2007, p. 23.

Chapter 5 Style, form and history in Australian mini-series

1. The history of the lOBA tax legislation and issues surrounding it are presented in accessible form in Susan Dermody and Elizabeth Jacka, *The Screening of Australia, Vol. 1: Anatomy of a Film Industry*, Currency Press, Sydney, 1987, pp. 211–16. See also *Film Assistance: Future Options*, Allen & Unwin, Sydney, 1987, p. 2.
2. For more detailed accounts of the institutional history of the mini-series, see Paul Ken, 'The Origins of the Mini-Series', *Broadcast*, 12 March 1979, pp. 16–17, and 'A Little Plot in Colorado', *Time Out*, 25–31 May 1979, pp. 20–1; Bart Mills, 'Washington Behind Closed Doors', *Stills*, April–May 1984, pp. 26–8; and Henry Castleman and Walter Podrazik, *Watching TV: Four Decades of American Television*, McGraw-Hill, New York, 1982, pp. 262–76. For Australian background as well as international antecedents, see Ewan Burnett, 'Mini-Series', *Cinema Papers*, 44/45, 1984, pp. 32–6; and Albert Moran, *Images and Industry: Television Drama Production in Australia*, Currency Press, Sydney, 1985.
3. John Caughie, 'Progressive Television and Documentary Drama', in Tony Bennett et al. (eds), *Popular Television and Film*, BFI, London, 1981, p. 346.
4. Tom Ryan, 'Historical Films', in Scott Murray (ed.), *The New Australian Cinema*, Nelson, Melbourne, 1980, pp. 122–5.
5. Colin MacCabe, 'Memory, Phantasy, Identity: *Days of Hope* and the Politics of the Past', in Tony Bennett et al. (eds), *Popular Television and Film*, BFI, London, 1981.
6. See, for example, Jodi Brooks, 'Dismissing', *Media Papers*, no. 19, New South Wales Institute of Technology, 1983.
7. Albert Moran, *Images and Industry*, p. 207.
8. See Andrew Goodwin et al. (eds), *Documentary Drama*, BFI, London, 1983, for accounts of these and other significant controversies around documentary drama.
9. See Australian Broadcasting Tribunal, 'Ratings of Australian Drama, Mini-Series, Films and Telemovies', *Australian Content Inquiry Discussion Paper*, ABT, Sydney, March 1988.

10 Ewan Burnett, 'Mini-Series', pp. 32–6; See also the following chapters from *The Imaginary Industry*: Elizabeth Jacka, 'The Industry'; 'Films'; Stuart Cunningham, 'Kennedy–Miller: "House Style" in Australian Television', in Susan Dermody & Elizabeth Jacka (eds), *The Imaginary Industry: Australian Film in the Late '80s*, AFTRS, North Ryde (Sydney), 1988.

11 Cited in Peter MacGregor, 'Australian Teachers Curriculum Package on *The Last Bastion*'. On the two earlier mini-series, see the comments of their co-scriptwriter: Ian Jones, 'The Historical Mini-Series – Problems and Priorities', in Anne Hutton (ed.), *The First Australian History and Film Conference Papers 1982*, AFTS, North Ryde, Sydney, 1982, pp. 73–88.

12 Michael Dunn, *Australia and the Empire: From 1788 to the Present*, Fontana, Sydney, 1984, especially chapter 6.

13 For a much fuller treatment of *The Last Bastion*, see the well-argued piece by Geoff Mayer, one of the very few that engages with questions of both style and representation: '*The Last Bastion*: History or Drama?', *Cinema Papers*, 48, 1985, pp. 38–41, 87.

14 Drew Cottle, '*The Petrov Affair* – Constructing the Right Past?', paper to the Fourth History and Film Conference, University of Queensland, December 1987.

15 See Freud's distinction between 'mourning' and 'melancholia', which this point follows: 'Mourning and Melancholia', in *On Metapsychology*, Penguin, Harmondsworth, 1984, pp. 245–68. Within a social psychology framework, the point is developed brilliantly by Alexander Mitscherlich and Margarete Mitscherlich, *The Inability to Mourn*, Grove, New York, 1975.

16 Terry Hayes, interview with Keryn Curtis, 6 February 1988. For more detail, see the chapter '*The Dismissal* and Australian Television', in Stuart Cunningham et al., *The Dismissal: Perspectives*, AFTS, North Ryde, Sydney, 1984, pp. 1–6.

17 'Comments from the Producer', in *Melba* Investment Prospectus, 1985.

18 Raymond Evans, 'Heroes Often Fail: "Shout!", Johnny O'Keefe and Another Australian Legend', *Cinema Papers*, 71, 1989, pp. 38–42.

19 Ina Bertrand, 'From Silence to Reconciliation', paper to the Fourth History and Film Conference, University of Queensland, December 1987.

20 For more detail, see Stuart Cunningham, 'Jewel in the Crown', *Filmnews*, 17, no. 4, 1987, pp. 8–9.

Chapter 6 Kennedy–Miller: 'House-style' in Australian television

1 For a brief but useful overview of this tradition of analysis, see Pam Cook, *The Cinema Book*, Pantheon, New York, 1985, pp. 10–24. One of the best works in this tradition is Nick Roddick, *A New Deal in Entertainment*, BFI, London, 1983.

2 Hugh Fordin, *The World of Entertainment: Hollywood's Greatest Musicals*, Doubleday, New York, 1975; David Pirie, *A Heritage of Horror: The English Gothic Cinema 1946–1972*, Gordon Frazer, London, 1973.

3 Charles Barr, *Ealing Studios*, Cameron and Taylor, London, 1977, and John Ellis, 'Made in Ealing', *Screen*, 16, no. l, Spring 1975.

4 See, for example, Graham Murdock and James D. Halloran, 'Contexts of Creativity in Television Drama: An Exploratory Study in Britain', in Heinz-Deitrich Fischer and Stefan Reinhard Melnick, *Entertainment: A Cross-Cultural Examination*, Hastings House, New York, 1979. Manuel Alvarado and John Stewart, *Made for Television: Euston Films Limited*, BFI, London, 1985, and Jane Feuer, Paul Kerr and Tise Vahimagi (eds), *MTM 'Quality Television'*, BFI, London, 1984, are the two studies mentioned. See also Albert Moran, *Making a TV Series: The Bellamy Project*, Currency Press/AFI, Sydney, 1982; and *Images and Industry: Television Drama Production in Australia*, Currency Press, Sydney, 1985.

5 Barbara Samuels, 'The movies, mate: Part Three. Inside Kennedy Miller', *Cinema Canada*, no. 113, December 1984, p. 26.

6 ibid.

7   'George Miller', in Sue Mathews, *35 mm Dreams*, Penguin, Ringwood, 1984, p. 270; and Irina Dunn, '*The Witches of Eastwick*: The film is really about Nicholson the actor', *Encore*, 8, October 1987.
8   Suellen O'Grady, 'Making character exploration an art form', *Weekend Australian Magazine*, 2 March 1985, p. 8, a review of *Cowra Breakout*; and Phillip Adams, 'The dangerous pornography of death', *Bulletin*, 1 May 1979, a review of *Mad Max*.
9   George Ogilvie, quoted in Samuels, 'Inside Kennedy Miller', pp. 26–7.
10 By 'comparable' I mean that Kennedy–Miller is able to secure pre-sales that ensure investors' and the company's break-even point, usually around 30–40% of budget. Thus, in the most relevant example, *Dirtwater Dynasty*'s $7,300,000 budget was 'met' by a $3,500,000 network pre-sale.
11 Patrice Fidgeon, 'Dynasty down under', *TV Week*, 7 March 1987.
12 'George Miller', in *35 mm Dreams*, pp. 233–4.
13 For perhaps the most fulsome effort to identify in similar terms the 'mythmaking' processes of these films, see Ross Gibson, 'Yondering: A Reading of *Mad Max Beyond Thunderdome*', *Art & Text*, no. 19, October–December 1985, pp. 25–33.
14 'George Miller', in *35 mm Dreams*, p. 234.
15 Historians routinely 'expose' what they consider to be the superficialities and inadequacies of historical analysis offered by mini-series, forgetting the quite different order of discourse to that of academic history within which they operate. Consider here, the extraordinarily illiterate denunciations of mini-series by eminent academic historians such as A.G. L. Shaw and Geoffrey Serle, in *Historical Studies* (1979), pp. 502–9, and *Australian Historical Association Bulletin* no. 49, December 1986, pp. 9–10, respectively. The Fourth History and Film Conference in 1987 also had more than its share of such denunciation.
16 Margaret Kelly, quoted in Samuels, 'Inside Kennedy Miller', p. 30.
17 Ross Gibson, 'Yondering', p. 31.
18 For further detail see Chapter 5 and my 'Textual Innovation in the Australian Historical Mini-Series', in John Tulloch and Graeme Turner (eds), *Australian Television Reader*, Allen & Unwin, Sydney, 1989.
19 Terry Hayes, interview with Keryn Curtis, 6 February 1988.
20 Crawford's chief executive Ian Bradley, on the 'realities' of internationalisation: 'Those are the realities these days. It's a shame, but obviously we'd never make *The Dismissal*, which I thought was terrific . . .' 'Ian Bradley Does His Sums', *Cinema Papers*, no. 69, May 1988, p. 19. Note also the way *True Believers* advertised itself as 'before the dismissal', with the famous 'Kerr's cur' footage prefacing its series trailer.
21 Terry Hayes, quoted in Fiona Manning, '1975 revisited: It will cause a stir', *Sunday Telegraph*, 23 January 1983, p. 43.
22 Stephen Crofts, Stuart Cunningham and Sylvia Lawson, '*The Dismissal*', *Filmnews*, April/May 1983, pp. 10–11; Stephen Crofts, Stuart Cunningham, Sylvia Lawson and Jennifer Craik, '*The Dismissal* in Circulation: A Trilogy', *Australian Journal of Cultural Studies*, December 1983, pp. 83–100 (also as *The Dismissal: Perspectives*, AFTRS, North Ryde, 1984); Jodi Brooks, 'Dismissing', *Media Papers*, no. 19, New South Wales Institute of Technology, September 1983.
23 'George Miller', in Sue Mathews, *35 mm Dreams*, p. 262.
24 Jodi Brooks, 'Dismissing', p. 18.
25 John Fiske and John Hartley, *Reading Television*, Methuen, London, 1978, ch 6. These authors speak of the bardic function of television corresponding to the anthropological category of 'ritual condensation', terms analogous to mine. They offer seven summary aspects of the bardic function, of which the central three are: to articulate the main lines of the established cultural consensus about the nature of reality; to implicate the individual members of the culture into its dominant value system; and to celebrate, explain, interpret and justify the doings of the culture's individual representatives in the world out there (p. 88).

26 See John Caughie, 'Progressive Television and Documentary Drama', in Tony Bennett et al. (eds), *Popular Television and Film*, BFI, London, 1981, pp. 341–2.
27 Philip Derriman, 'Replay of *Bodyline* series warms up dramatically at the Sydney Cricket Ground', *Sydney Morning Herald*, 20 October 1983.
28 Phil Derriman, '*Bodyline*', *Sydney Morning Herald Guide*, 16 July 1984, pp. 1, 3.
29 See, among many examples, John Stevens, '*Bodyline*: the moan of a routed kangaroo', *The Age*, 10 June 1984, p. 7.
30 'Cricket, lovely cricket!', *Sun Herald*, 15 July 1984, p. 53.
31 Derriman, '*Bodyline*', p. 3.
32 'Cricket, lovely cricket!', p. 53.
33 Robin Oliver, 'Bodyline breaks our TV rules', *Daily Telegraph*, 16 July 1984, p. 19.
34 'Bowled over!', *Daily Mirror*, 6 July 1984, p. 14.
35 *Bodyline* publicity package by Kennedy–Miller for Network Ten.
36 Suellen O'Grady, 'Making character exploration an art form', *Weekend Australian Magazine*, 2 March 1985, p. 8 (review of *Cowra Breakout*).
37 One strand of criticism of the series pursues this sense of its departure from the Kennedy–Miller signature: '*Bodyline* might have appealed to the C'mon Aussie set, but for anybody else it must have been too long, too caricatured and, sadly, rather amatuerish' (Richard Coleman, '*Bodyline*: sadly, all its balls weren't malapert Yorkers', *Sydney Morning Herald*, 21 July 1984, p. 16).
38 For examples among many, see 'Cowra comedy', *Sun* (Sydney), 14 March 1985, and Clement Semmler, 'Drama reduced by strains on credulity', *Bulletin*, 5 March 1985, pp. 58–9.
39 For a sample, see Suellen O'Grady, 'Making character exploration an art form', and James Cunningham, 'A classic case of doomed heroism', *Sydney Morning Herald Guide*, 4 March 1985, p. 3.
40 Suellen O'Grady, 'Making character exploration', p. 8.
41 Edward Bullough, 'Psychical Distance as a Function in Art and the Aesthetic Principle', quoted in Geoff Mayer '"The Last Bastion": History or Drama?', *Cinema Papers*, no. 50, February–March 1985, p. 39.
42 John Ellis, *Visible Fictions*, Routledge and Kegan Paul, London, 1982, Part II.
43 The title of Moran's chapter on soap opera, in *Images and Industry*, ch. 10.
44 Terry Hayes, quoted in Robin Oliver, 'Dynasty down under', *Sydney Morning Herald Guide*, 4 April 1988, p. 6.
45 Terry Hayes, interview with Keryn Curtis, 6 February 1988.
46 For a discussion of the 'modularity' of modern nationalism, see Benedict Anderson, *Imagined Communities*, Verso, London, 1983, especially ch. 6.
47 See Meaghan Morris, 'Tooth and Claw: Tales of Survival, and Crocodile Dundee', *Art & Text*, no. 25, June–August 1987, pp. 36–68.
48 Phillip Adams, 'Theatre of the Absurd comes to the small screen', *Weekend Australian*, 8 April 1988.
49 Terry Hayes, quoted in Oliver, 'Dynasty down under', p. 6.
50 Phillip Adams, 'Theatre of the Absurd'.
51 Tom O'Regan, 'The Enchantment with Cinema: Australian Film in the 1980s', in Albert Moran and Tom O'Regan (eds), *The Australian Screen*, Penguin, Ringwood, 1989.

Chapter 7 Australian television in world markets

1 Toby Miller, 'When Australia Became Modern' (review of *National Fictions* 2nd edn), *Continuum*, vol. 8, no. 2, 1994, pp. 206–14.
2 Andrew Milner, *Contemporary Cultural Theory*, Allen & Unwin, Sydney, 1991.
3 John Caughie, Playing at Being American: Games and Tactics', in Patricia Mellencamp (ed.), *Logics of Television: Essays in Cultural Criticism*, Indiana University Press, Bloomington and Indianapolis, 1990, pp. 44–58.

4   William Shawcross, *Rupert Murdoch: Ringmaster of the Information Circus*, Random House, Sydney, 1992.
5   Catharine Lumby and John O'Neil, 'Tabloid Television', in Julianne Schultz (ed.), *Not Just Another Business: Journalists, Citizens and the Media*, Pluto Press and Ideas for Australia, Marrickville, 1994, pp. 149–66.
6   Geoff Lealand, '"I'd Just Like to Say How Happy I Am To Be Here in the Seventh State of Australia": The Australianisation of New Zealand Television', *Sites*, no. 21, Spring, pp. 100–12, 1990.
7   Els De Bens, Mary Kelly and Marit Bakke, 'Television Content: Dallasification of Culture?', in Karen Siune and Wolfgang Truetzschler (eds) for the Euromedia Research Group, *Dynamics of Media Politics: Broadcast and Electronic Media in Western Europe*, Sage, London, 1992.
8   Ian Craven, 'Distant Neighbours: Notes on Some Australian Soap Operas', *Australian Studies*, no. 3, December 1989, pp. 1–35.
9   Alessandro Silj et al., *East of Dallas: The European Challenge to American Television*, British Film Institute, London, 1989.
10 Minette Marin, *The Daily Telegraph*, 10 March 1994, p. 18, quoted in Mallory Wober and S. Fazal, 'Neighbours at Home and Away: British Viewers' Perceptions of Australian Soap Operas', *Media Information Australia*, no. 71, February 1989, pp. 78–88.
11 *Trader*, 6 April 1987.
12 Silj et al., *East of Dallas*.
13 Mallory Wober and S. Fazal, 'Neighbours at Home and Away'.
14 Kate Bowles, in Catherine Taylor, 'Squeaky-clean soap, export quality', *Australian*, 28 May 1993, p. 13.
15 Neil Shoebridge, 'Village Goes Global with Low-Risk TV', *Business Review Weekly*, 7 May 1993, pp. 10–11.
16 For a derisively dismissive New Zealand account, see Diana Wichtel, 'Ain't it a beach', (New Zealand) *Listener*, 28 August 1993, p. 71.
17 Peter Schembri and Jackie Malone, *Paradise Beach* Reconsidered', *Cinema Papers*, nos 97/98, April 1994, pp. 30–33.
18 James McNamara (Chief Executive Officer and President, New World Entertainment), Thea Diserio (Senior Vice-President, New World International) and Phil Oldham (Executive Vice President, Genesis Entertainment), interview with Stuart Cunningham, New York, March 1994.
19 Stephen Crofts, 'Global Neighbours', in Robert C. Allen (ed.), *To be continued . . .*, Routledge, New York, 1995, pp 98-121.
20 A. J. Nieuwenhuis, 'Media Policy in the Netherlands: Beyond the Market, *European Journal of Communication*, 7, 2, 1992, pp. 195–218.
21 Ien Ang, *Desperately Seeking the Audience*, Routledge, London and New York, 1991.
22 Ria van Essen (Head of Acquisitions, VARA), interview with Elizabeth Jacka, Hilversum, October 1992.
23 Louise Tollen-Worth (Head of Program Buying, NOS), interview with Elizabeth Jacka, Hilversum, November 1992.
24 Hedy von Bochove (Production Head, JE Productions), interview with Elizabeth Jacka, Aalsmeer, October 1992.
25 Edward Said, *Orientalism: Western Concepts of the Orient*, Penguin, London, 1991.
26 BIE (Bureau of Industry Economics), *Audiovisual Industries in Australia: A Discussion Paper*, BIE, Canberra, April 1994.
27 Jock Given, 'Australian Content, Broadcasting and Export Opportunities', paper for the 1993 Australian Broadcasting Summit, 11 November 1993.
28 Department of Industry, Technology and Regional Development (DITARD), *Media Developments in Asia and Implications for Australia: A Discussion Paper*, Audiovisual Task Force, DITARD, March 1994.

29 John Milne, 'Overcoming Australia's Regional Image Problem: A Personal View', in Don Grant and Graham Seal (eds), *Australia in the World: Perceptions and Possibilities*, pp. 283–90, 1993.
30 Mary de Jabrun, 'French Adolescents' Perceptions of Australia', in Don Grant and Graham Seal (eds), *Australia in the World: Perceptions and Possibilities*, Black Swan Press, Perth, 1993, pp. 102–7.
31 Ian Craven, 'Distant Neighbours: Notes on Some Australian Soap Operas', 1989.
32 Andrew McCathie, 'Europe tunes in to "new-look" Australia', *Financial Review*, 3 September 1991, p. 32.
33 Graeme Turner, 'The End of the National Project? Australian Cinema in the 1990s', in Wimal Dissanayake (ed.), *Questions of Nationhood in Asian Cinema*, Indiana University Press, Bloomington, 1994.
34 Tom O'Regan, 'The Rise and Fall of Entrepreneurial TV: Australian TV, 1986–90', *Screen*, 32, 1, Spring, pp. 94–108. Reprinted in Graeme Turner (ed.), *Nation, Culture, Text: Australian Cultural and Media Studies*, Routledge, London, 1993, pp. 91–105.
35 Roland Barthes, *Mythologies*, Paladin, London, 1973.

Part 3

Introduction

1 Compelling works of Australian cultural analysis are coming out of these intersections. Some examples are: Ghassan Hage, *White Nation: Fantasies of White Supremacy in a Multicultural Society*, Pluto Press, Sydney, 1998; *Against Paranoid Nationalism: Searching for Hope in a Shrinking Society*, Pluto Press, Annandale, 2003; Ghassan Hage (ed.), *Arab-Australians Today: Citizenship and Belonging*, Melbourne University Press, Carlton South, 2002; Jon Stratton, *Race Daze: Australia in Identity Crisis*, Pluto Press, Sydney, 1998; Ien Ang et al. (eds), *Alter/Asians: Asian-Australian Identities in Art, Media and Popular Culture*, Pluto Press, Sydney, 2000; S. Poynting, G. Noble, P. Tabar and J. Collins, *Bin Laden in the Suburbs: Criminalising the Arab Other*, Federation Press/Institute of Criminology, Sydney, 2004; I. Ang, J. Brand, G. Noble and J. Sternberg, *Connecting Diversity: Paradoxes of Multicultural Australia*, Special Broadcasting Services Corporation, Artarmon, 2006. In the specific case of the Vietnamese, which is the subject of Chapter 9, there is a strong intersection with anthropology (Mandy Thomas, *Dreams in the Shadows: Vietnamese-Australian Lives in Transition*, Allen & Unwin, St Leonards, NSW, 1998) and political science (Nancy Viviani, *The Indochinese in Australia, 1975–1995: From Burnt Boats to Barbecues*, Oxford University Press, Melbourne, 1996).
2 John Frow and Meaghan Morris (eds), 'Introduction', in *Australian Cultural Studies: A Reader*, Allen & Unwin, St Leonards, NSW, 1993, p. viii.

Chapter 8 Theorising the diasporic audience

1 Stuart Cunningham and John Sinclair (eds), *Floating Lives: The Media and Asian Diasporas*, University of Queensland Press, St Lucia, 2000.
2 Jürgen Habermas, 'The public sphere', *New German Critique*, vol. 1, no. 3, 1974, pp. 49–55; and Jürgen Habermas, *The Structural Transformation of the Public Sphere: An Inquiry in a Category of Bourgeois Society*, Polity Press, Cambridge, 1962, 1989.
3 Nicholas Garnham, 'The Media and the Public Sphere', in C. Calhoun (ed.), *Habermas and the Public Sphere*, MIT Press, Cambridge, MA, 1992.
4 See H. Schiller, *Culture Inc: The Corporate Takeover of Public Expression*, Oxford, New York, 1989.
5 John Hartley, *Uses of Television*, Routledge, London, 1999, pp. 217–18.

6   Charles Husband, 'Differentiated Citizenship and the Multi-ethnic Public Sphere', *Journal of International Communication*, vol. 5, nos 1 and 2, 1998, pp. 134–48.
7   Jim McGuigan, 'What Price the Public Sphere?', in Daya Kishan Thussu (ed.), *Electronic Empires: Global Media and Local Resistance*, Arnold, London, 1998, pp. 91–107.
8   Jim McGuigan, 'What Price the Public Sphere?', p. 98, quoting Garnham, 'The Media and the Public Sphere', p. 274.
9   Todd Gitlin, 'Public Sphere or Public Sphericules?', in T. Liebes and J. Curran (eds), *Media, Ritual and Identity*, Routledge, London, 1998, pp. 175–202.
10 ibid., p.173.
11 Nancy Fraser, 'Rethinking the Public Sphere', in C. Calhoun (ed.), *Habermas and the Public Sphere*, MIT Press, Cambridge, MA, 1992.
12 John Hartley and Alan McKee, *The Indigenous Public Sphere*, Oxford University Press, Oxford, 2000.
13 ibid., pp. 3, 7.
14 John Sinclair, Audrey Yue, Gay Hawkins, Pookong Kee and Josephine Fox, 'Chinese Cosmopolitanism and Media Use', in Stuart Cunningham and John Sinclair (eds), *Floating Lives: The Media and Asian Diasporas*, University of Queensland Press, St Lucia, 2000.
15 Stuart Cunningham and Tina Nguyen, 'Popular Media of the Vietnamese Diaspora', in Stuart Cunningham and John Sinclair (eds), *Floating Lives: The Media and Asian Diasporas*, University of Queensland Press, St Lucia, 2000.
16 Manas Ray, 'Bollywood Down Under: Fiji Indian Cultural History and Popular Assertion', in Stuart Cunningham and John Sinclair (eds), *Floating Lives: The Media and Asian Diasporas*, University of Queensland Press, St Lucia, 2000.
17 Deborah Wong, '"I Want the Microphone": Mass Mediation and Agency in Asian-American Popular Music', *TDR* (The Drama Review), vol. 38, no. 3, Fall 1994, pp. 152–67.
18 Hamid Naficy, *The Making of Exile Cultures: Iranian Television in Los Angeles*, University of Minnesota Press, Minneapolis, 1993.
19 D. Kolar-Panov, *Video, War and the Diasporic Imagination*, Routledge, London, 1997.
20 ibid., p. 31.
21 John Hartley, *Uses of Television*, p. 84.
22 Mandy Thomas, *Dreams in the Shadows: Vietnamese-Australian Lives in Transition*, Allen & Unwin, St Leonards, 1999, p. 149.
23 Ghassan Hage, *White Nation: Fantasies of White Supremacy in a Multicultural Society*, Pluto Press, Annandale, and West Wickham, Comerford and Miller Publishers, 1998, p. 10.
24 John Hartley, *Uses of Television*, p.143.

Chapter 9 Actually existing hybridity

1   Hamid Naficy, *The Making of Exile Cultures: Iranian Television in Los Angeles*, University of Minnesota Press, Minneapolis, 1993.
2   Dona Kolar-Panov, *Video, War and the Diasporic Imagination*, Routledge, London, 1997.
3   Ashley Carruthers, 'National Identity, Diasporic Anxiety and Music Video Culture in Vietnam', in Yao Souchou (ed.), *House of Glass: Culture, Modernity and the State in Southeast Asia*, ISEAS, Singapore, 2001.
4   To Van Lai, interview conducted by Tina Nguyen and Stuart Cunningham, Westminster, CA, May 1996.
5   Ashley Carruthers, 'National Identity, Diasporic Anxiety and Music Video Culture in Vietnam'.
6   Trang Nguyen, personal communications and research notes, June 1997.
7   Ashley Carruthers, 'National Identity, Diasporic Anxiety and Music Video Culture in Vietnam'.
8   ibid.
9   ibid.
10 Kolar-Panov, *Video, War and the Diasporic Imagination*.

11 Pham Duy, *Musics of Vietnam*, 1973, p. 118.
12 Terry Rambo, 'Black Flight Suits and White *Ao-dais*: Borrowing and Adaptation of Symbols of Vietnamese Cultural Identity', in Truong Buu Lam (ed.), *Borrowings and Adaptations in Vietnamese Culture*, South East Asia Paper No. 25, Centre for South East Asian Studies, School of Hawaiian, Asian and Pacific Studies, University of Hawaii at Manoa, 1987.
13 Ashley Carruthers, 'National Identity, Diasporic Anxiety and Music Video Culture in Vietnam'.
14 Graeme Turner, *Making It National: Nationalism and Australian Popular Culture*, Allen & Unwin, St Leonards, 1994, pp. 124–5 (internal quotes Stuart Hall, 'Culture, Community, Nation', *Cultural Studies*, vol. 7, no. 3, 1993).
15 Trang Nguyen, personal communications and research notes, June 1997.

Part 4

Introduction

1 Tony Bennett, *Culture: A Reformer's Science*, Allen & Unwin, St Leonards, 1998.
2 Jim McGuigan, *Rethinking Cultural Policy*, Open University Press, Buckingham, 2004; Justin Lewis and Toby Miller (eds), *Critical Cultural Policy Studies: A Reader*, Blackwell, Malden, MA, 2003; Toby Miller and George Yúdice, *Cultural Policy*, Sage Publications, London and Thousand Oaks, 2002; George Yúdice, *The Expediency of Culture: Uses of Culture in the Global Era*, Duke University Press, Durham, 2003.

Chapter 10 Cultural studies from the viewpoint of cultural policy

1 Meaghan Morris, 'Banality in Cultural Studies', in Patricia Mellencamp (ed.), *Logics of Television*, British Film Institute, London, 1990.
2 John Kelly, 'Iron lady in a nanny's uniform', *Times Higher Education Supplement*, 9 December 1988.
3 See, for example, the British journal *Screen*'s new editorial policy debate in vol. 31, no. 1 and Richard Collins, *Television: Policy and Culture*, Unwin Hyman, London, 1990.
4 See Manuel Alvarado and John O. Thompson (eds), *The Media Reader*, British Film Institute, London, 1990. See also Fred Inglis, *Media Theory: An Introduction*, Blackwell, Oxford, 1990.
5 Elizabeth Jacka, 'Australian Cinema – An Anachronism in the '80s?', in Susan Dermody and Elizabeth Jacka (eds), *The Imaginary Industry: Australian Film in the Late '80s*, Australian Film, Television and Radio School, Sydney, 1988, p. 118.
6 For discussion, see Stuart Cunningham, 'Figuring the Australian Factor', *Culture and Policy*, vol. 2, no. 1, 1990.
7 Julie James-Bailey, 'Communicating with the decision makers: the role of research, scholarship and teaching in film and media studies', staff seminar, Griffith University, 20 October 1989.
8 John Docker, 'Popular culture versus the state: an argument against Australian content regulation for TV', unpublished attachment to Federation of Australian Commercial Television Stations (FACTS) submission to ABT Inquiry into Australian Content on Commercial Television, 16 August 1988 (Document D020B, ABT Inquiry File). A shorter version is published as 'Popular culture versus the state: an argument against Australian content regulations for TV', *Media Information Australia*, vol. 59, 1991. For further discussion, see Stuart Cunningham, Jennifer Craik, Tony Bennett and Ian Hunter, 'Responses to Docker', *Media Information Australia*, vol. 59, 1991.
9 Graeme Turner, '"It Works for Me": British Cultural Studies, Australian Cultural Studies, Australian Film', in L. Grossberg et al. (eds), *Cultural Studies*, Routledge, New York, 1992.

10   Industries Assistance Commission, *International Trade and Services*, Report no. 418, AGPS, 30 June 1989, p. 202.
11   Graham Shirley and Brian Adams, *Australian Cinema: The First Eighty Years*, Angus & Robertson/Currency Press, Sydney, 1983; Albert Moran, *Images and Industry: Television Drama Production in Australia*, Currency Press, Sydney, 1985.
12   Phillip Lynch, 'Advance Australia', *Bulletin*, 2 February 1982.
13   Gary Sturgess, 'The Emerging New Nationalism', *Bulletin*, 2 February 1982.
14   Stephen Alomes, *A Nation at Last? The Changing Character of Australian Nationalism 1880–1988*, Angus & Robertson/Currency Press, Sydney, 1983; Albert Moran, '"Peculiarly Australian" – The Political Construction of Cultural Identity', in Sol Encel and Lois Bryson (eds), *Australian Society*, 4th edn, Longman Cheshire, Melbourne, 1984; Noel King and Tim Rowse, '"Typical Aussies": Television and Populism in Australia', *Framework*, vol. 22–3 (Autumn 1983).
15   Kathy Myers, *Understains – The Sense and Seduction of Advertising*, Comedia Publishing Group, London, 1986.
16   William Leiss, Stephen Kline and Sut Jhally, *Advertising as Social Communication: Persons, Products and Images of Well-Being*, Methuen, Toronto, 1986.
17   John Fiske, *Reading the Popular*, Unwin Hyman, Boston, 1989, p. 179.
18   Christopher Ham and Michael Hill, *The Policy Process in the Modern Capitalist State*, Harvester Press, Brighton, 1984.
19   Donald Home, *Think – or Perish! Towards a Confident and Productive Australia*, Occasional Paper no. 8, Commission for the Future, June 1988; and *The Public Culture*, Pluto Press, Sydney, 1986.
20   Graham Murdock and Peter Golding, 'Information Poverty and Political Inequality: Citizenship in the Age of Privatised Communications', *Journal of Communication*, vol. 39, no. 3, Summer 1989, pp. 180–95.
21   Aramand Mattelart, Xavier Delcourt and Michele Mattelart, *International Image Markets*, Comedia, London, 1984.
22   For example, Toby Miller, 'Film and Media Citizenship', *Filmnews*, February 1990; Trevor Barr, 'Reflections on Media Education: The Myths and Realities', *Metro Media and Education Magazine*, vol. 82, Autumn 1990; Tony Bennett, 'Putting Policy into Cultural Studies', in L. Grossberg et al. (eds), *Cultural Studies*, Routledge, New York, 1992.
23   Geoff Hurd and Ian Connell, 'Cultural Education: A Revised Program', *Media Information Australia*, vol. 53, August 1989, pp. 23–30.
24   Trevor Barr, 'Reflections on Media Education', p. 16.
25   *Windows onto Worlds: Studying Australia at Tertiary Level*, AGPS, Canberra, 1987, p. 18.

Chapter 11 Re-framing culture

1   Jennifer Craik, 'One Flew Out of the Cuckoo's Nest', *Filmnews*, November 1992, p. 20.
2   Meaghan Morris, 'Theorising Pragmatism', *Australian Left Review*, September 1992, pp. 38–40.
3   Anthony May, 'The Magnetics of Policy: Stuart Cunningham's *Framing Culture*', *New Researcher*, nos 1/2, 1992, pp. 116–21.
4   Gay Hawkins, 'Suiting the Critics', *Australian Left Review*, September 1992, pp. 40–2.
5   See Boris Frankel, *From the Deserts Prophets Come: The Struggle to Reshape Australian Political Culture*, Arena Publishing, North Carlton, 1992; Chris Healy, 'It Doesn't Matter If It's True, Is It Useful?', *Australian Book Review*, September 1992, pp. 24–5; Bronwen Levy, 'Ruffling the Feathers of the Cultural Polity', *Meanjin*, vol. 51, no. 3, 1992, pp. 552–5; David McKie and Michael Bennett, 'Chaos, Cultural Studies and Cosmology', *Meanjin*, vol. 51, no. 4, Summer 1992, pp. 785–94.
6   MacKenzie Wark, 'After Literature: Culture, Policy, Theory, and Beyond', *Meanjin*, vol. 51, no. 4, Summer 1992, p. 677.

7   Stuart Cunningham, 'The Cultural Policy Debate Revisited', *Meanjin*, vol. 51, no. 3, 1992, pp. 533–42.
8   Michael Pusey, *Economic Rationalism in Canberra: A Nation-Building State Changes Its Mind*, Cambridge University Press, Melbourne, 1991.
9   John Frow, 'Rationalisation and the Public Sphere', *Meanjin*, vol. 51, no. 3, 1992, p. 506.
10 Hester Eisenstein, *Gender Shock: Practising Feminism on Two Continents*, Allen & Unwin, Sydney, 1991, p. 33.
11 Boris Frankel, *From the Deserts Prophets Come*.
12 John Hartley, 'Popular Reality: A (Hair)Brush with Cultural Studies', *Continuum*, vol. 4, no. 2, 1991, p. 11.
13 Toby Miller, 'Culture with Power: The Present Moment in Cultural Policy Studies', *South East Asian Journal of Social Sciences*, vol. 22, 1994, pp. 264–82.
14 Meaghan Morris, 'A Gadfly Bites Back', *Meanjin*, vol. 51, no. 3, 1992, p. 526.
15 Tim Rowse, 'Searching for Cultural Connections: A Review of *Framing Culture*', *Media Information Australia*, no. 68, May 1993, pp. 100–5.

Part 5

Introduction

1   Jeremy Rifkin, *The Age of Access: How the Shift from Ownership to Access Is Transforming Modern Life*, London, Penguin, 2000.

Chapter 12 The creative industries after cultural policy

1   Marion Jacka, *Broadband Media in Australia: Tales from the Frontier*, Australian Film Commission, Australian Key Centre for Cultural and Media Policy, and Creative Industries Research and Applications Centre, Sydney, 2001.
2   Stuart Cunningham, 'Policies and Strategies', in K. Harley (ed.), 'Australian Content in New Media: Seminar Proceedings', Network Insight, RMIT, Sydney, 2002, pp. 39–42.
3   John Howkins, *The Creative Economy: How People Make Money From Ideas*, Allen Lane, London, 2001.
4   See Stuart Cunningham, 'From Cultural to Creative Industries: Theory, Industry, and Policy Implications', *Media Information Australia Incorporating Culture & Policy*, no. 102, February 2002, pp. 54–65; and Tom O'Regan, *Cultural Policy: Rejuvenate or Wither?*, Griffith University Professorial Lecture, 2001 <http://www.gu.edu.au/centre/cmp/mcr1publications.html#tom>.
5   Damien Tambini, 'The New Public Interest', Australian Broadcasting Authority Conference, Canberra, May 2002.
6   See: Ben Goldsmith, Julian Thomas, Tom O'Regan and Stuart Cunningham, *The Future for Local Content? Options for Emerging Technologies*, Australian Broadcasting Authority, Queen Victoria Building, NSW, June 2001; and Ben Goldsmith, Julian Thomas, Tom O'Regan and Stuart Cunningham, 'Asserting Cultural and Social Regulatory Principles in Converging Media Systems', in Marc Raboy (ed.), *Global Media Policy in the New Millennium*, University of Luton Press, London, 2002.
7   Brian Arthur, 'Increasing Returns and the New World of Business', in J. Seely Brown (ed.), *Seeing Differently: Insights on Innovation*, Harvard Business Review Books, Boston, 1997, pp. 3–18; Paul Romer, 'The Origins of Endogenous Growth', *Journal of Economic Perspectives*, vol. 8, no. 1, Winter 1994, pp. 3–22; and Paul Romer, interview with Peter Robinson, *Forbes*, vol. 155, no. 12, 1995, pp. 66–70.
8   Australian Labor Party, *An Agenda for the Knowledge Nation: Report of the Knowledge Nation Task Force*, Canberra, Chifley Research Centre, 2001 <http://www.alp.org.au/download.html?filename=federal/repoprts/kn_report_020701.pdf>; Department of Information and

the Information Economy, *R&D Strategy Paper*, 2002 <www.iie.qld.gov.au/research/strategy.html>; *Developing National Research Priorities: An Issues Paper* <http://www.dest.gov.au/sectors/research_sector/publications_resources/national_research_priorities/>.
9   Organisation for Economic Co-operation and Development (OECD), *Content as a New Growth Industry*, OECD, Paris, 1998.
10 Creative Industries Task Force (CITF), 2001 <http://www.culture.gov.uk/creative/mapping.html>.
11 Jeremy Rifkin, *The Age of Access: the New Culture of Hypercapitalism, where All of Life is a Paid-For Experience*, JP Tarcher/Putnam, New York, 2000.
12 John Howkins, *The Creative Economy: How People Make Money from Creative Ideas*, Allen Lane, London, 2001.
13 Scott Lash and John Urry, *Economies of Signs and Space*, Sage, London, 1994.
14 Rifkin, *The Age of Access*.
15 ibid., p. 52.
16 Greg Hearn, Tom Mandeville and D. Anthony, *The Communication Superhighway: Social and Economic Change in the Digital Age*, Allen & Unwin, Sydney, 1998.
17 C. P. (Charles Percy) Snow, *The Two Cultures and the Scientific Revolution*, Cambridge University Press, Cambridge, 1959.

Chapter 13 What price a creative economy?

1   Richard E. Caves, *Creative Industries: Contracts between Art and Commerce*, Harvard University Press, Cambridge, Mass., 2000.
2   John Holden, *Capturing Cultural Value: How Culture Has Become a Tool of Government Policy*, Demos, London, 2004, available at <http://www.demos.co.uk/catalogue/culturalvalue/>, accessed 10 April 2006.
3   For an excellent short overview, see Terry Flew, *New Media: An Introduction*, Oxford University Press, Oxford, 2002, ch. 6. A more detailed introduction is provided by John Hartley (ed.), *Creative Industries*, Blackwell Publishing, Malden, MA, 2005.
4   It is probable, however, that the term was originally used in Australia in 1994 by Terry Cutler and Roger Buckeridge, *Commerce in Content: Building Australia's International Future in Interactive Multimedia Markets*, a report for the Department of Industry, Science and Technology, CSIRO and the Broadband Services Expert Group, Department of Industry, Science and Technology, Canberra, available at <http://www.nla.gov.au/misc/cutler/cutlercp.html>, accessed 10 April 2006.
5   See <http://www.culture.gov.uk>, accessed 10 April 2006.
6   For a fuller account, see Stuart Cunningham, 'The Humanities, Creative Arts and International Innovation Agendas', in Jane Kenway, Elizabeth Bullen and Simon Robb, *Innovation and Tradition: The Arts, Humanities and the Knowledge Economy*, Peter Lang, New York, 2004, pp. 113–24.
7   See <www.mct.go.kr/english/section/vision>, accessed 10 April 2006, and *The Third Master Plan for Informatization, 2002–2006*, Ministry of Information and Communication, Korea, 2006.
8   See Dooboo Shim, 'Hybridity and the Korean Wave', *Media, Culture and Society*, vol. 28.1, 2006, pp. 25–54.
9   For a summary of Taiwan's creative industry policy, see *Challenge 2008: The Six-Year National Development Plan*, available at <http://www.gio.gov.tw/taiwan-website/4-oa/20020521/2002052101.html>, accessed 10 April 2006. See also Tsai Wen-ting, 'Cultural and Creative Industries: Wedding Commerce with Culture', *Sinorama*, no. 4, 2004, p. 6.
10 *Baseline Study on Hong Kong's Creative Industries*, Centre for Cultural Policy Research, University of Hong Kong, 2003; and Hong Kong Trade Development Council, *Creative Industries in Hong Kong*, 2002, available at <http://www.tdctrade.com/econforum/tdc/tdc020902.htm>, accessed 10 April 2006.

NOTES

11 For an overview of Singapore's policies and links to a number of key policy documents, see <http://www.mica.gov.sg/mica_business/b_creative.html>, accessed 10 April 2006.
12 For an overview of New Zealand's policies, see 'Developing Creative Industries in New Zealand', available at <http://www.nzte.govt.nz/section/11756.aspx#overview> and <http://www.nzte.govt.nz/common/files/ses-creative05.pdf>, accessed 10 April 2006.
13 See, for example, Nicholas Garnham, 'From Cultural to Creative Industries: An Analysis of the Implications of the "Creative Industries" Approach to Arts and Media Policy Making in the United Kingdom', *International Journal of Cultural Policy*, vol. 11, 2005, pp. 15–29.
14 See <http://www.gov.cn/english/2005-11/26/content_109854.htm>, accessed 10 April 2006.
15 See J. O'Connor, 'A New Modernity? The Arrival of "Creative Industries" in China', and D. Hui, 'From Cultural to Creative Industries – Strategies for Chaoyang District, Beijing', *International Journal of Cultural Studies*, vol. 9.3, 2006.
16 See <www.cep.culture.gov.uk>, accessed 10 April 2006.
17 See UK Creative Industries Minister James Purnell, 4 November 2005, available at <www.culture.gov.uk/global/press_notices/archive_2005/147_05.htm>, accessed 10 April 2006.
18 See <www.sdi.qld.gov.au/dsdweb/v3/guis/templates/content/gui_cue_cntnhtml.cfm?id=2223>, accessed 10 April 2006.
19 See Cutler and Company, *Commerce in content : building Australia's international future in interactive multimedia markets : a report for the Department of Industry, Science and Technology, CSIRO, and the Broadband Services Expert Group*, Department of Communications, Information Technology and the Arts, Canberra, 1994; Coopers & Lybrand, Multimedia Industry Group report, *Excellence in Content: The Focus for Australian Investment in Multimedia Content*, Sydney, June 1995; *Networking Australia's Future: The Final Report of the Broadband Services Expert Group*, Australian Government Publishing Service, Canberra, 1995; *Creative Nation: Commonwealth Cultural Policy*, Department of Communications, Information Technology and the Arts, Canberra, 1994.
20 For a detailed account of this history, see Tom O'Regan and Mark David Ryan, 'From Multimedia to Digital Content and Applications: Remaking Policy for the Digital Content Industries', *Media International Australia incorporating Culture & Policy*, no. 112, 2005, pp. 28–49.
21 Creative Industries Cluster Study, Department of Communications, Information Technology and the Arts (DCITA), Canberra, 2004, available at <www.cultureandrecreaton.gov.au/cics/>; Digital Content Industry Action Agenda, available at <http://www.dcita.gov.au/arts/film_digital/digital_content_industry_action_agenda>; Prime Minister's Science, Engineering and Innovation Council (PMSEIC) Working Group, *The Role of Creativity in the Innovation Economy*, 2005, available at <http://www.dest.gov.au/NR/rdonlyres/B1EF82EF-08D5-427E-B7E4-69D41C61D495/8625/finalPMSEICReport_WEBversion.pdf>, accessed 10 April 2006.
22 *Creativity Is Big Business: A Framework for the Future*, Department of State Development, Trade and Innovation, available at: <http://www.sdi.qld.gov.au/dsdweb/v3/documents/objdirctrled/nonsecure/pdf/2698.pdf>, accessed 10 April 2006.
23 See <http://www.ozco.gov.au/news_and_hot_topics/news/creative_innovation/files/3375/CIS%20public%20FINAL.pdf>, accessed 8 May 2006.
24 See also Stuart Cunningham, 'Match Seller or Sparkplug? The Human Sciences and Business', *B-HERT (Business–Higher Education Round Table) News*, issue 22, July 2005, pp. 8–10.
25 John Howkins, *The Creative Economy: How People Make Money from Ideas*, Penguin, Harmondsworth, 2001, p. 85.
26 Richard Florida, *The Rise of the Creative Class: And How It's Transforming Work, Leisure, Community and Everyday Life*, Basic Books, New York, 2002.
27 See Terry Cutler's foreword to the Australian edition of Richard Florida's *Rise of the Creative Class*, Pluto Press, North Melbourne, 2002, pp. vii–xi.

28. See 'How big are the Creative Industries in Australia? The interim findings' and 'Taking the ruler to the Creative Industries: How, why and to what effect', at <wiki.cci.edu.au/confluence>. See also P. Higgs and others, *The Ecology of Queensland Design*, CIRAC, QUT, 2005, available at <http://eprints.qut.edu.au/archive/00002410/>, accessed 10 April 2006, and CIRAC and SGS Economics and Planning, *Mapping Queensland's Creative Industries: Economic Fundamentals*, CIRAC, QUT, 2005, available at <http://eprints.qut.edu.au/archive/00002425/>, accessed 10 April 2006.
29. See <http://cultureandrecreation.gov.au/cics/>, accessed 10 April 2006.
30. See the survey in Margaret Bruce and Lucy Daly, *International Evidence on Design: Near Final Report for the DTI*, Manchester Business School, University of Manchester, 2005.
31. David Throsby, *Economics and Culture*, Cambridge University Press, Cambridge, 2001, p. 112.
32. David Throsby, *Does Australia Need a Cultural Policy?*, Platform Paper No. 7, Currency House, Sydney, 2006, p. 39.
33. The ABC secured an additional $88 million over three years in the 2006 budget for Australian and digital content production. This will contribute to its ability to innovate.
34. 'The End of Serious Journalism?', in Jonathan Mills (ed.), *Barons to Bloggers: Confronting Media Power*, The Alfred Deakin Debate, vol. 1, Miegunyah Press, Melbourne, 2005, p. 67.
35. See <http://www.carnegie.org/reporter/10/news/index.html>, accessed 10 April 2006.
36. Richard Caves, *Creative Industries*, pp. 2ff.
37. Arthur De Vany in his *Hollywood Economics: How Extreme Uncertainty Shapes the Film Industry*, Routledge, London & New York, 2004.
38. J. Stanley Metcalfe, *Evolutionary Economics and Creative Destruction*, Routledge, London & New York, 1998; B. J. Loasby, *Knowledge, Institutions and Evolution in Economics*, Routledge, London & New York, 1999; Jason Potts, *The New Evolutionary Microeconomics: Complexity, Competence and Adaptive Behaviour*, Edward Elgar Publishing, London, 2000.
39. See J. Stanley Metcalfe and Ian Miles (eds), *Innovation Systems in the Service Economy: Measurement and Case Study Analysis*, Kluwer Academic, Boston, 2000; and Mark Boden and Ian Miles (eds), *Services and the Knowledge-Based Economy*, Continuum, London & New York, 2000.
40. See <http://www.mmu.ac.uk/h-ss/mipc/foci/mission.htm>, accessed 10 April 2006.
41. CIRAC, QUT and Cutler & Co., *Research and Innovation Systems in the Production of Digital Content*, Report for the National Office for the Information Economy, September 2003, available at <http://www.cultureandrecreation.gov.au/cics/Research_and_innovation_systems in_production_of_digital_content.pdf>, accessed 10 April 2006, and CIRAC, QUT and Cutler & Co., *Research and Innovation Systems in the Production of Digital Content and Applications*, Creative Industries Cluster Study, vol. 3, DCITA, Canberra, 2004, pp. 9–67. A summary version was published as Stuart Cunningham and others, 'From "Culture" to "Knowledge": An Innovation Systems Approach to the Content Industries', in Caroline Andrew and others (eds), *Accounting for Culture: Thinking through Cultural Citizenship*, University of Ottawa Press, Ottawa, 2005, pp. 104–23.
42. See John Holden, *Capturing Cultural Value: How Culture Has Become a Tool of Government Policy*, Demos, London, 2005, and *Cultural Value and the Crisis of Legitimacy: Why Culture Needs a Democratic Mandate*, Demos, London, 2006, available at <http://www.demos.co.uk/catalogue/culturallegitimacy/>, accessed 10 April 2006.
43. George Steiner, *Language and Silence: Essays 1958–1966*, Penguin Books, Harmondsworth, 1969; John Carey, *What Good Are the Arts?*, Faber & Faber, London, 2005.
44. Richard Florida, *Rise of the Creative Class*, ch. 17.

Index

Adams, Brian, 11, 32
Adams, Phillip, 99, 120
adaptation to environment, white people and, 12–13
administrative law, 208–9
Adorno, Theodore, 212
Adventures of Barry McKenzie, The, 65
advertising, 188–92
advocacy, xxv–xxvi, 195, 207
Against the Wind, 73, 84, 86
Age of Access (Rifkin), 225
Alien Years, The, 74, 85
All the Way, 74, 84, 91
Allen, Robert, 25–6, 30
Alvin Purple, 65
Anderson, Benedict, 51
animation industry,
    Flash software and, 253
    Korea, 235
anti-Vietnam War protests, 208
Anzacs, 74, 84, 85
Apollonius and Dionysus in the Antipodes, 50–60
Armstrong, Gillian, 2
art cinema, 61, 111
    1960s, 18
arts,
    myth of subsidies, 232
    value of, 242, 264–5
    workers and skills, xxxv, 243–8, 255–6, 261, 263
ASIA Productions, 165, 167, 176
Asia TV, 126, 138–42
'Asianisation', 140
audience fragmentation across media industries, 213–14
audio-visual industry, export potential, 142, 145
    see also, content creation; creative industries
Australia Council, 240–1, 251
Australia Television, 72, 128, 139–42
    government pressures on, 139–40
Australian Broadcasting Corporation (ABC), xxxviii, 71, 126
    Australia television in Asia, 138–42
    government pressures on, 139
    nation building role, 126
    role of in new economy, 251–2
Australian Broadcasting Tribunal, 187–8, 213
Australian Centre for the Moving Image, xxiv
Australian cinema,

Chauvel and, 34–49
histories of, 30–4
imperialism and, 4–5, 19,32–4
innovative, 10–17
Second World, 33–4, 51–2
television market and, 123
    see also Australian film industry
Australian Labor Party (ALP), 223–4
Australian literature, xxiii–xxiv, 84
Australian Research Council (ARC) Centre of Excellence for Creative Industries and Innovation, 245, 259–60, 261
Australian television,
advertising and national culture, 188–92
benefits and drawbacks of internationalisation, 142–6
case studies of international successes and failures, 128–42
content rules, 187–8
international markets and, 122–46
mini-series exports, 122
modernity and, 125
post-colonial cultures and, 124–6
production costs, 123
Australia-United States Free Trade Agreement, 251

Babe films, 70
Back of Beyond, 12–14
Bangkok Hilton, 144
Barr, Charles, 95
Barthes, Roland, 144, 190, 193
Bastard Boys, 71–2
Baxter, John, 30, 36, 38, 39
Beecher, Eric, 194, 254
Bellamy, 96
Bennett, Tony, 183, 184
Beyond 2000, 135
Bhangra music, 158
Bich Chieu, 175
Bildungsroman model, 80–3
Birdsville Track mailman, 12–13
Bishop, Julie, xxiii
Bitter Spring, 12, 19
Blair government, 234
Bligh, Captain William, 55–6
Blundell, Graeme, 114
Bodyline, 74, 78, 79, 80, 83, 85, 94, 97, 103, 104, 107–10
Bollywood, 158
Bordwell, David, 26, 29, 44–5
Bradman, Don, 78, 107–10

287

INDEX

Breaking of the Drought, The, 36
Brides of Christ, 128
Bridgstock, Ruth, xxxviii
Britain
    communications law reform, 221
    creative industry revival, 236, 237–8
    Creative Industries Taskforce, 234–5, 258
British Broadcasting Corporation
    (BBC), 127–8, 131, 253
British documentary movement, 10–11, 28
British film industry, 6–7
British television, 125–6, 127–8, 131, 253
broadband communications, future of television and, 220–1
Broadband Services Expert Group, 238
broadcasting
    British, 125–6, 127–8, 131, 253
    commercial, 187–92, 205, 213, 250–1, 263
    public, xxvi, 145–6, 250–1
    see also, Australian Broadcasting Corporation (ABC); Australian television;
bureaucratic reform
    cultural policy and studies and, 208–10
    feminist critique and, 192–3, 195
    social democrats and, 197, 209
Buscombe, Edward, 26, 29

Capitalism, Socialism and Democracy (Schumpeter), xxxiv–xxxv
Captain James Cook, 74, 84, 91
Captain Thunderbolt, 12
Captives of Care, 100
Carruthers, Ashley, 166, 169, 176
Caswell, Robert, 89, 97
Caughie, John, 81, 107, 125
Caves, Richard E. 232, 254, 257, 259
Challenge, The, 81, 84, 91
Chauvel, Charles, xxv, 2, 7–10, 12, 16, 25–49
    biographical "legend" of, 43, 44–5
    how his works and been classified, 34–42
    melodrama and nationality, 45–9
    Pacific peoples, dystopia and, 52, 55–60
    phases of his career, 42–4
    travelogue-drama, 50, 52–60
Chauvel, Elsa, 37–8, 43, 52, 53
Chauvel, Susanne, 53
China, 236–7
Chinese communities
    popular cultures in, 158–9
    sub groupings in, 155
cinema revival, xxi, 2, 61–4
Cinesound, 6, 8, 32, 46
citizen journalism, 253
citizenship, cultural policy and knowledge, 196–7
civil societies, 152
    ethno-specific sphericules and, 156–7156–7

Clarke, Edith, 103, 109–10
Clean Machine, The, 94, 102
colonialism and film industry, xxvi, 1–2, 5–10
    Australian innovation, 1940s–50s, 10–17
    Australians in the Pacific, 50–60
    Chauvel and, 39–41, 58–60
    Hurley and, 52–5
    Sylvia Lawson on, 32
    Tulloch on, 32–3
Commerce in Content, Excellence in Content, 238
commercial broadcasters,
    advertising, 188–92, 205
    Australian content, 187–8, 213
    content rules 187–8
    protection of, 250–1
commercials, 18–19, 188–92
content creation,
    Australian Council strategy, 240–1
    Australian versus foreign, 186–92, 213
    Britain, 221
    broadcasters and, 263
    media format convergence and, 220–3, 263
    policy development, 218–20, 261–2
    regulation and new forms of entertainment culture, 216–17, 221–2
    size of industry, 220
convergence, 220–3, 250–1, 263
cool Britannia, 235
Coombs, H.C. 197
Cooper, Ross, 22, 54
cosmopolitanism, nationalism and, 157
Country Practice, A, 129, 143
Cowra Breakout, 74, 77, 78, 79, 80, 81, 85, 88, 94, 102, 110–12
Crawfords, xxxvii, 138
creative class, xxxix, 243–4
creative destruction, xxxv
Creative Digital Industries in Australia, 245
creative economy, xxxiv
    Australian policy developments, 238–41
    Australian policy ideas, 261–4
    cultural identity and social empowerment, 242–3
    international recognition and developments in, 233–8
    measuring and valuing, 242–8, 260
creative industries, xxxi–xxxv, 233–4
    cultural policy and, 218–30
    economic innovatory thinking and, 254–60
    employment skills and, xxxiv, xxxv, 243–8, 263–4
    mapping, 245
    policy development for, 215–17
    research and development in, 222–9
    skills taught and valued, xxxv–xxxix, 232–3
    valuing and expanding, 242–8
    United Kingdom, 234

INDEX

Creative Industries Cluster Study, 239
Creative Industries Taskforce (UK), 234–5, 258
creative innovation, Australia Council strategy, 240–1
creative production, 225, 254–5
creativity, 241, 260–1
creativity index, 243–4
Croatian video, 156, 171
Crocodile Dundee, 100
cross-cultural challenges, TV, 141, 143
Culotta, Nino, 22–4
cultural consumption, xxix, 153, 225–6, 242
  driver of innovation, 252–3
  nationalism and, 192, 217
cultural critique and policy, 187, 206–7
  feminism and, 192–3, 195, 209
  see also cultural policy
cultural imperialism, 4–5, 19, 32–3, 127, 190–1
cultural industries, 143–6, 211
  see also, arts, creative industries
cultural nationalism, xxvi
  Chauvel, 38, 40–2, 45–9
  creative industries and, 215–17
  cultural studies curricula and, 199, 205
  international TV sales and 143–4
  mini-series and, 79, 91
  1970–80s films, 62–4
  Vietnam and, 114–15
  Vietnamese, 168–73
  world trade rules and, 219–20
cultural negotiation, Chinese-Vietnamese, 173–6
cultural policy, 183
  ABC and, 252
  citizenship, knowledge and, 196–7
  content regulation as, 213, 219–20
  cultural critique and, 187, 195–201
  curricula and, 199, 205–6
  economics of, 248–52
  feminism and reform, 192–3, 195, 209
  industry policy and, 211, 217, 248–52, 261–4
  international perspectives and debate, 184
  media ownership and, 192–3
  pay television, 213
  political realignments, 185–7
cultural studies
  and cultural policy, 183, 185–201, 205
  as interdiscipline, 147–8
  Australianising, 199–200
  British model, 199–200
  critique and development of policy, 2–5–14
  developing curricula with policy as focus, 198–200
  left-right continuum and, 185
  political and cultural power, 194–201

citizenship and activism, 208–9
cultural understanding, television and, 143
Current TV, 253
Cutler & Company, 239, 261

Dad and Dave series, 7
Dawkins, Richard, 2
De Vany, Arthur, 257
Dead Calm, 94
Death of a Princess, 83
dependency theory, 33–4
deregulation, 213
  convergence and, 221–2, 251
Dermody, Susan, 32
design, 260
diasporas
  and media use, 147–8, 154–60
  homeland and, 168–73
  nationalism and, 157
  Vietnamese and music video, 161–82
Diggers in Blighty, 7
digital storytelling, 253
digital television, 220–1
Dirtwater Dynasty, 74, 85, 89, 94, 100, 103, 104, 113, 116–21
Dismissal, The, 72, 74, 76, 78, 79, 80, 81, 94, 97
  getting it on, 103–4
  way of telling a complex story, 81, 84, 86, 87–8, 102, 103–7, 118
DIY cultures, xxx, 253
Docker, John, 188
documentaries, 18
  see also, British documentary movement
documentary-dramas, 81, 83–92
Don's Party, 114
Donavan, Jason, 143
Dreyer, Carl-Theodor, 44–5
Duigan, John, 63, 94, 97, 98
Dunera Boys, The, 74, 85
Dunn, Michael, 86–7
Duy Quang, 175
Dyer, Richard, 65, 66

Ealing Studios, 11, 14–15, 19, 95
economic values, capturing, 241–2
economics, xxvi
  creative industries, valuing and expanding, 243–8
  cultural, shifting rationale for, 248–52
  emerging varieties of, 256–60
  seismic shift in drivers of, 254–5
Economics and Culture (Throsby), 249
education services, export of, 142, 231, 261
electronic games, 217
Ellis, John, 95, 115
Elsaesser, Thomas, 14

employment
    creative, importance of to the
        economy, xxxvii, 243–8
    enhancing and encouraging in creative
        industry, 263–4
    incomes, 247–8
    precarious, xxxiv, xxxvi
enlightenment values, questioning, 186–7, 209–10
enterprise xxxiv
    and the state, xxxvii, 208–9, 261–4
    creative economy and, 254–60
Eureka Stockade, 12, 15, 19
Eureka Stockade (mini-series), 74, 78, 81, 84
evolutionary economics, 257–9
experimentation, 1940s–50s, 12
exports, creative sector, 231–2, 262–3

fandom, 185
Fanon, Franz, 28, 51
Far East, 62, 63
Farewell Saigon, 165, 170–3
feminist cultural theory
    bureaucratic reform and, 192–3, 195, 209
Film Australia, xxvii
Finnane, Francine, 97, 103
Fiske, John, xxx
    bardic function of TV, 105
    resistance and change, 196
Flash software, 253
Florida, Richard, 243–5, 265
Flying Doctors, 72, 128, 129, 135–8, 143
For the Term of His Natural Life, 84
Forgotten Cinema, 30
Fortunate Life, A, 74, 76, 78–9, 84
Forty Thousand Horsemen, 12, 37
40,000 Years of Dreaming, 70
fragmentation
    of audiences, 213–14
    of cultures, 152, 153
Fragments of War, 94
Framing Culture (Cunningham), xxxi, 183, 203–4
    critiques of, 205–14
From the Prophets Deserts Come (Frankel), 210–12
frontier society, 12–13
Frow, John, xxvii
future culture, 254–5

Garnham, Nicholas, xxx, xxxi, xxxii, 150
Gaumont-British, 7
Gauntlett, David, xxxix
German expressionism, 28
Getting of Wisdom, The, 77, 78
Gia Biet Saigon, 165, 170–3
Gibbs, Barbara, 97, 103

Gibson, Ross, 12–13
Gitlin, Todd, 152, 153
globalisation, 204, 214, 219–20, 251
graduates, with skills in creative
    industries, xxxv–xxxix, 261, 263
Gramsci, Antonio, 28
Greater Union, 6, 11, 18
Greenhide, 46
Grundy Productions, 127

Habermas, Jurgen 149–51, 214
habitus, 160
Hall, Ken, 8, 11, 16
Hall, Stuart, 186
Hammer Productions, 95
Happy Feet, 70
Hard Road to Renewal (Hall), 186
Hartley, John,
    bardic function of TV, 105
    civil societies and counterpublics, 152, 153
    cultural studies and activists, 212
    mediasphere, 150–1, 152
    political economy of consumption, xxx
    teaching, xxxvi
    valuing popular culture, xxv
Hawks, Howard, 17
Hayes, Terry, 88, 97–8, 101, 102
    Dirtwater Dynasty and classic
        storytelling, 116–18
Hayseeds, 7
Heatwave, 64
Heritage, 7, 8
Heyer, John, 12
Hill, John, 36–7, 39
His Royal Highness, 7
Ho Chi Minh, 169
Ho, Don, 177, 180
Hogan, Paul, 100
Holden, John, 232–3, 264
Hollywood,
    Australian revival and commercial
        filmmaking, 61–8
    dominant by 1930s, 6
    film history and, 29–30
Home and Away, 122, 129–31, 143
homeland and diaspora, 168–73
Hong Kong cinema, 158
Hopkins, Harold, 120
Horkheimer, Max, 212
Horne, Donald, 197
Hound of the Deep, The, 50
Howkins, John, 220, 225, 227, 241–2
Hoyts, 18
Hurley, Frank, xxv, 2, 50, 52–5
hybridity, 124, 148
    new wave assertive, 177–81
    Vietnamese video, 161–82

290

INDEX

immigration, from Vietnam, 181–2
import cultures, 204
In the Grip of the Polar Pack Ice, 50
In the Wake of the Bounty, 7, 8, 38, 42, 46, 50, 52, 55–60
Indian popular culture, 158–9
Indigenous peoples,
    Australia as interesting because of, 124–5
    counterpublics, 152
    first and second world dominance and, 51
industry model, exports and, 142–6, 231
industry policy, 211–12, 217
    broadcasting, 145–6, 250–1
    content industries and research and development, 222–9, 261–4
    see also, creative industries; cultural policy
information and communications technology (ICT), 235–6, 242
information society, xxxi–xxxii
innovation,
    as driver of economy, 254–60, 264–5
    Australia Council statement, 240–1
    Australian creative industries, 217, 218, 239, 261
    Australian film history, 10–17
    Australian mini-series, 103–7
    broadcasters and, 263
    drivers of, 252–6
    knowledge economy and, 223
    Vietnamese popular music, 175
Iranian video, 156, 163
Irishman, The, 77
It Isn't Done, 8–10
Italian neo-realism, 28
ITV, 127, 129

Jacka, Liz, 72, 122–43, 187
James-Bailey, Julie, 188
Japanese voices, in *Cowra Breakout*, 110–13
Jardine, Douglas, 78, 108–10
Jedda, 12, 115
Jhally, Sut, 192, 193
Jungle Woman, The, 50, 52

kabuki, 105, 106
Kangaroo, 11, 19
Keating, Paul, 146
Kellaway, Cecil, 8–9
Kelly Gang, The, 32
Kelly, Paul, 76
Kennedy, Byron, 96
Kerr, Sir John, 106
Keynesianism, xxxiv
Khanh Ly, 164, 176
Kid Stakes, The, 35
Kidman, Nicole, 89, 103
King, Noel, 192

Kingsford-Smith, Charles, 78
Kline, Stephen, 192, 193
Knowledge Nation, 223–4
knowledge-based economy, 217, 218–19, 222–9
Kolar-Panov, D, 156, 158, 163, 171

Lace, 116–17
Lancaster-Miller Affair, 74, 85
Last Bastion, The, 74, 76, 77, 78, 79–80, 85, 86–7
Last Frontier, The, 89, 100, 117, 144
Last Outlaw, The, 84, 86
Lawson, Sylvia, 11, 32, 39
Leaving of Liverpool, 144
Legends of the Screen (Tulloch), 32, 39, 41–2
Leiss, William, 192, 193
libertarianism, 200
literary adaptations, 84
localism and globalism, 157, 214, 219–20
location shoots, Chauvel's commitment to, 48
Long Way From Home, A, 144
Longford, Raymond, 32, 35–6, 39, 42
Longley, Victoria, 103, 119
Lorenzo's Oil, 70
Lovers and Luggers, 7
Lucinda Brayford, 84
Luke's Kingdom, 73
Luu Bich, 174, 175

McGuigan, Jim, 151, 152, 160, 184
McKee, Alan, xxviii–xxix, 152, 153
McLelland, Diamond Jim, 114–15
McRobbie, Angela, xxxvi
Mad Max films, 62, 63–4, 70, 94, 96, 101, 103, 104, 128
Madonna, 178, 179
Magistrate, The, 144
Malone, Jackie, 133
Man from Snowy River, The, 62
Mango Tree, The, 77
mapping creative industry, 245
Mapping Queensland's Creative Industries, 245
marginalised groups, 51, 124–5, 152, 184, 186, 204
media imperialism, 4–5, 19, 32–3
media ownership and cultural power, 193–4
Melba, 74, 78, 85, 88–90, 117
melodrama, 20
    and nationality, Chauvel and, 45–9
    documentary and, 55–60
Melodramatic Imagination, The (Brooks), 47
Menzies government, 11
metropole-colony relations, 6–10, 58–60, 123
MGM, 56, 95
microeconomic reform, 232
    see also, bureaucratic reformism; economics

INDEX

Mike and Stefani, 12, 17
Miller, George, 70, 96–7, 101
Miller, Toby, xxxi, xxxiii, 184, 212
mini-series
    dramaturgy and narrative, 80–3
    hybrid form, 75
    Kennedy-Miller and, 79, 97–121
    number made in early to mid 1980s, 74
    quality television, 76–7
    style form and history in Australia, 73–93
    world market success, 122
Minogue, Kylie, 143
Moffatt, Tracy, xxv
Molloy, Bruce, 11, 39, 42
Moran, Albert, 82, 96
Morris, Meaghan, xxiv, 2, 117, 185–6, 206, 210
Moth of Moonbi, The, 46
MTM, 95
Mudrooroo, xxv
multiculturalism, xxxvi, 23–4, 144, 195
multiperspectivism, 79–80
Murdoch, Rupert, 70, 126, 254, 260
music video
    new wave assertive hybridity, 177–81
    piracy in Vietnam, 166
    Vietnamese, 155, 161–82
musicals, 2–3, 64–8
Musics of Vietnam (Pham) 170, 174
Mutiny on the Bounty, 56
My Brilliant Career, 78

Naficy, Hamid, 156, 163
Nancy Wake, 85, 89, 117
narrowcasting, ethno-specific audiences, 156
national cinemas, 27–30
nationalism,
    cosmopolitanism and ethnic diaspora, 157
    Chauvel and, 45–9, 53
    nostalgia and, 62–4
    cultural studies curricula and, 199, 205
    Hurley and, 53
    Kennedy-Miller storylines and, 79
    new Europe and, 157
    response to imperial industry, 6
    Sword of Honour and, 91
    television advertising and, 190–2
    World War II and, 10–12
Nehm, Kristina, 119
Neighbours, 72, 122, 128, 129–31
    international image of Australia and, 143
neo-Marxism, xxvi, 28, 186, 187, 196–7, 204
new wave, Vietnamese diaspora, 177–81
Newsfront, 114
Nguyen, Tina, 155, 161–82
1915, 83, 84
Noonan, Chris, 97
Now You're Talking, 30

Noyce, Phil, 97, 98
Numero Deux, 185

O'Grady, John, 22–3
O'Regan, Tom, xxii, 2, 121, 143–4
ockerism, 65
Ogilvie, George, 97, 98, 99
O'Keefe, Johnny, 88–90
On The Beach, 11, 19
Overlanders, The, 12, 14–17, 19
Papua and New Guinea, Hurley's filmmaking, 50–5
Paradise Beach, 72, 128, 132–4
Parer, Damien, 94, 114
Paris By Night series, 164–5, 168–9, 177–8
Parnell, James, 237–8
participatory cultures, 253
Passionate Industry, The, 30, 35
Patrick, 63
pay television, 213
Pearls and Savages, 50, 52–5
period film, 77, 78
Petersen, 65
Petrov Affair, 85, 86, 87–8
Pham Duy, 170, 174
Phur Lap, 62–3
Phuong, Elvis, 164, 174, 175
Picnic at Hanging Rock, 78
Pictures That Moved, 30, 35
Pike, Andrew, 11, 22, 31
    on Chauvel, 38–9
    on Hurley, 54
Pitcairn Island, 55–60
popular culture, xxi, xxiv–xxix
    semiotic resistance citizenship, 196–7, 199–200
    diaspora, 157–9
    Vietnamese, 161–82
popular music, Vietnam ,174–6
post-colonial society, 124–5
post-industrial societies, 153, 253
postmodernism, 187, 204
post-structuralism, 187
Potts, Jason, 257
power, media ownership and, 193–4
Power Without Glory, 74, 84
Prisoner: Cell Block H, 129
Prospero and Caliban (Mannoni), 51
public service broadcasting, xxx
    see also, Australian Broadcasting Corporation (ABC); broadcasting
public sphere, 149–50
    commercial media and, 150–1
    entertainment and its formation, 151–2
    fragmenting, 152, 153, 213–14
Pure Shit, 64
Pusey, Michael, 207–9

Race for the Yankee Zephyr, 63
Radio Australia, 138–9
Rafferty, Chips, 15–16, 19, 23, 50
Rats of Tobruk, 16, 37, 42
Ray, Manus, 155–6
Reade, Eric, 30, 38
Reading the Popular (Fiske), 196
reality television, 251
Red River, 17
Red Shoes, 67
regulation
    Australian culture and, 219–20
    format convergence and, 221–2, 250–1, 263
    of Australian content, 187–92, 205, 213, 216
    US model, 221
research and development, 218, 222–6
    Korea, Taiwan and UK, 233–6
    need for more in content industries, 226–9, 261–4
    public broadcasters and new economy, 251–2
Restless and the Damned, 19, 20–1, 50
Return to Eden, 84, 117, 143
Richmond Hill, 129
Riddle of the Stinson, The, 94
Rifkin, Jeremy, 217, 225
Road Games, 63
Roadshow Coote and Carroll, 128
Robbery Under Arms, 84
Robinson, Lee, 19, 50
Ross, Andrew, xxxvi
Routt, Bill, 39, 40, 46, 57
Rowse, Tim, 192, 213
Royal Commission into the Moving Picture Industry (1927–8), 6
    Chauvel's evidence to, 42, 43, 53
Rush, 77

Said, Edward, 140
Savieri, Grace, 54
Schultz, Carl, 97
Schumpeter, Joseph, xxxiv
Scorsese, Martin, 90
Screen Producers' Association, 98
Screen Writers' Guild, 97
semiosphere, 151
semiotic resistance and change, 196–7, 199–200
Sentimental Bloke, The, 31
service industries, policy development, 217, 220–2, 226–7
Seven Network, 73
Shiralee, The, 19
Shirley, Graham, 11, 32
Shout!, 84, 88–90
Siege of Pinchgut, 19
Silence of Dean Maitland, 7

Sinclair, John, xxvii, 154
soap opera exports, 129–35
    US competition and, 133–5
Soap Opera Weekly (magazine), 134
Sons of Matthew, 12, 17, 36
Southern International Co, 19
Soviet cinema, 28
Special Broadcasting Service (SBS), 251–2
Spence, Bruce, 119–20
sphericule, ethno-specific diasporic, 153–4, 156–7
Spielberg, Stephen, 94
Splendid Fellows, 7
Sportz Crazy, 94
Star TV, 126
Starstruck, 2, 64–8
Stone, 64
Stork, 65
storytelling, 101, 116–18
Stowaway, The, 19, 20, 50
Stretton, Hugh, 197
Strictly Ballroom, 2–3
structuralism, 187
Sullivans, The, 77, 81, 129
Summer of the Seventeenth Doll, 19
sunrise industries, 236
Sword of Honour, 84, 90–1

tabloid television, 126–7
Tales of Hoffman, 67
Talkies Era, The (Reade), 30
Tambini, Damien, 221
tax legislation, and mini-series production, 74
technocracy, 210
techo-music, 180–1
teen magazines, 134
television,
    Australian on world markets, 122–46
    British, 125–6, 127–8
    classic serials, 77
    convergence and its future, 220–1
    corporate strategy in new economy, 251
    impact on film production, 18
    history of mini-series production, 73–93
    mini-series as Australian genre, 69–72
    mini-series as quality programming, 76–7
    Murdoch and, 126–7
    New Zealand, 127
    see also Australian television; broadcasting; Australian television
Ten Network, 70, 80, 100, 103
Thatcherism, 186, 199–200
They're a Weird Mob, 19, 22–4
Third World
    cinema of, 27
    depiction in film, 51, 58–60
    reception of western film, 27

INDEX

This Day Tonight, 114
This Fabulous Century, 81
Thousand Skies, A, 78
Three In One, 12
Thuy Nga, 164–5, 167, 169
Thuy Nga Productions, 164–6, 167
Timeless Land, The, 84
To Van Lai, 164–5, 173
Town Like Alice, A, 74, 81, 84
Tracy, 84
trade unions, 100, 208, 211
True Believers, 74, 85
Tuan Ngoc, 174, 175
Tulloch, John, 4, 5, 32–3, 39
   on Chauvel, 41–2
Tunstall, Jeremy, 190
Turner, Graeme, xxvi, xxviii, xxix, xxxi, 143, 188
Turner, Tina, 103
Twilight Zone, The, 94, 98
Two Minutes Silence, 7

Uncivilised, 7, 8, 37, 38, 46, 55
UNESCO, 197
Unmaking of Gough, The (Kelly), 76
utopias
   Starstruck and, 66–7
   Wake of the Bounty and, 55–60

video
   ethnic minority, 156, 158, 163–82
   historical compilations, 168–73
   Vietnamese Paris by Night series, 164–5, 168–9, 177–8
Viet Kieu, 163
Vietcong, 172
Vietnam
   anti-war protest, 208
   diaspora performers and, 175–6
   Doi Moi policies and video piracy, 166
   folksongs, 167, 171–2
Vietnam, 77, 79, 80–1, 84, 89, 90–2, 94 102, 103, 104, 113–16
Vietnamese diaspora, 155, 159
   anti-communism, 167–8
   cultural negotiation, 173–6
   English-Vietnamese lyrics, 177–8
   heritage maintenance, 168–73
   homeland audiences, 176
   music video, 155, 161–82
   new wave assertive hybridity, 176–81
   Southern California, 163–5, 177–9
   visiting Vietnam, 169
   western pop, 177–81
   westernised, 163, 175–6
Vietnamese opera, 170

Village Roadshow, 132
Visible Fictions (Ellis), 115

Walk Into Paradise, 19, 20, 50
Walkabout (Chauvels), 48
War Game, The, 83
Ward, Ian, xxiii
Water Under the Bridge, 84
Waterfront, 74, 76
Watt, Harry, 12, 14
We of the Never Never, 78
Wealth of Networks (Benkler), xxx
Weaving, Hugo, 119
web 2.0, 215, 216
Webby, Elizabeth, xxiii
Weekly's War, 85
Whitlam, Gough, 76, 81, 92, 106
wikipedia, 253
Williams, Raymond, 68
Williamson, David, 79–80, 86, 98
Windsors, The, 77
Witches of Eastwick, 70, 94, 98
   With the Headhunters of Unknown Papua, 50
Wolf Creek, 3
Women of the Sun, 85
working class culture, television content rules and, 188
Wretched of the Earth, The (Fanon), 51

Year My Voice Broke, The, 94, 98
Yoram Gross Studios, 135